10.09

W9-BGK-813

THE NEW NATIONS IN THE UNITED NATIONS, 1960-1967

NUMBER EIGHT

Columbia University Studies
in International Organization

EDITORS

Leland M. Goodrich
William T. R. Fox

THE

New Nations

IN THE

UNITED
NATIONS,
1960-1967

by DAVID A. KAY

COLUMBIA UNIVERSITY PRESS

New York and London
1970

David A. Kay is Associate Professor of Political Science at Barnard College and Graduate Faculties, Columbia University.

Copyright © 1970 Columbia University Press
ISBN: 0-231-03350-8
Library of Congress Catalog Card number: 71-115223

Printed in the United States of America

COLUMBIA UNIVERSITY STUDIES
IN INTERNATIONAL ORGANIZATION

This series of monographs was initiated to provide for the publica-
tion under University auspices of studies in the field of international
organization undertaken and carried out, in whole or in part, by
members of the Columbia Faculties or with the assistance of funds
made available under research programs of the University. Work in
this field has been substantially assisted by grants from the Rocke-
feller and Ford Foundations.

The series is not intended to provide a systematic coverage of the
field of international organization nor is it anticipated that volumes
will appear with any set regularity. The value of the contribution
which the monograph makes to knowledge and understanding of the
role of international organization and its functioning in the world in
which we live will be the dominant consideration in determining
inclusion. The series is published under the joint editorship of
Leland M. Goodrich and William T. R. Fox, with Andrew W. Cordier
and Louis Henkin acting in an advisory capacity.

The other books in this series are *Controls for Outer Space*, by
Phillip C. Jessup and Howard J. Taubenfeld, *The United Nations
Emergency Force*, by Gabriella Rosner, *UN Administration of Eco-
nomic and Social Programs*, edited by Gerard J. Mangone, *The UN
Secretary-General and the Maintenance of Peace*, by Leon Gordenker,
The United Nations Economic and Social Council, by Walter R.
Sharp, *Legal Effects of United Nations Resolutions*, by Jorge Cas-
tañeda (translated by Alba Amoia), and *Dag Hammarskjold's United
Nations*, by Mark W. Zacher.

Foreword

BY LELAND M. GOODRICH

The United Nations today is a different organization in many respects from the one which was envisaged by those primarily responsible for writing the Charter. What one is perhaps most inclined to emphasize in discussing differences between the San Francisco Organization and the one which we see today is the fact that in the performance of its function of maintaining international peace and security the emphasis is not placed on enforcement but rather on consent. This consent is too often lacking because of the disagreements among the major powers and the opportunity thus offered to the smaller powers to exploit the conflicting aims and interests of the great powers in the advancement of their own conflicting interests. The emphasis on peace-keeping operations in contrast to peace-enforcement suggests the change that has taken place.

In a real sense, however, equally if not more important than this important difference is the change that has taken place in the priorities of the Organization with respect to its purposes and the methods employed for achieving them as the result of the expansion of membership. At San Francisco the older states, primarily Western in culture and tradition, were in the saddle. Though the emergence of the Soviet Union as a superpower and the ideological challenge that it offered prevented the new Organization from having the homogeneity that the League had originally possessed, there was nevertheless general agreement on the priority to be accorded to the maintenance of international peace and security in the work of the Organization. The confrontation between East and West was over issues of this nature, and this confrontation—the "cold war"—had one of its manifestations in the deadlock over membership.

While the breaking of this deadlock by the "package deal" of 1955 did not result immediately in a radical change in the nature of the membership of the Organization or of its activities, this did prepare the way for another "membership explosion" of a different character: the admission on a large scale and with unexpected suddenness of new states—largely African possessions that until only recently had been colonies of European member states. The attitudes of these new members towards the Organization and its activities were the product of different experiences from those of the older members of the United Nations. Being new states, economically underdeveloped and only recently the colonial possessions of Western powers, they brought into the Organization strong views regarding the evils of colonialism, and an equal strong desire to share in the material well-being which until then had been denied, so they believed, by their colonial masters. Furthermore, being of different racial stock than their former colonial masters and conscious of having suffered from racial discrimination, they were insistent upon recognition of their equality and the elimination of racial discrimination wherever it existed. With these special interests, they were not particularly concerned with issues of international peace and security, or more particularly, the conflicts of the "cold war", except as they might be exploited to serve their more immediate interests.

It is the analysis of the impact of these new members upon the Organization that David Kay undertakes in this book. Not content with relying on intuition or common-sense observation, he has used quantitative data, including statistics on voting and participation in debates in the General Assembly and the Main Committees, to demonstrate the influence of the new members in establishing priorities in the work of the United Nations and in determining the decisions that are taken. This study is a major contribution to our understanding of the new United Nations and the changes in the Organization that have resulted from the more than doubling of its membership.

Acknowledgments

During the course of writing this study I have had the benefit of the constant encouragement and friendship of Leland M. Goodrich. Both as a teacher and a scholar he has profoundly shaped my interest in the study of the politics of international organization. I also wish to acknowledge my appreciation to Louis Henkin, Donald Puchala and Ruth Russell for their valued advice and comments on the study. I also owe a belated vote of thanks to the staff of the United States Mission to the United Nations with whom it was my privilege to serve during 1967-1968 as an Advisor on International Organization Affairs. The opportunity to participate in the political process of the United Nations made an important contribution to my understanding of this process. The views expressed in this study are, of course, solely those of the author.

The assistance of the Library of the Carnegie Endowment for International Peace and, particularly, its Director, Vivian Hewitt, is cheerfully acknowledged. For all who must labor with United Nations documentation, this library serves as a model of friendliness and effectiveness.

The labor of turning my dissertation into the present manuscript occurred in the stimulating environment of the Department of Political Science of The University of Wisconsin. To my colleagues there I owe a vote of thanks for their advice and encouragement.

Finally, I owe a large debt to my wife, Jane, not only for the expenditure of so much of her own time in the mundane tasks of preparing a manuscript but, more importantly, for her unfaltering encouragement and good humor during the project.

David A. Kay

Contents

THE NEW NATIONS IN THE UNITED NATIONS, 1960-1967

Chapter I

INTRODUCTION

The fifteenth session of the General Assembly of the United Nations, which convened in New York in September 1960, marked an important turning point in the history of the Organization. The United Nations had been created primarily through the efforts of states with a European or European-derived political and social culture, possessing a common history of political involvement at the international level. During its first ten years the Organization was dominated by the problems and conflicts of these same states. However, by 1955 the process of decolonization, which has marked the post-1945 political arena, began to be reflected in the membership of the United Nations. In the ten years preceding the end of 1955, ten new nations devoid of experience in the contemporary international arena and struggling with the multitudinous problems of fashioning coherent entities in the face of both internal and external pressures joined the Organization.[1] By 1960 the rising tide of decolonization had reached flood crest with the entry in that one year of 17 new nations—16 of which were African.

The United Nations at its present stage of development is a political system of formally coordinate members, each able to place before the Organization the demands that flow from its own national policy. The United Nations is forced to respond to its environment and the demands emanating from that environment.[2] One can expect

[1] These states are Burma, Cambodia, Ceylon, Indonesia, Laos, Libya, Pakistan, Philippines, Israel, and Jordan.
[2] Ernst B. Haas, "Dynamic Environment and Static System: Revolutionary Regimes in the United Nations," in Morton A. Kaplan (ed.), *The Revolution in World Politics* (New York: John Wiley & Sons, 1962), 267–309.

1

that a stable environment will yield a stable pattern of demands on the United Nations political system. Similarly, a change in the environment—the major components of which are the nation-states—can be expected to change the pattern of demands made on the political system of the Organization. It is on just such a change that the present study proposes to focus. By 1960 the admission of 33 new nations to the United Nations had substantially altered its environment and the inputs being placed into its political system. It is suggested here that these changes were so substantial that they altered the nature of the political process of the Organization. This study sets out to examine the nature of this changed political process from the point of view of the demands the new nations have made upon the system and the political influence that they have attempted to exercise to achieve these demands. Concern will be focused successively upon determining the areas in which the new nations have made new demands upon the system, the pattern of interaction within the Organization in the course of their exercise of political influence, their degree of success in achieving their demands, and finally, the general nature of the political process as it has evolved under the impact of the new nations.

It was following the sudden increase in the number of independent African states during 1960 that the new nations first became a significant component of the United Nations. As shown in Table I. 1, in that year alone the number of new nations in the Organization more than tripled, while as a group they composed slightly more than a third of it. By 1968 more than 45 percent of the Members had achieved independence since 1945 and over 25 percent have been independent for less than five years.

". . . the United Nations must be described as a multiphase system, whose characteristics and evolutionary potential must be specified in terms of the changing environment in which it operates. Environments, in turn, are made up of the totality of policies, aims, expectations, fears, hopes, and hatreds funneled into the institutional structure and its political processes, the 'system' proper." (p. 270) And later—"The UN system is hyperdependent on its environment." (p. 280)

See also, Ernst B. Haas, "The Comparative Study of the United Nations," World Politics, 12, No. 2 (Jan. 1960), 298–322. Haas has further suggested that the construction of an empirical theory of international organization can best be approached through the examination of the system in each phase in which the pattern of inputs changes because of change in the environment. Such an examination would explain the evolution of the system "in terms of the global tasks and programs which devolve upon it because of the tensions in the policies of the members." (p. 303) For a parallel suggestion with regard to political systems in general, see David Easton, A Framework for Political Analysis (Englewood Cliffs, N.J.: Prentice-Hall, 1965), 115–16.

TABLE I.1

Growth of New Nation Representation in the United Nations

Year	Total United Nations Membership	New Nations in United Nations	Percentage of United Nations Composed of New Nations
1950	60	5	8.33
1955	76	10	13.15
1960	99	33	33.33
1961	104	37	35.57
1962	110	43	39.09
1963	113	46	40.70
1964	115	48	41.73
1965	118	51	43.3
1966	122	55	45.0
1967	123	56	45.5

The new nations with which this study is concerned are those states that have achieved independence since 1945. The states meeting this criterion are set forth in Table I. 2. India is the only questionable exclusion from this list. While India did not achieve independence until August 15, 1947, it was a founding Member of both the League of Nations and the United Nations. On the other hand, Pakistan is included in this grouping of new states. This inclusion follows from the decisions of the Security Council and the General Assembly in 1947 at the time of the partition of the Indian subcontinent. At that time the Organization took the view that the government of India represented the state of India which was an original signatory of the Charter, but that Pakistan was a new state which would have to be admitted to the United Nations as a new member.

Political influence along with power is probably the most pervasive concept in the literature of political analysis. Any discussion of the political process of a given system must inevitably deal with the manner in which political power or influence is wielded in the system.[3] Indeed, in this present study the exercise of political influence lies at the very heart of the analysis. And while the process through

[3] Much of this discussion of the problems of measuring political influence is derived from the extremely cogent analysis in Robert A. Dahl, *Modern Political Analysis* (Englewood Cliffs, N.J.: Prentice-Hall, 1963), 39–54.

TABLE I.2

New Nations in the United Nations 1960–1967

Country	Former Status	Date of Independence or Coming into Existence	Date of United Nations Membership
Africa			
Algeria	French	3 Jul 1962	8 Oct 1962
Botswana	British	30 Sep 1966	17 Oct 1966
Burundi	Belgian Trusteeship	1 Jul 1962	18 Sep 1962
Cameroon	French Trusteeship	1 Jan 1960	20 Sep 1960
Central African Republic	French	13 Aug 1960	20 Sep 1960
Chad	French	1 Aug 1960	20 Sep 1960
Congo (Brazzaville)	French	15 Aug 1960	20 Sep 1960
Congo (Leopoldville)	Belgian	30 Jun 1960	20 Sep 1960
Dahomey	French	11 Aug 1960	20 Sep 1960
Gabon	French	17 Aug 1960	20 Sep 1960
Gambia	British	18 Feb 1965	21 Sep 1965
Ghana	British	6 Mar 1957	8 Mar 1957
Guinea	French	2 Oct 1958	12 Dec 1958
Ivory Coast	French	7 Aug 1960	20 Sep 1960
Kenya	British	12 Dec 1963	16 Dec 1963
Lesotho	British	4 Oct 1966	17 Oct 1966
Libya	British Trusteeship	24 Dec 1951	14 Dec 1955
Madagascar	French	26 Jun 1960	20 Sep 1960
Malawi	British Protectorate	6 Jul 1964	1 Dec 1964
Mali	French	22 Sep 1960	28 Sep 1960
Mauritania	French	28 Nov 1960	27 Oct 1961
Morocco	French	2 Mar 1956	12 Nov 1956
Niger	French	3 Aug 1960	20 Sep 1960

a Tanganyika became a Member on 14 December 1961 and Zanzibar on 16 December 1963. Following the ratification of articles of union between Tanganyika and Zanzibar on 26 April 1964; the United Republic of Tanganyika and Zanzibar continued as a single Member of the United Nations, later changing its name to the United Republic of Tanzania.

b Indonesia withdrew from the United Nations effective 1 March 1965 (Documents A/5857 and Corr. 1 and S/6157).

c On 16 September 1963, Sabah (North Borneo) and Sarawak joined with the Federation of Malaya (which had become a United Nations Member on 17 September 1957) to form Malaysia.

TABLE I.2 *(continued)*

Country	Former Status	Date of Independence or Coming into Existence	Date of United Nations Membership
Nigeria	British	1 Oct 1960	7 Oct 1960
Rwanda	Belgian Trusteeship	1 Jul 1962	18 Sep 1962
Senegal	French	20 Aug 1960	28 Sep 1960
Sierra Leone	British	27 Apr 1961	27 Sep 1961
Somali Republic	Italian Trusteeship	1 Jul 1960	20 Sep 1960
Sudan	Anglo-Egyptian Condominium	1 Jan 1956	12 Nov 1956
Tanganyika[a]	British Trusteeship	9 Dec 1961	14 Dec 1961
Togo	French Trusteeship	27 Apr 1960	20 Sep 1960
Tunisia	French	20 Mar 1956	12 Nov 1956
Uganda	British Protectorate	9 Oct 1962	25 Oct 1962
Upper Volta	French	5 Aug 1960	20 Sep 1960
Zambia	British Protectorate	24 Oct 1964	1 Dec 1964
Zanzibar[a]	British Protectorate	9 Dec 1963	16 Dec 1963
Americas			
Barbados	British	30 Nov 1966	9 Dec 1966
Guyana	British	26 May 1966	20 Sep 1966
Jamaica	British	6 Aug 1962	18 Sep 1962
Trinidad and Tobago	British	31 Aug 1962	18 Sep 1962
Asia			
Burma	British	4 Jan 1948	19 Apr 1948
Cambodia	French	8 Nov 1949	14 Dec 1955
Ceylon	British	4 Feb 1948	14 Dec 1955
Indonesia[b]	Netherlands	28 Sep 1949	28 Sep 1950
Laos	French	19 May 1949	14 Dec 1955
Malaysia[c]	British and Malaya	16 Sep 1963	17 Sep 1957
Maldive Islands	British	26 Jul 1965	21 Sep 1965
Mongolia	Under Chinese Suzerainty	5 Jan 1946	27 Oct 1961
Pakistan	British	15 Aug 1947	30 Sep 1947

TABLE I.2 *(continued)*

Country	Former Status	Date of Independence or Coming into Existence	Date of United Nations Membership
Philippines	United States	4 Jul 1946	24 Oct 1945
Singapore	British	9 Aug 1965	21 Sep 1965
Europe			
Cyprus	British	16 Aug 1960	20 Sep 1960
Malta	British	31 May 1964	1 Dec 1964
Middle East			
Israel	British Mandate	14 May 1948	11 May 1949
Jordan	British Mandate	17 Jun 1947	14 Dec 1955
Kuwait	British Protectorate	19 Jun 1961	13 May 1963
South Yemen	British	30 Nov 1967	14 Dec 1967

which influence is exercised can be observed and described, the measurement of the extent of influence possessed or used involves one of the most difficult conceptual problems of political analysis. As a matter of principle, there is no difficulty in accepting Dahl's definition of influence as "a *relation among actors* in which one actor induces other actors to act in some way they would not otherwise act."[4] The confusion and difficulty arise not from the definition but from the practical need to use the definition to compare the relative influence of different actors in a political system. Riggs in attempting to measure the influence of the United States in the General Assembly has said that ". . . influence is expressed in terms of positions fought for and won, positions compromised, positions abandoned, and a few fought for and lost."[5] However, this approach raises many difficulties. It is often impossible to know the initial positions of the various actors and how much they have actually changed.

In the United Nations states sometimes assume extreme positions

[4] *Ibid.*, p. 40.
[5] Robert E. Riggs, *Politics in the United Nations, A Study of United States Influence in the General Assembly* (Urbana, Ill.: The University of Illinois Press, 1958), p. 4.

for bargaining purposes, for the purpose of ending up with a compromise that is close or identical to their real but concealed initial position. One of the most important skills in diplomacy is the ability to detect a bargaining position and to determine how much it diverges from the opposing state's "real" position. The converse of this skill is the diplomat's ability to conceal his real position and to create credibility in his bargaining position. An additional problem with this type of scale for measuring influence is that it is often difficult to determine whether any one change in position is larger or smaller than any other change. If State X is only able to exert sufficient influence to convince State A to abstain on a vote on colonialism, while State Y has enough influence to convince State B to vote yes on the same issue, can you therefore say that State Y's influence is greater than that of State X? Although the change of position of State B is greater than that of State A, nothing has been said of the value either A or B placed on a vote on colonialism. If to B such a vote is a matter of indifference, but to A it is a matter of intense concern involving a long history of support for the opposite side, more influence might have been involved in its decision to abstain than in B's decision to vote yes.

To avoid this failure to measure the "psychological distance" involved in change, an attempt can be made to determine the "subjective psychological cost of compliance."[6] This involves taking into account the fact that "a seeming equal change in the 'objective' positions of two different actors may actually require quite different amounts of subjective change."[7] For example, in the United Nations it is clearly recognized that more influence is required to secure United States support for an anticolonial resolution than is required to secure the support of Mexico for the same resolution. However, in the actual practice of measuring influence over a broad spectrum of issues it is not always possible to calculate the real psychological costs of compliance. But informed guesses—and very often they can be little more than that—about the assumptions concerning subjective cost can do much to elucidate the problem of measuring the extent of influence.

Another promising method of measuring the extent of influence

[6] Dahl, *Modern Political Analysis*, p. 43.   [7] *Ibid.*

involves determining the difference in the probability of compliance. If it is known that on any given resolution proposed by the new nations in the United Nations 23 other states will support the resolution without any influence being applied, then the amount of influence wielded can be measured by determining how many states in excess of this base figure supported any particular resolution. Thus, if on a hypothetical resolution the new nations sponsoring the resolution were able to secure 50 votes in addition to their own, one could measure their influence with 27 states. However, it is very difficult to know the number of states that can be counted on without the exertion of any influence. The calculation of reasonably accurate probabilities requires either a random number or a large number of past occurrences of equivalent events, and neither of these requirements is likely to be met in politics. Additionally, this method fails to measure the two previous dimensions: the absolute change in position and the subjective cost of compliance.

Unfortunately, all of these methods of measuring influence have limitations and present several serious conceptual problems. Rather than depend on any one measure of influence, this study will attempt to spread the risk by using all three where appropriate. Absolute changes in positions, votes won and lost, and the size of differences in the probability of compliance all lend themselves to quantitative techniques, which will be used. On the other hand, estimates on the subjective cost of compliance are more readily handled by descriptive techniques. Regardless of which method is used in measuring influence, two injunctions will hopefully not be violated. First, it must be recognized that, especially in a multipurpose organization such as the United Nations, discussions of influence must always be coupled with a reference to the scope of the Organization's activities. Political influence is a discrete quantity that cannot be expected to be the same over the broad spectrum of activities in which the United Nations is involved. Second, when discussing influence an attempt will be made always to be explicit about the specific basis used for judging both the influence and the dimensions that are absent from the measurement because of the technique used.

An analysis centered upon the exercise of influence in the United Nations raises an additional conceptual problem. Political influence exercised in the United Nations can be broken down according to its target into two dimensions. The first dimension, and the most obvious, is directed at shaping the policy outputs of the Organization, that is, passing or defeating resolutions and amendments, advancing or opposing candidates for positions of leadership in the Organization, and affecting the budget of the Organization. A second dimension of influence concerns shaping the policy of states in the environment external to the United Nations. The second dimension, in other words, concerns the extent of influence exercised over states that are the objects or targets of United Nations resolutions and decisions. It is thus quite possible to exercise a potent influence on the outputs of the United Nations and yet to wield a considerably lesser amount of influence on the adherence or compliance of states with these same resolutions. Or the reverse could be the case. In the analysis that follows, the impact of the new nations along these two dimensions will have to be considered separately.

This study is organized into four sections. In the first section attention is devoted to a process analysis of the methods available to the new nations for pressing their demands on the Organization. The main concern is to determine the roles played by missions, delegations, caucusing groups, committees, negotiations, and voting.

The judging of the extent to which the new nations have successfully exercised their influence in the United Nations demands a knowledge of the goals they have pursued and their relative evaluation of each. The second section of this study is thus devoted to an examination of the pattern of concerns revealed in the conduct of the new nations in the Organization.

The United Nations is a multipurpose organization called to consider and act on a broad range of topics. On the other hand, political influence is a highly discrete quality that cannot be expected to remain uniform over a broad range of issues. These two factors—the multipurpose nature of the United Nations and the discrete nature of political influence—ensure that the extent of the influence exercised by the new nations cannot be determined from a study of two or three major issues. While the extended case study on colonialism that follows in the fourth section is able to demonstrate the methods and means of exercising influence, it does not go very far in demonstrating either the scope of this influence or the consistency with which it is exercised. To obtain this depth and perspective, the multitude of issues dealt with by the United Nations has been separated into five categories. The third section of this study is devoted to a consideration of these issue categories with particular reference to determining the demands the new nations have placed before the United Nations and their development in relation to the alternatives advocated by the new nations.

Following this, the analysis shifts to a detailed study of a case in which the new nations were engaged in the active exercise of political influence. This case involves the 1960 General Assembly Declaration on Colonialism and the 1961 decision to establish a Special Committee to examine the implementation of the Declaration.[8] While this certainly is not a typical case in that the new nations manifested a greater than average interest in its outcome, this active involvement should be more revealing of the methods of influence employed by the new nations than would be a study of a more typical case. It is hoped that a clearer understanding will be gained of the role of the new nations in the United Nations political process and of the process itself from this case study than would otherwise be available from an analysis solely of the tools of influence.

[8] With regard to the correct form of the titles of United Nations organs and resolutions, this study has followed the practice of the UN Monthly Chronicle, United Nations Office of Public Information, and the Yearbook of the United Nations, United Nations Office of Public Information. Also in this study the general practice has been to use the shortened form of such titles as set forth in the above publications.

Chapter II

INSTRUMENTS OF INFLUENCE IN THE
UNITED NATIONS POLITICAL SYSTEM

Before turning to an examination of the pattern of demands that the new nations have made on the United Nations and their success in achieving these demands, the instruments through which demands are made and influence is exercised within the United Nations will be examined. These are the instruments that are used to influence the framing of the policy of the Organization. This section is intended to provide a survey of the instruments through which a nation makes its demands known and strives to make good these demands, rather than a detailed analysis of the effect of each of these instruments on the political process of the Organization.

Missions and Delegations

It is with the permanent missions of the Member States that the immediate responsibility for the advancement of national policy in the United Nations rests.[1] The establishment by members of permanent representation at the headquarters of an international organization is a relatively recent innovation in diplomatic practice. In

---

[1] During the plenary sessions of the General Assembly and the Economic and Social Council, states are represented by delegations specially accredited to the particular session of the body. The composition of these special delegations varies from country to country. Many states choose to compose them of prominent members of the government, while others tend to draw heavily upon their permanent mission when making such appointments. As a general rule the new nations tend to follow the latter practice. Regardless of the composition of the special delegations, they are dependent upon the permanent missions for staff work and expertise in the politics of the Organization. Unless otherwise noted, the author has followed the practice in this section of using the term "missions" to cover the activity of the specially accredited delegations as well as the permanent missions.

spite of the initial negative reaction of the League Secretariat, permanent delegations—League terminology for what is now called a permanent mission—first put in a large-scale appearance at Geneva. Although as many as 40 permanent delegations were accredited to the League of Nations at the height of its activity, their impact appears to have been slight. The leading historian of the League, F. P. Walters, asserts flatly that "the system of Permanent Delegations was of no serious significance in League history."[2]

While the Charter of the United Nations made no mention of a system of permanent missions accredited to the Organization by the Members States, the tempo of postwar diplomacy as well as the fact that the Organization was not located in the capital of one of the Members soon dictated the establishment of such a system.[3] Forty-one of the then 58 Members had established by 1948 permanent missions in New York; by January 1968 this figure had risen to 122 of the 123 Members. Walters' assessment of permanent missions during the League period would be repeated by few, if any, observers of the role played by such missions in the United Nations.

Within the United Nations political system at least four distinct functions as instruments of political influence are performed by the permanent missions.[4] The feverish activity that constantly surrounds each mission can be functionally differentiated according to its contribution to (1) national policy formation; (2) the design and execution of the tactics of parliamentary diplomacy; (3) the collection and reporting of information; and (4) the dissemination of propaganda.

Although each permanent mission serves as its government's

[2] F. P. Walters, A History of the League of Nations (London: Oxford University Press, 1952), p. 199.

[3] The only hint of such a system is in Article 38(1), which states: "The Security Council shall be so organized as to be able to function continuously. Each member of the Security Council shall for this purpose be represented at all times at the seat of the Organization."

[4] There are very few studies of the role played by permanent missions in the political system of the United Nations. See James N. Hyde, "United States Participation in the United Nations," International Organization, 10, No. 1 (Feb. 1956), 22–34; Richard F. Pedersen, "National Representation in the United Nations," International Organization, 15, No. 2 (Spring 1961), 256–66. Under the direction of John Goormaghtigh, the Centre Européen de la Dotation Carnegie in 1965 established a Groupe d'Étude sur l'Organization Internationale. The group's first research project, which is still in progress, is a broad study of the role and functions of permanent missions to international organizations. The work of this group of 24 distinguished scholars promises to be the first systematic study of this new diplomatic institution.

advisor on United Nations affairs, this does not automatically assure that the mission's views will be given decisive weight in the determination of national policy. The foreign policy process today has become such a complicated and interrelated web that what seems decisive in New York may not seem so in London or Cairo. An additional handicap under which all the missions struggle in influencing the course of national policy is that their geographical isolation from the national capitals where the broad policy is determined severely limits their personal intervention in the policy-making process, where personal influence is often significant. Even as articulate a mission head as Adlai Stevenson found that the 200 miles separating New York and Washington was sufficient to keep him out of touch with decision-making in Washington.[5]

The very nature of United Nations diplomacy with its heavy emphasis on the drafting of resolutions, amendments, and reports to be voted on by one or the other of its numerous organs ensures that the execution of the tactics of parliamentary diplomacy will be a principal focus of the activity of the permanent missions. An unceasing round of private negotiations is the most pervasive form of this activity. It is in the design and execution of the tactics of parliamentary diplomacy that the permanent missions excel. As Pedersen has noted,

. . . a delegation's role in the formulation of tactics and in the precise manner of implementing policy is usually decisive. The tactical situation varies so rapidly from day to day, and the calculation of probable voting and of the attitudes of other countries is so crucial in achieving a successful result, that tactics must be left reasonably flexible. Even such a question as when to inform other delegations of a country's policy can be a critical decision. Such factors as the order in which various people are approached, the concessions which a delegation can make within the limits of its authorization, and the level and timing of moves are best judged as closely to the necessary action as possible, both in time and distance.[6]

Of course, when dealing with a system in which new issues are constantly arising and the terms of old ones are constantly shifting,

[5] Theodore C. Sorensen, *Kennedy* (New York; Harper & Row, 1965), pp. 287–88.

[6] Richard F. Pedersen, "National Representation in the United Nations," *International Organization*, 15, No. 2 (Spring 1961), 260. For a similar assessment, see John G. Hadwen and Johan Kaufmann, *How United Nations Decisions Are Made* (2d ed. rev. New York: Oceana Publications, 1962), p. 34.

the mission's acknowledged control over the tactics to be followed often results in its having *de facto* control of policy as well. Few missions operate under detailed instructions as to tactics, and even in regard to policy the guide lines are usually broad enough to allow the mission a certain amount of discretion. As one might imagine, this inability to exercise detailed control is often the despair of home governments. The sentiments once echoed by Prime Minister Macmillan are probably generally shared in many capitals.

. . . the [resolutions] come flooding in, they are very long and complicated and, with the best will in the world, they really do present quite a difficulty to the delegations in New York and to Governments overseas.

This is, of course, not made easier by the time factor, and the curious rules of procedure which are not, like ours, worked out after many generations. Amendments are moved in New York of which we in the capital cities have hardly seen the context—perhaps we get it on the telephone—and in situations in which we are unable to appreciate the full implications. Many of the member Governments, I can assure the House, have given up the task in despair and give no instructions to their representatives. Some have given permanent instructions to their representatives to abstain.[7]

A third function of the permanent mission is the constant collection and reporting of information on the wide range of questions that face the Organization. Every mission desires to know the probable line of conduct of the over 120 other Members, and all of them would like to stay at least one step ahead of any likely crisis issue. The exchange of information on issues and policies with other missions and the reporting of this information take a considerable proportion of the time of each mission. In addition to collecting and exchanging information with other missions, they must maintain contact with the Secretariat for the same purposes.

Finally, every mission is engaged in public relations campaigns directed to the other missions, the Secretariat, foreign governments, and foreign and domestic public opinion. One major difficulty is that these various campaigns directed at different audiences must be waged simultaneously, and what may be suitable for one audience may not be for another. Indicative of the extent of this public relations effort is the fact that the verbatim records of the General As-

---

[7] Great Britain, *Hansard's Parliamentary Debates* (5th Series). (Commons), 653, Feb. 5, 1962, 53–54.

sembly and its subsidiary organs now exceed 40,000 pages a year.[8] In addition to speeches, most missions consider it necessary to hold periodic press conferences and to issue a stream of press releases on the views of their governments on the questions before the United Nations.

The growth of the permanent mission system has both reflected and assisted the evolution of the United Nations into a continuous diplomatic conference. As the Organization has acquired more operational tasks, permanent missions have become essential instruments for constantly monitoring and influencing these activities. Permanent missions also serve a psychological function as a token of a Member's concern and interest in the Organization. However, the principal function of the missions remains at the present time the advancement of national policy aims through the United Nations.

By the early 1960's when the majority of new nations had entered the Organization, the permanent mission system was already well established, and it was assumed that as a matter of course they would also establish missions in New York. In general, this expectation was followed, and at the end of 1967 Gambia was the only new nation to remain without a permanent mission for more than one year.[9] However, as even a cursory glance at Tables II.1 and II.2 will show, these missions tended to be quite small. For example, the average number of diplomatic personnel in all the missions of the new nations in 1960 was only 3.6, and by 1967 this figure had risen to only 5.64. This contrasts with the average size[10] of the Latin American missions for October 1962, which was 7.3. The figure for the new nations is somewhat overstated, since it was a common practice for the new nations to appoint their Ambassadors to the United States as heads of their permanent missions. In 1961 seventeen of the 37 new nations listed their Ambassadors to the United States as heads of their permanent missions, and as late as 1967 fifteen of the 56 new nations still followed this practice. Even with great exertion on their part, most such heads of delegations forced to fill two key posts are only able to maintain close contact with United

[8] Richard P. Hunt, "At the U.N.—13,000,000 Words a Year," *New York Times Magazine*, Dec. 9, 1962, 31–33.

[9] Until 1963 Libya followed the curious policy of appointing a permanent mission but of not maintaining a New York office for the mission.

[10] United Nations, *Permanent Missions to the United Nations*, No. 148, Oct. 1962.

TABLE II.1

Size of New Nations' Permanent Missions
to United Nations 1960–1964[a]

State	1960	1961	1962	1963	1964
Algeria			4[h]	4	7
Burundi			3[h]	2	1
Cameroon	_[d]	3[e]	2	4	5
Central African Republic	4[h]	3[e]	5	2	2
Chad	_[d]	3[e]	3[e]	3[e]	2
Congo (Brazzaville)	_[d]	3[e]	4[e]	3[e]	1[e]
Congo (Leopoldville)	_[d]	2	4	4	4
Dahomey	_[d]	2[e]	2[e]	3[e]	5[e]
Gabon	3[h]	4[e]	2	2	3[e]
Ghana	5	6	9	11	11
Guinea	2	3	3	3	3
Ivory Coast	_[d]	4	4	6	6
Kenya				_[d]	2
Libya	1[e, f]	2[e, f]	2[e, f]	2[g]	3
Madagascar	1[g]	3[e]	3[e]	4[e]	6[e]
Malawi					_[d]
Mali	1[h]	3[e]	4	7	5
Mauritania		3[e]	3[e]	2[e]	3[e]
Morocco	3[e]	6	3	5	5
Niger	_[d]	2[e]	2[e]	4[e]	5[e]
Nigeria	5[g]	8	9	17	16
Rwanda			2[h]	2	2
Senegal	3	3[e]	3[e]	3[e]	3[e]
Sierra Leone		3[h]	3	7	5[e]
Somali Republic	_[d]	2	3	4	4
Sudan	5	5	5	5	5

a Unless otherwise indicated, the figure given is for September of the year in question. The source of these figures is United Nations, *Permanent Missions of the United Nations*.

b Tanganyika became a Member on 14 December 1961, and Zanzibar on 16 December 1963. Following the ratification of articles of union between Tanganyika and Zanzibar on 26 April 1964, the United Republic of Tanganyika and Zanzibar continued as a single Member of the United Nations, later changing its name to the United Republic of Tanzania. The size of mission given for Tanganyika is for the merged State.

c On 16 September 1963, Sabah (North Borneo) and Sarawak joined with the Federation of Malaya to form Malaysia.

d No Permanent Mission to the United Nations.

e Head of Permanent Mission is also the Ambassador to the United States.

f Permanent Mission has no New York office.

g Figure is for November.

h Figure is for December.

TABLE II.1 *(continued)*

State	1960	1961	1962	1963	1964
Tanganyika[b]		_d	6	5	8
Togo	1[g]	1[e]	1[e]	1	5[e]
Tunisia	3[e]	4[e]	4	6	5
Uganda			4[h]	5	7
Upper Volta	_d	2[e]	3	3[e]	3[e]
Zambia					_d
Zanzibar				_d	
Jamaica			2[h]	4	6
Trinidad and Tobago			1[h]	3	3
Burma	6	7	6	7	7
Cambodia	3[e]	3[e]	4[e]	5[e]	5
Ceylon	5	4	3	3	3
Indonesia	11	7	10	11	12
Laos	2	2	2	2[e]	2[e]
Malaysia[c]	4[e]	4[e]	4[e]	6[e]	6[e]
Mongolia		3	6	4	5
Pakistan	6	6	6	6	5
Philippines	26	28	21	19	15
Cyprus	1[g]	2	5	5[e]	5[e]
Malta					_d
Israel	9	10	10	8	7
Jordan	2	4	4	6	8
Kuwait				1	6
Average Size	3.67	4.37	4.35	4.76	4.94

Nations affairs during the annual sessions of the General Assembly —and in some cases not even then.

There are several reasons for the small size of the permanent missions of the new nations. One manifestation of economic under-development and social backwardness is a shortage of trained personnel. This shortage has meant that the new nations have in general tried to keep most of their talented personnel at home to staff key ministries and departments and to ration the remainder out among various international commitments. Important limits have been placed upon the size of missions by the shallowness of the pool of available talent. Another limiting factor on the size of these missions has been their financial cost. Stoessinger in his study of United Nations financing calculated the average cost of maintaining a mis-

TABLE 11.2

*Size of New Nations' Permanent Missions
to the United Nations 1965–1967*[a]

State	1965	1966	1967
Algeria	9	8	12
Botswana			2e
Burundi	3	3	4e
Cameroon	5	6	5e
Central African Republic	2e	3e	3e
Chad	2e	2e	2e
Congo (Brazzaville)	3e	3e	3e
Congo (Democratic Republic of)	5	10	9
Dahomey	4e	4e	2
Gabon	4	6	5
Gambia	_d	_d	_d
Ghana	12	11	11
Guinea	2	3	3
Ivory Coast	6	6	5
Kenya	7	8	10e
Lesotho			2e
Libya	3	6	7
Madagascar	5e	5e	5e
Malawi	3	3	5
Mali	4	5e	6e
Mauritania	3e	4e	5
Morocco	7	5	6
Niger	3	3	1
Nigeria	17	19	14
Rwanda	2	2	3e
Senegal	3	5e	5e
Sierra Leone	5e	6e	7
Somali Republic	2	2	2
Sudan	6	6	7
Tanganyikab			
Tanzania	7	8	6

a Unless otherwise indicated, the figure given is for September of the year in question. The source of these figures is United Nations, *Permanent Missions to the United Nations.*

b Tanganyika became a Member on 14 December 1961, and Zanzibar on 16 December 1963. Following the ratification of articles of union between Tanganyika and Zanzibar on 26 April 1964, the United Republic of Tanganyika and Zanzibar continued as a single Member of the United Nations, later changing its name to the United Republic of Tanzania. The size of mission given for Tanganyika is for the merged state.

c On 16 September 1963, Sabah (North Borneo) and Sarawak joined with the Federation of Malaya to form Malaysia.

d No Permanent Mission to the United Nations.

e Head of Permanent Mission is also the Ambassador to the United States.

TABLE II.2 (continued)

State	1965	1966	1967
Togo	4e	4e	4e
Tunisia	5	5	6
Uganda	8	8	6
Upper Volta	2e	1	2
Zambia	4	4	5
Zanzibarb			
Barbados			6
Guyana			6
Jamaica	7	7	6
Trinidad and Tobago	5	4	6
Burma	7	6	7
Cambodia	4	5	6
Ceylon	3	4	3
Indonesia			8
Laos	3e	3e	3e
Malaysiac	5	6	4
Maldive Islands		1	2
Mongolia	3	3	4
Pakistan	6	6	6
Philippines	14	19	23
Singapore		3	3
Cyprus	5e	6e	6e
Malta	1	3	5
Israel	6	8	11
Jordan	8	8	10
Kuwait	9	7	5
South Yemen			_d
Average Size	4.88	5.06	5.64

sion in New York at $100,000.[11] That this figure is probably much closer to a minimum than to an average is indicated by Stoessinger's own use of Indonesia's and Mexico's annual expenditures of $270,000 to illustrate the cost of a small mission.[12] Whatever the true minimum cost of a mission, many new nations have believed the cost of a large establishment in New York to be greater than any potential benefits and have kept the size of their missions very small.

[11] John G. Stoessinger, et al., Financing the United Nations System (Washington, D.C.: Brookings Institution, 1964), p. 71.
[12] Ibid., The average size of the Mexican and Indonesian missions during Stoessinger's study was 11.

The more interesting questions relate not strictly to the size of the missions of the new nations but to how they have functioned in the political system of the United Nations. One would expect that to the extent that the permanent mission system represents a functional response to requirements of the United Nations political system the tasks performed by the new nations' missions would duplicate those performed by the missions of other nations. With certain important variations, this has been the case. As was noted earlier, each mission in its capacity as its government's advisor on United Nations affairs plays an important role in shaping the foreign policy of its government. While this is as true for the new nations as for the other Members of the United Nations, there are certain significant distinctions. For the older and generally larger nations with a longer history of diplomatic involvement and consequently more international commitments, the United Nations is seldom the dominant concern of their foreign policy. Recommendations from the missions of these older nations must contend with the recommendations from other elements of their national foreign policy-making apparatus.

Most of the new nations, however, face a significantly different situation. Having been independent for a shorter period, they generally have fewer international commitments. More importantly, for the vast majority of the new nations the United Nations forms both the chief arena and the major instrument of their foreign policy; it is only within the United Nations confines that they can speak and vote on a basis of equality with the world's larger powers. This tends to give a much greater weight in the determination of policy to the advice emanating from the missions of the new nations. This tendency is greatly re-enforced by the limited size of the foreign offices of these new states which, when combined with their geographic separation from New York, effectively limits the scope of their supervision of the missions. In general, the missions of the new nations have significantly fewer instructions as to policy and tactics and consequently have greater latitude of action than the other missions.[13] This degree of discretion does vary, however, according to the nature of the issue under consideration. On colonial issues and questions of economic aid and development, only the vaguest of in-

---

[13] Riggs, *Politics in the United Nations*, p. 20. Hayward R. Alker, Jr., and Bruce M. Russett, *World Politics in the General Assembly* (New Haven, Conn.: Yale University Press, 1965), 218–19. Thomas Hovet, Jr., *Africa in the United Nations* (Evanston, Ill.: Northwestern University Press, 1963), 218–22.

structions are issued to these missions. On the other hand, when the issue involved is one with significant East-West overtones, the missions of most new nations seek to obtain instructions from their governments or, if this is impossible, they abstain. Thus, the missions of the new nations play a much larger role than the missions of other states in determining the shape of their national policy as expressed in the United Nations.

Faced with only limited diplomatic representation abroad, many of the new nations have broadened the traditional function of the permanent mission in collecting and reporting information into a distinctly new function. Unable to afford the costs in money and trained manpower needed to maintain diplomatic representation in over a hundred capitals, these new nations have used the opportunity provided by the concentration in New York of diplomatic representatives from most members of the international community to complete their diplomatic network. The head of a typical mission from a new state may find himself also serving as his country's Ambassador to the United States and de facto representative to 80 or more other states.

Public relations is an important function of all missions, and the new nations provide no exception. In fact, for many new nations the importance of this function is considerably greater than for other states. The United Nations provided these nations with their first opportunity to place before the world, on the basis of equality, their views on the panorama of issues that confront the international community. Before independence they were, in most cases, subjects of racial and political domination with little or no opportunity for expressing their opinions on these issues. The United Nations provided this opportunity, and the new nations have used it with an enthusiasm that threatens to engulf the Organization with new problems and demands. Certainly never before in diplomatic history have the major powers been forced to listen to such a sustained outpouring of the problems, fears, ambitions, and demands of the less powerful nations as has taken place since the new nations entered the United Nations.

The strain placed on the small missions of the new nations is obvious. With, on the average, only slightly more than five diplomatic personnel, these missions must shoulder the burden of representing their nation, in a quite literal sense, before the world. The audience, both governmental and private, available to a permanent mission of a new nation in New York is larger than that in any of the world's capitals. In addition to this heavy representational burden, this mission of a typical new nation bears the responsibility for the successful advancement of its nation's foreign policy in the United Nations as well as advising the government on future policy. The heavy and time-consuming schedule of plenary and committee meetings during Assembly sessions is followed by an almost equally heavy load of *ad hoc* committees when the Assembly is not in session. In all of these tasks the permanent missions of most new nations are not only grossly understaffed in New York but are inadequately backstopped at home with research and other assistance.

Caucusing Groups

Preceding the surge of new nations to membership in the United Nations was the emergence of a rather extensive system of caucusing groups. As early as the San Francisco Conference the pressures of having to decide which states were to serve on the limited-membership organs of the United Nations had resulted in an inchoate system of geographical groupings.[14] By the 1950's under the impetus of an expansion in the concerns of the Organization and the pressures inherent in parliamentary diplomacy toward frequent voting, these informal groupings of Member States were caucusing for periodic discussions of issues before the United Nations.[15] It is these caucus-

[14] Writing in 1961, M. Margaret Ball noted: "The specter of bloc voting has haunted the United Nations since the Charter was first debated at San Francisco. Since then, the influence of certain groups of states in affecting the outcome of elections has occasioned considerable comment, and it has been suggested that the same groups have been inordinately powerful in deciding substantive issues." M. Margaret Ball, "Bloc Voting in the General Assembly," *International Organization*, 5, No. 1 (Feb. 1951), **3.**

[15] Thomas Hovet, Jr., who has done much of the pioneering work in this area, draws a distinction between blocs and caucusing groups. He applies the term bloc only to "a group of states which meets regularly in caucus and the members of which are bound in their votes in the General Assembly by the caucus decision." Only the Soviet group meets Hovet's criteria of a bloc. The other groups which meet regularly in caucus but lack bloc discipline are referred to by Hovet as caucusing groups. Thomas Hovet, Jr., *Bloc Politics in the United Nations* (Cambridge, Mass.: Harvard University Press, 1960), 31–32. However, as both terms refer to states engaged in the same activity, i.e., periodic meetings within some degree of organizational structure, the more inclusive term "caucusing group" is used in this study to cover both the Soviet bloc and the other caucusing groups. For a discussion of the confused terminology in this area, see Arend Lijphart, "The Analysis of Bloc Voting in the General Assembly: A Critique and a Proposal," *The American Political Science Review*, 57, No. 4 (Dec. 1963), 902–904.

ing groups which possess varying degrees of organization but meet with some degree of regularity for the purpose of discussing United Nations issues that form the principal element of the group system in the United Nations political process.[16]

At least four functions of the caucusing groups in the political process of the United Nations can be discerned. A principal function of these groups remains the selection of candidates for election to the limited-membership organs of the United Nations. In an examination of 12 years of the Assembly's electoral practice, Norman J. Padelford found that group association and the concerted political action associated with it played a decisive role in the process.[17] Operating in the context of the "gentlemen's agreements" that have developed for the allocation of many of the elective posts of the Organization, the caucusing groups in their elective function have fulfilled a quasi-official role in the structure of the Organization. Certainly, as the United Nations has grown larger, the only thing preventing the *de facto* disenfranchisement of a large number of Members with respect to the limited-membership organs has been the development of indirect representation through the caucusing groups.

Caucusing groups have also functioned in the United Nations as convenient centers for the exchange and, to varying extents, the harmonization of view on issues before the Organization. Particularly as the cultural, economic, and ideological diversity of the United Nations increased, these groups began to function as important arenas for the preliminary consideration of issues among states possessing a broadly similar outlook. Of decisive importance in the caucusing groups' development of this function was the pressure inherent in the majority voting rules of parliamentary diplomacy to accent the resolution-passing power of the Assembly. As long as resolutions were rare and their passage required unanimity, as in the League, there was little point in engaging in extensive preliminary

---

[16] Various special interest groups, ranging from land-locked states to economically underdeveloped states, may temporarily coalesce for a particular resolution, but as these groupings do not consider the broad range of issues before the United Nations, it seems more appropriate to consider these special interest groups as a normal product of the negotiations process.

[17] Norman J. Padelford, *Elections in the United Nations General Assembly, A Study in Political Behavior* (Cambridge, Mass.: Center for International Studies, Massachusetts Institute of Technology, 1959), 67.

consideration of issues among one's friends. But when these conditions changed, such consideration became incumbent for the effective exercise of political influence.

As greater emphasis was placed on passing Assembly resolutions, the caucusing groups began to assume responsibilities for the initiation and coordination of efforts to obtain action on issues of special interest to their group. Thus, the move at the seventh session to add for the first time to the General Assembly's agenda the question of apartheid in South Africa was initially made in the Afro-Asian caucus, and the accompanying draft resolution was a product of the caucus.[18] To a limited extent this emerging function of the caucusing groups compensates for the lack of clearly defined leadership centers within the Assembly.

Starting with the large membership increases of 1955, the caucusing groups began to play an important tutorial function in the political process of the United Nations. Upon their admission to the Organization, the new Members found themselves immediately welcomed into an ongoing group of similar states, which seemed far less imposing than the Organization as a whole. In exercising this function the caucusing groups contributed significantly to the inculcation of the new Members with the mores and procedures of United Nations diplomacy. More importantly in terms of the exercise of political influence, the caucusing groups helped structure the activity of the new Members. Left to themselves the overworked missions of many of these new Members, when faced with the plenitude of issues dealt with each year, might have diluted their influence in a flurry of undirected activity. Although in no sense able to prevent all of the confusion that inevitably surrounds first immersion into the diplomacy of the Organization, the caucusing groups have fulfilled an important socialization function in assisting the adjustment of new Members to this political process.

As instruments in the exercise of political influence, the caucusing groups had by 1960 developed important functions in regard to elections to United Nations organs, the preliminary discussion of issues, initiating and coordinating action on issues of special interest, and the initiation of new Members into the political mores and folkways

[18] United Nations Documents A/2183, Sept. 15, 1952; A/AC.61/L.8/Rev. 2, Nov. 19, 1952.

of United Nations diplomacy. Although they varied greatly in structure and frequency of meetings, nine caucusing groups[19] could be identified in the United Nations by the beginning of 1960.

The beginnings of the Asian-African group can be traced back to the search by these states in early 1951 for a basis of negotiations to end the Korean conflict.[20] After the Bandung Conference of 1955 and the Suez crisis of 1956, the process of caucusing among the Asian, Arab, and African members of the Organization had developed sufficiently for these states to be identified as a caucusing group.[21] During Assembly sessions the group normally meets at least once a week with the chairmanship rotating alphabetically among the members.[22] Formal organization from the beginning was kept to a minimum with the emphasis being placed upon informal discussions.

The African group emerged as a result of the Accra Conference of Independent African States held in April 1958. The Conference directed the eight African countries who were then United Nations Members to instruct their permanent missions to consult together on matters of common concern.[23] Great pains were taken to emphasize the fact that the African group was remaining in the Asian-African

[19] *Asian-African Group* (29 members, 15 new nations): Afghanistan, Burma, Cambodia, Ceylon, Ethiopia, Ghana, Guinea, India, Indonesia, Iran, Iraq, Japan, Jordan, Laos, Lebanon, Liberia, Libya, Malaya, Morocco, Nepal, Pakistan, Philippines, Saudi Arabia, Sudan, Thailand, Tunisia, Turkey, United Arab Republic, and Yemen.
Arab Group (10 members, 5 new nations): Iraq, Jordan, Lebanon, Libya, Morocco, Sudan, Saudi Arabia, Tunisia, United Arab Republic, and Yemen.
African Group (9 members, 6 nations): Ethiopia, Ghana, Guinea, Liberia, Libya, Morocco, Sudan, Tunisia, and United Arab Republic.
Benelux Group (3 members): Belgium, Luxembourg, and the Netherlands.
Commonwealth Group (10 members, 4 new nations): Australia, Canada, Ceylon, Ghana, India, Malaya, New Zealand, Pakistan, Union of South Africa, and the United Kingdom.
Latin American Group (20 members): Argentina, Bolivia, Brazil, Chile, Colombia, Costa Rica, Cuba, Dominican Republic, Ecuador, El Salvador, Guatemala, Haiti, Honduras, Mexico, Nicaragua, Panama, Paraguay, Peru, Uruguay, and Venezuela.
Scandinavian Group (4 members): Denmark, Iceland, Norway, and Sweden.
Soviet Group (9 members): Albania, Bulgaria, Byelorussian Soviet Socialist Republic, Czechoslovakia, Hungary, Poland, Rumania, Ukrainian Soviet Socialist Republic, and the U.S.S.R.
Western European Group (5 members): Belgium, France, Italy, Luxembourg, and the Netherlands.
[20] Geoffrey Goodwin, "The Expanding United Nations, I.—Voting Patterns," *International Affairs* (London), 36, Apr. 1960, 181.
[21] Israel, China, and South Africa were excluded from the beginning.
[22] Hovet, *Bloc Politics in the United Nations*, pp. 84–85. Samaan Boutros Farajallah, *Le Groupe Afro-Asiatique Dans le Cadre des Nations Unies* (Genève: Libraire Droz, 1963), pp. 13–41.
[23] Hovet, *Africa in the United Nations*, p. 75. Farajallah, *Le Groupe Afro-Asiatique dans le Cadre des Nations Unies*, pp. 41–71. The eight initial members were Ethiopia, Ghana, Liberia, Libya, Morocco, Sudan, Tunisia, and the United Arab Republic.

group and was only constituting a separate group for the purpose of discussing strictly African affairs. Unlike the Asian-African group, the African group chose to establish an elaborate organization bearing the unlikely title of The Informal Permanent Machinery.[24] The Informal Permanent Machinery provides for a Coordinating Body, composed of the permanent representatives of all the African United Nations Members, and a Secretariat, composed of four of the African states elected for two-year terms. Although the procedures of the African group are in theory more precise and formal than those of the larger group, in operation the practice has been so informal "that some of the newer African Members of the United Nations, especially those with small delegations, may be completely unaware that they are part of the formally organized Informal Permanent Machinery."[25]

At the start of 1960 the new nations composed 50 percent or more of the Asian-African group, the African group, and the Arab group, while in the Commonwealth the new nations were just one shy of having a majority. The extent to which the surge of new nations between 1960 and 1968 was funneled into the Afro-Asian and African groups is apparent from the fact that, while in 1959 the Asian-African group comprised only 35.4 percent of the United Nations membership, by the beginning of 1968 this figure had risen to 52 percent. Indicative of the increased African influence on the combined caucus is the shift in names after 1960 from the Asian-African group to the Afro-Asian group. This sharp rise in the size of these two caucusing groups resulting from the admission of the new nations has certainly increased the potential of the Afro-Asian and African caucusing groups to serve as effective instruments of political influence.

Limited-Membership Organs

While the three councils, Security, Economic and Social, and Trusteeship, played a significant role in the political process of the

---

[24] Hovet, *Africa in the United Nations*, pp. 80–82.

[25] *Ibid.*, p. 82. Both Hovet and Farajallah provide in the pages cited excellent discussions of the formal mechanisms and divisions that have developed in these groups. As this present study is devoted primarily to an analysis of the demands made by the new nations on the United Nations and their record in achieving these demands, this subject will not be discussed again here.

United Nations from the very beginning, it was only as the Organization undertook an increased number of tasks and its membership grew that other limited-membership organs gained a significant role in its political process.[26] For the United Nations, limited-membership organs, whether they be called councils, commissions, committees, or subcommittees, provide an effective means of ensuring that certain problems receive continuous attention. It was for this purpose that such bodies as the Committee on South-West Africa and the Eighteen Nation Committee on Disarmament were established by the Assembly. Limited-membership organs also provide an effective means of securing expert advice on technical subjects for the Assembly. Both the Assembly and the Economic and Social Council have been responsible for the proliferation of a host of select bodies, such as the International Law Commission, the Population Commission, and the Statistical Commission, all designed to gain expert opinion on technical questions. While the practice varies as to whether such experts sit in their individual capacity or as representatives of governments, few would argue that nationality plays a minor role in the selection of such bodies.

The General Assembly, the only United Nations organ in which all Members are represented, has been loath to make use of limited-membership bodies to expedite its work while it is in session. In spite of a doubling in its size in 20 years, the Assembly's main committees still remain committees-of-the-whole. This reluctance to approve a large-scale use of select committees during the Assembly's session stems from the understandable desire of many states to protect their "sovereign equality" in the one body of the United Nations in which all states are represented. However, the Assembly's aversion to limited-membership organs is strictly limited to the period in which it is in session. The necessity of providing continuous attention to sensitive subjects and the need for expert advice has forced the Assembly to spawn numerous limited-membership organs.

As instruments of influence within the political process of the Organization, these limited-membership organs play two noteworthy functions. The very fact that such organs are established in order to provide continuous attention to a particular subject ensures

[26] Catherine Senf Manno, "Problems and Trends in the Composition of Nonplenary U.N. Organs," *International Organization*, 19, No. 1 (Winter 1965), 37–55.

TABLE II.3

New Nations' Representation in United Nations Limited-Membership Organs, 1960

State	Security Council	ECOSOC	Trusteeship Council	Subsidiary UN Organs[d]
Cameroun[a]				
Central African Republic[a]				
Chad[a]				
Congo (Brazzaville)[a]				
Congo (Leopoldville)[a]				
Dahomey[a]				1
Gabon[a]				
Ghana				2
Guinea				
Ivory Coast[a]				
Libya				
Madagascar[a]				
Mali[a]				
Morocco				
Niger[a]				
Nigeria[b]				1
Senegal[c]				1
Somali Republic[a]				
Sudan		1		3
Togo[a]				1
Tunisia	1			2
Upper Volta[a]				

[a] Became a Member as of 20 September 1960.
[b] Became a Member as of 7 October 1960.
[c] Became a Member as of 28 September 1960.
[d] Subsidiary UN Organs:
Advisory Committee on Administrative and Budgetary Questions (9)
Committee on Contributions (10)
Commission of Conciliation for the Congo (6)
Sub-Committee on the Situation in Angola (5)
Committee on the Peaceful Uses of Outer Space (24)
UN Commission for Rwanda-Urundi (3)
Special Commission for Rwanda-Urundi (3)
Committee on South West Africa (9)
Committee on Information from Non-Self-Governing Territories (7)
Working Group to Examine Administrative and Budgetary Procedures of UN (15)
Statistical Commission of ECOSOC (15)
Social Commission of ECOSOC (18)
Commission on Human Rights (18)
Commission on the Status of Women (18)
Technical Assistance Committee (24)
Governing Council of Special Fund (18)
International Law Commission (21)
Source: United Nations Yearbook, 1960.

TABLE II.3 *(continued)*

State	Security Council	ECOSOC	Trusteeship Council	Subsidiary UN Organs[d]
Burma			1	1
Cambodia				
Ceylon	1			1
Indonesia				3
Laos				
Federation of Malaya				1
Pakistan				5
Philippines				2
Cyprus[a]				
Israel				1
Jordan				
Total	2	1	1	25
Positions Available	6	18	5	223
Percentage Held by New Nations	33.3	5.6	20.0	11.2

that their members will have a greater opportunity to exercise influence than those states that are not members. For example, when the Committee on South-West Africa was established in 1953 to conduct negotiations with the South African Government and to submit annual reports to the Assembly on conditions in South-West Africa, it was obvious to all that the members of the Committee would play a central role in the United Nations handling of the question. Certainly, as Catherine Manno has noted, the heated arguments in the Assembly over the composition of these limited-membership organs is significant evidence that the Member States believe the bodies wield significant influence.[27]

Not only do these limited-membership organs by their continuous attention to a problem provide greater opportunities for influence, but as they have taken upon themselves the preliminary formulation of United Nations programs and policies they have become useful instruments for influencing the course of final United Nations action. The Commission on Human Rights is but one of many available examples of a limited-membership organ constantly called upon to

[27] *Ibid.*, p. 37.

TABLE II.4

New Nations' Representation in United Nations Limited-Membership Organs, 1961

State	Security Council	ECOSOC	Trusteeship Council	Subsidiary UN Organs[d]
Cameroun				
Central African Republic				
Chad				
Congo (Brazzaville)				
Congo (Leopoldville)				
Dahomey				1
Gabon				
Ghana				3
Guinea				1
Ivory Coast				2
Libya				
Madagascar				2
Mali				1
Mauritania[a]				
Morocco				1
Niger				4
Nigeria				2

[a] Became Member as of 27 October 1961.
[b] Became Member as of 28 September 1961.
[c] Became Member as of 14 December 1961.
[d] Subsidiary UN Organs:
Advisory Committee on Administrative and Budgetary Questions (9)
Committee on Contributions (11)
ENDC (18)
Special Committee of Seventeen (17)
Committee of Conciliation for the Congo (6)
Subcommittee on the Situation in Angola (5)
Committee on the Peaceful Uses of Outer Space (23)
Committee on a UN Capital Development Fund (25)
Five-Member UN Commission for Rwanda-Urundi (5)
UN Special Committee for South West Africa (7)
Committee on Information from Non-Self-Governing Territories (8)
Special Committee of Seven on Territories under Portuguese Administration (7)
Working Group to Examine Administrative and Budgetary Procedures of United Nations (15)
Population Commission of ECOSOC (15)
Social Commission of ECOSOC (18)
Commission on Human Rights (18)
Commission on the Status of Women (18)
Commission on International Commodity Trade (18)
Technical Assistance Committee (24)
Committee for Industrial Development (30)
Governing Council of Special Fund (18)
International Law Commission (21)
Source: *United Nations Yearbook, 1961.*

TABLE II.4 *(continued)*

State	Security Council	ECOSOC	Trusteeship Council	Subsidiary UN Organs[d]
Senegal				
Sierra Leone[b]				
Somali Republic				1
Sudan				5
Tanganyika[c]				1
Togo				2
Tunisia				3
Upper Volta				
Burma			1	4
Cambodia				1
Ceylon	1			4
Indonesia				2
Laos				
Federation of Malaya				2
Mongolia[a]				
Pakistan				7
Philippines				4
Cyprus				1
Israel				3
Jordan		1		2
Total	1	1	1	59
Positions Available	6	18	5	336
Percentage Held by New Nations	16.7	5.6	20.0	17.6

draft preliminary programs for the consideration of the parent body. Since its establishment in 1946 the Commission, composed of only 18 representatives, has prepared for Assembly consideration the Universal Declaration on Human Rights; draft covenants on civil and political rights and on economic, social, and cultural rights; and a series of objective and general comments, conclusions, and recommendations on the status of human rights in the world. The ability of the parent body to amend or to disregard totally its offspring's recommendations remains unquestioned, but the fact remains that those states represented on such organs have the greatest opportunity to exercise influence during the formative stages of drafting a program or a policy.

TABLE II.5

New Nations' Representation in United Nations Limited-Membership Organs, 1962

State	Security Council	ECOSOC	Trusteeship Council	Subsidiary UN Organs[d]
Algeria[a]				1
Burundi[b]				
Cameroun				1
Central African Republic				1
Chad				1
Congo (Brazzaville)				
Congo (Leopoldville)				
Dahomey				1
Gabon				
Ghana	1			2
Guinea				3
Ivory Coast				1
Libya				
Madagascar				3
Mali				3
Mauritania				1
Morocco				1
Niger				
Nigeria				5

[a] Became Member as of 8 October 1962.
[b] Became Member as of 18 September 1962.
[c] Became Member as of 25 October 1962.
[d] Subsidiary UN Organs:
Advisory Committee on Administrative and Budgetary Questions (12)
Committee on Contributions (10)
Committee on Peaceful Uses of Outer Space (28)
Committee of 17 (17)
Preparatory Committee for a United Nations International Co-operation Year (12)
Special Committee on the South African Government's Policies of *Apartheid* (11)
Special Committee on Preparing Plans to Celebrate the Fifteenth Anniversary of the Universal Declaration of Human Rights (20)
UN Special Committee for South West Africa (7)
Committee on Information from Non-Self-Governing Territories (only elected members) (8)
Special Committees on Territories under Portuguese Administration (7)
Statistical Commission of ECOSOC (18)
Social Commission of ECOSOC (21)
Commission on Human Rights of ECOSOC (21)
Commission on International Commodity Trade of ECOSOC (21)
Technical Assistance Committee (30)
Committee for Industrial Development (18)
Governing Council of the Special Fund (18)
Preparatory Committee of UNCTAD (30)
International Law Commission (25)
Source: *United Nations Yearbook, 1962.*

TABLE II.5 (continued)

State	Security Council	ECOSOC	Trusteeship Council	Subsidiary UN Organs[d]
Rwanda[b]				
Senegal		1		4
Sierra Leone				1
Somali Republic				2
Sudan				4
Tanganyika				1
Togo				1
Tunisia				3
Uganda[c]				
Upper Volta				2
Jamaica[b]				
Trinidad and Tobago[b]				
Burma				1
Cambodia				1
Ceylon				6
Indonesia				2
Laos				
Federation of Malaya				3
Mongolia				1
Pakistan				6
Philippines				4
Cyprus				2
Israel				3
Jordan		1		4
Total	1	2	0	75
Positions Available	6	18	2	334
Percentage Held by New Nations	16.7	11.1	0	22.4

Because of their continuing concern with selected problems and their role in the preliminary formulation of United Nations programs and policies, the subsidiary organs are important instruments in the exercise of political influence in the United Nations. The subsidiary organs offered the greatest opportunity for a rapid increase in the representation of the new nations. The membership patterns of the principal organs had been largely set before the entry of the majority of the new nations, and significant changes in these patterns had to wait the enlargement of the principal organs by Charter amendment.

TABLE II.6

New Nations' Representation in United Nations Limited-Membership Organs, 1963

State	Security Council	ECOSOC	Trusteeship Council	Subsidiary UN Organs[d]
Algeria				2
Burundi				
Cameroun				2
Central African Republic				2
Chad				1
Congo (Brazzaville)				
Congo (Leopoldville)				
Dahomey				3
Gabon				1
Ghana	1			5
Guinea				1
Ivory Coast				2
Kenya[a]				
Libya				
Madagascar				5
Mali				2

[a] Became Member as of 16 December 1963.

[b] On 16 September 1963 Sabah and Sarawak joined with the Federation of Malaya (which had become a UN Member on 17 September 1957) to form Malaysia.

[c] Became Member as of 13 May 1963.

[d] Subsidiary UN Organs:

International Law Commission (25)
Advisory Committee on Administrative and Budgetary Questions (12)
Committee on Contributions (10)
Committee on the Peaceful Uses of Outer Space (28)
Committee of 24 (24)
Committee for the International Co-operation Year (12)
Special Committee on the South African Government's Policies of *Apartheid* (11)
UN Fact-Finding Mission to South Viet-Nam (7)
Ad Hoc Committee on Oman (5)
Committee on a United Nations Capital Development Fund (24)
Committee on Information from Non-Self-Governing Territories (elected members only) (7)
Special Committee on Principles of International Law concerning Friendly Relations and Co-operation among States (27)
Population Commission of ECOSOC (21)
Social Commission of ECOSOC (21)
Commission on Human Rights of ECOSOC (21)
Commission on Status of Women (21)
Commission on International Commodity Trade (21)
Technical Assistance Committee (30)
Committee for Industrial Development (30)
Governing Council of Special Fund (18)
Ad Hoc Committee on Co-ordination of Technical Assistance Activities (10)
Preparatory Committee of UNCTAD (32)
  Source: *United Nations Yearbook, 1963.*

TABLE II.6 (continued)

State	Security Council	ECOSOC	Trusteeship Council	Subsidiary UN Organs[d]
Mauritania				
Morocco	1			2
Niger				
Nigeria				8
Rwanda				
Senegal		1		5
Sierra Leone				2
Somali Republic				1
Sudan				3
Tanganyika				1
Togo				
Tunisia				4
Uganda				
Upper Volta				1
Zanzibar[a]				
Jamaica				
Trinidad and Tobago				
Burma				1
Cambodia				1
Ceylon				4
Indonesia				5
Laos				
Malaysia[b]				4
Mongolia				1
Pakistan				5
Philippines	1			6
Cyprus				1
Israel				3
Jordan		1		4
Kuwait[c]				
Total	3	2	0	88
Positions Available	6	18	1	424
Percentage Held by New Nations	50.0	11.1	0	21.3

As shown in Table II.3, the new nations were only sparsely represented on these subsidiary organs in 1960. While the new nations in 1960 composed 33.3 percent of the Organization, they composed in that year only 11.2 percent of the subsidiary organs. During the next four years, as can be seen in Tables II.4 through II.7, the rep-

TABLE II.7

New Nations' Representation in United Nations
Limited-Membership Organs, 1964

State	Security Council	ECOSOC	Trusteeship Council	Subsidiary UN Organs[d]
Algeria		1		4
Burundi				
Cameroun				1
Central African Republic				2
Chad				1
Congo (Brazzaville)				
Congo (Leopoldville)				
Dahomey				1
Gabon				1
Ghana				5
Guinea				2
Ivory Coast	1			2
Kenya				
Libya				
Madagascar				4
Malawi[a]				1
Mali				1
Mauritania				1
Morocco	1			

[a] Became Member as of 1 December 1964.

[b] Following the ratification of articles of union between Tanganyika and Zanzibar on 26 April 1964, the United Republic of Tanganyika and Zanzibar continued as a single Member of the United Nations, later changing its name to the United Republic of Tanzania.

[c] Subsidiary UN Organs:
Advisory Committee on Administrative and Budgetary Questions (12)
Committee on Contributions (10)
Committee on the Peaceful Uses of Outer Space (28)
Committee of 24 (24)
Committee for the International Cooperation Year (12)
Special Committee on the South African Government's Policies of Apartheid (11)
Ad Hoc Committee on Oman (5)
Committee on a United Nations Capital Development Fund (24)
Commission on Human Rights (21)
Commission on International Commodity Trade (21)
Commission on the Status of Women (17)
Population Commission (18)
Social Commission (21)
Statistical Commission (18)
Technical Assistance Committee (30)
Committee for Industrial Development (30)
Committee on Housing, Building, and Planning (21)
Governing Council of Special Fund (24)
Source: United Nations Yearbook, 1964.

TABLE II.7 (continued)

State	Security Council	ECOSOC	Trusteeship Council	Subsidiary UN Organs[d]
Niger				
Nigeria				7
Rwanda				
Senegal		1		4
Sierra Leone				3
Somali Republic				2
Sudan				2
Tanzania[b]				1
Togo				
Tunisia				5
Uganda				
Upper Volta				
Zambia[a]				
Jamaica				
Trinidad and Tobago				
Burma				1
Cambodia				1
Ceylon				1
Indonesia				2
Laos				5
Malaysia				2
Mongolia				1
Pakistan				4
Philippines				5
Cyprus				1
Malta[a]				
Israel				2
Jordan				1
Kuwait				
Total	2	2	0	74
Positions Available	6	18	1	347
Percentage Held by New Nations	33.3	11.1	0	21.0

resentation of the new nations on these bodies increased to slightly over 20 percent, but it lagged significantly behind their proportion of the total membership, which increased to approximately 40 percent during this period. In several of the subsidiary organs dealing with topics of vital interest to the new nations, new nations' representation has even lagged behind the over-all figures. For example, in the last year of its operation, 1963, the Committee on Information from Non-Self-Governing Territories had 14 members of which only 2, or 14.3 percent, were new nations. In 1964 the twenty-one-member Commission on Human Rights numbered among its membership only 2 new nations. The Technical Assistance Committee is a standing committee of the Economic and Social Council responsible for approving the yearly activities of the Expanded Program of Technical Assistance, reviewing its progress and originating the legislation that governs the program. However, in spite of the general interest of the new nations in the operation of the Expanded Program of Technical Assistance, in 1964 only 4 members, or 13.3 percent, of the Technical Assistance Committee's membership of 30 states were new nations. The new nations, because of their under-representation, faced serious obstacles in using many of the subsidiary organs as instruments of political influence.

As for three of the limited-membership organs that are also principal organs of the United Nations—the Security Council, the Economic and Social Council, and the Trusteeship Council—only in the Security Council did the proportion of new nations among the elected members ever reach or exceed their proportion in the Organization. As can be seen from Tables II.3 through II.7, new nations were totally absent from the Trusteeship Council in three of the five years examined. Similarly, the number of new nations that were members of the Economic and Social Council during this period was at best a token representation.

Negotiations

In the assertion of demands and in exercising influence to obtain them, negotiations play a central role. The very nature of United Nations diplomacy with its heavy emphasis on the drafting of resolutions, amendments, and reports to be voted on by one or the other of its organs ensures this key role for negotiations.[28] In spite of the heavy schedule of public meetings associated with United

---

[28] "The public debate, and the decisions reached gain added significance when the attitudes presented in public result from practically uninterrupted informal contacts and negotiations. Thus, it does not belittle the importance of the formal proceedings in the General Assembly, the Councils, and other United Nations organs if it is understood that, to an increasing extent, their role has come to provide for public confrontation of views which have developed in negotiations under other forms, and for the registration of a resulting consensus, or, when this has not been achieved of a

Nations activity, the negotiating process is overwhelmingly private. Hadwen and Kaufmann in discussing the role of personal relations in the private meetings in which most negotiations are conducted wrote,

In such meetings personal relations are paramount. If a delegate is to be effective, it is necessary for him to know and approach the right person in the right delegation at the right time. If this approach is made under conditions of pressure and decisions are urgent, close personal understanding between the individuals concerned is of special importance.[29]

The private nature of the negotiation process reflects the desire of the participants to ensure their freedom of maneuver. However, the ability of any of the participants even in private negotiations to force an issue to a public test of strength through the simple device of pushing for a vote on the question gives to United Nations negotiation an element of openness not always found in diplomatic negotiation outside the confines of the Organization. Regardless of a nation's devotion to private negotiation, the possibility of an ultimate public test makes it incumbent upon all states to maintain a rather close correlation between public and private positions for fear of inviting such a public test, which would publicize the discrepancy.

Negotiations are strongly influenced by the orientation of most activity toward the ultimate adoption of a resolution. A general tendency toward compromise emanates from the fact that, with the exception of a few matters, the United Nations can only make recommendations. Those who favor a given course of action desire to see it supported by the largest number of states possible in order that the recommendation may have the maximum weight behind it. On the other hand, those opposed to a given course of action would prefer, in most cases, not to be forced to take a public stand against the majority of the United Nations. These two factors combine to produce an inherent bias toward compromise in the negotiation process of the Organization.

---

difference of opinion with the relative support apparent from the votes." United Nations General Assembly *Official Records*, 14th Session, Supplement No. 1A (A/4132/Add. 1, Aug. 1959), "Introduction to the Annual Report of the Secretary-General on the Work of the Organization, June 16, 1958–June 15, 1959," p. 2.

[29] Hadwen and Kaufmann, *How United Nations Decisions Are Made*, p. 36. These authors, both of whom served as members of permanent missions, lay heavy emphasis on the private, informal nature of United Nations negotiations. This opinion is shared by all observers of this aspect of United Nations diplomacy. Also see Pederson, "National Representation in the United Nations," *International Organization*, 15, No. 2 (Spring 1961), 264.

In the negotiating process the new nations, in common with other small powers, lack the resources to pose creditable threats of direct action vis-a-vis other states as a means of gaining support within the Organization. Also, there is little in the way of tangible benefits outside the Organization that the new nations can offer in exchange for support. However, there are two potent bargaining devices that the new nations do have in the negotiating process. First, on many issues in the Assembly the new nations have the opportunity to play the great powers off against each other. The reasoning behind this strategy is usually that, if the West (East) does not support resolution X and the East (West) does, then the West (East) will suffer a permanent loss of influence with the new nations. Secondly, the large number of votes commanded by the new nations on those issues on which they are relatively united provides them with a strong bargaining device. It has become very much a quixotic effort to oppose the new nations flatly on questions such as decolonization and economic development where they already have sufficient votes to secure the adoption of their proposals. The wiser negotiating strategy for the other Members has been to support these initiatives of the new nations while bargaining on the details of the proposal. The ultimate appeal to numbers in the parliamentary process of the Organization provides the new nations with a strong negotiating position on those issues on which they are united.

With the rapid expansion of United Nations membership produced by the sudden emergence of the new nations, negotiations became more important and at the same time more difficult. With larger membership the public bodies of the Organization became submerged in their own debate, and concerted action could be arranged only through private negotiations. The effective use of private negotiations as an instrument of political influence requires, however, an intimate knowledge of the personnel and positions of the other missions. This knowledge can only be gained through prolonged contact. Many of the new missions operating with fewer than five people simply have lacked the personnel to acquire this experience. On the other hand, even the large missions of the older states have found this sudden inflow of so many new states difficult to cope with in terms of developing the personal contacts necessary for private negotiations.

Resolutions and Voting

The remaining two instruments of influence to be surveyed in this chapter exist in tandem in the United Nations political system. In the final analysis it is the procedure of adopting formal conclusions embodied in a resolution through some form of majority voting that distinguishes United Nations diplomacy from the diplomacy practiced in the various capitals of the world.

A draft resolution submitted either by a single state or a group of states represents in its clearest form the policy preferences of its sponsors. In the United Nations political system, resolutions are the necessary instruments for translating policy preferences into United Nations decisions and are viewed as the logical end toward which much of the activity of the Member States is directed. The activities of the permanent missions, the caucusing groups, and the various organs of the United Nations all bear the imprint of this ultimate "parliamentary test."

Most resolutions are drafted in New York on the basis of guide lines approved by the national governments with the right of final approval being held by the home government. While individual sponsorship allows a state to put forward a draft resolution without the necessity of accepting compromises in the drafting stage, the political impact gained from a long list of co-sponsors is such that few delegations, other than the major powers, are willing to submit a draft without at least a few co-sponsors.[30]

As an instrument of political influence a draft resolution has the advantage of shifting the terms of debate and negotiations toward the positions of the draft's sponsors and providing a bargainable commodity. Whereas United Nations discussions and negotiations tend to have an amorphous quality before the introduction of draft resolutions, they tend to take on something of the crass air of the market place after their introduction. Both qualities are to a large extent the products of parliamentary diplomacy. In the period before a draft is introduced, no state is willing to reveal fully its position for fear of robbing itself of potential bargaining power in the drafting process. On the other hand, once a draft or drafts are introduced

---

[30] For an interesting study of the strategy of sponsorship of General Assembly resolutions, see A. Glenn Mower, Jr., "The Sponsorship of Proposals in the United Nations General Assembly," *Western Political Quarterly*, 15 (Dec. 1962), 661–66.

the eventual necessity of obtaining a two-thirds majority "on important questions" for the adoption of any resolution exerts a strong force toward compromise. It is this drive to compromise in an atmosphere where "*the why* and *the how* is often much more important than *the what*" that gives a "nit-picking" air to much United Nations activity.[31]

Permeating all of this activity is the prospect of the ultimate "parliamentary test" in which all members of the Assembly have but one vote. When United Nations activity in the form of resolutions is viewed as the logical product of the Organization's political system, then each state's vote is its final instrument of influence within the system.

[31] Hadwen and Kaufmann, *How United Nations Decisions Are Made*, p. 49. Emphasis is that of the authors.

Chapter III

THE DIRECTION OF DEMANDS

With the fundamental rearrangement in the political composition of the Organization brought about by the emergence of the new nations, their concerns and the intensity with which they pursue them assume considerable importance.[1] Of course, the judging of the extent to which the new nations have successfully exercised their influence in the system demands a knowledge of the goals they have pursued and their relative evaluation of each.

However, an accurate determination of the demands articulated by the new nations and the strength of their commitment to these demands poses several problems. Sole reliance on extensive interviewing of mission personnel in order to determine these demands makes one all too dependent upon the fallible memories of heavily burdened personnel. This method also presents the monumental task of determining the extent of bias introduced by the personal perspectives of those interviewed. Were the responses unduly affected by the natural tendency of those interviewed to conceive of their own area of responsibility as the most important? To what extent is bias introduced by the tendency to give "correct replies" rather than actual positions?[2]

[1] As noted in Chapter I, Ernst Haas has stressed the importance to trend analysis of international systems and to the eventual construction of an empirical theory of international organization of more careful analysis of the shifting pattern of demands placed before international organizations as a result of environmental changes. Haas, "The Comparative Study of the United Nations," *World Politics*, 12, No. 2 (Jan. 1960), 278–303. David Easton has also selected the demands made on a political system as a key variable in his construction of a general theory of political systems. Of particular relevance are Easton, *A Framework for Political Analysis*, pp. 112–17; and David Easton, *A Systems Analysis of Political Life* (New York: John Wiley & Sons, 1965), pp. 37–40, 57–84.

[2] For a discussion of this problem in interviewing United Nations delegates, see

Another method of discerning the pattern and intensity of concern would be to examine the behavior of the Members as reflected in the number of times each state speaks in the Assembly and its main committees on a given topic.[3] This method rests on the proposition that a state will speak most often on those topics that concern it most. While this method avoids having to rely upon the memories of delegates, it is not a completely satisfactory solution. For the major powers, such as the United States and the U.S.S.R., who feel compelled to speak on everything that comes before the Organization, this index would probably fail to adequately discriminate between topics. Also some delegates are simply very loquacious and will talk on any and everything irrespective of their degree of concern for the topic.[4] While not completely satisfactory, and no method short of reading the cables and instructions for each mission is ever likely to be so, the index of intensity of demands derived from a speech count seems to be the least unsatisfactory.[5] It allows an observer to construct an index of intensity for any or all Members on the broad panorama of issues faced by the Organization and to compare changes over time without giving undue weight to the memory and bias of the participants.[6] Although un-

---

Jack Ernest Vincent, *The Caucusing Groups of the United Nations—An Examination of Their Attitudes toward the Organization* Arts and Sciences Studies, Social Studies Series, No. 12 (Stillwater, Okla.: Oklahoma State University, 1965), p. 139.

[3] This method was first applied to the United Nations in Bruce M. Russett, *Trends in World Politics* (New York: The Macmillan Company, 1965), pp. 70–71; and in Alker and Russett, *World Politics in the General Assembly*, pp. 191–217. Alker and Russett also constructed a more complicated measure of intensity based on whether a delegate spoke, how many times he spoke, whether he introduced resolutions or amendments on the topic. However, when they compared the results of this index with those of the speech count such a high correlation, $r = .88$, was found that the more complicated index was abandoned in favor of the speech count. *Ibid.*, pp. 192–93.

The reason for choosing the General Assembly and its main committees is that it is only in these bodies that all the Members are represented and hence have an opportunity to express their views.

[4] While not absent, the high correlation Alker and Russet obtained between the speech count and a more inclusive index indicates that the bias introduced by the personal loquaciousness of the delegates is not great.

[5] The speech count used in the present study is based on the *Official Records* of the General Assembly as indexed in *Index to Proceedings of the General Assembly*, Fifteenth–Twenty-first Sessions (New York: United Nations, 1961–1966). For purposes of this count, when a speech dealt with more than one topic, each topic was counted as a separate speech.

[6] As the membership and work load of the Organization have increased, it has become virtually impossible during the course of a single research project to conduct personal interviews with responsible officials from every mission. This index does provide a means around this obstacle. Unfortunately, this same increase in membership and work load has made the construction of this index more onerous.

doubtedly an abstraction of the actual pattern and intensity of concerns held by any nation or group of nations, this index provides an extremely useful tool for discerning the nature of the actual pattern and for measuring trends. It will be coupled with an analysis in the following chapter of the actual substantive demands made under each topic and the extent of success in achieving their adoption.

Topics of Concern

The priorities of the new nations are strikingly revealed in Tables III.1, III.2, III.3. Based on an analysis of all speeches made in plenary and main committee meetings of the fifteenth through twenty-first sessions of the General Assembly, this data reveals the extent to which the interest of these countries was focused upon essentially two demands, decolonization and economic aid and development.[7] At six of the seven sessions speeches on decolonization topics exceeded in number any other single topic. If one combines the closely related topics of decolonization and South Africa into one category, this dominance becomes quite impressive. For example, at the sixteenth session the number of speeches in this category, 1131, was more than four times as great as the nearest rival, and in fact, exceeded by approximately 35 percent the combined total of the other eight key issues. The relatively large concern with human rights questions indicated by a speech total that ranged during six sessions from approximately 20 to 65 percent of the decolonization level is partially deceptive. As will be seen in a subsequent chapter, where attention is focused upon the substantive demands made under each topic, much of the new nations' concern with human rights questions is directly related to their anticolonial drive.

The second priority demand of the new nations indicated by this method of analysis centers on economic aid and development. The interest in economic aid and development as measured by this method increased considerably during this period. Between the fifteenth and twenty-first sessions the number of speeches on economic aid and development increased by 75 percent. More significant

[7] The results obtained for the 19th session must be viewed with caution. The deadlock resulting from the Organization's financial crisis prevented the main committees from from meeting and focused the discussion that did take place largely on the Organization's inability to act.

TABLE III.1

Analysis of the Number of Speeches by the New Nations on Ten Key Issues at Three Sessions of the General Assembly[a]

Topic	Number of Speeches
	0 100 200 300 400 500 600 700 800 900 1000

Fifteenth Assembly

Topic	Number of Speeches
Decolonization	‖‖‖‖‖‖‖‖‖‖‖‖‖‖‖‖‖‖‖‖‖‖‖‖‖‖‖‖ 511
South Africa	‖‖‖‖‖‖‖‖ 156
Economic Aid	‖‖‖‖‖‖‖‖‖‖‖‖‖‖‖‖‖‖‖‖‖ 390
Congo	‖‖‖‖‖‖‖ 137
Human Rights	‖‖‖‖‖‖ 111
Rep. in UN Organs	‖‖‖‖‖‖ 106
Disarmament	‖‖‖‖ 75
Refugees	‖‖‖ 58
China	‖ 21
International Law	‖‖ 55

Sixteenth Assembly

Topic	Number of Speeches
Decolonization	‖‖ 928
South Africa	‖‖‖‖‖‖‖‖‖‖‖ 203
Economic Aid	‖‖‖‖‖‖‖‖‖‖‖‖‖‖ 264
Congo	‖‖‖ 62
Human Rights	‖‖‖‖‖‖‖‖‖‖ 179
Rep. in UN Organs	‖‖‖‖‖ 93
Disarmament	‖‖‖‖‖‖‖ 143
Refugees	‖‖‖‖ 70
China	‖‖ 40
International Law	‖‖ 44

Seventeenth Assembly

Topic	Number of Speeches
Decolonization	‖‖‖‖‖‖‖‖‖‖‖‖‖‖‖‖‖‖‖‖‖‖‖‖‖‖‖‖‖‖‖‖‖‖‖‖ 661
South Africa	‖‖‖‖‖‖‖‖‖‖‖ 203
Economic Aid	‖‖‖‖‖‖‖‖‖‖‖‖‖‖‖‖‖‖‖‖‖‖‖‖‖‖‖‖‖‖‖‖‖‖ 600
Congo	‖ 28
Human Rights	‖‖‖‖‖‖‖‖‖‖‖ 201
Rep. in UN Organs	‖‖‖ 66
Disarmament	‖‖‖‖‖‖‖‖ 161
Refugees	‖‖‖‖‖ 98
China	‖‖ 44
International Law	‖‖ 68

[a] Speech count includes all plenary and main committee meetings. See Appendix A for the speech count by State.

TABLE III.2

Analysis of the Number of Speeches by the New Nations on Ten Key Issues at Two Sessions of the General Assembly[a]

Topic	Number of Speeches
	0 100 200 300 400 500 600 700 800 900 1000
	Eighteenth Assembly
Decolonization	‖‖‖‖‖‖‖‖‖‖‖‖‖‖‖‖‖‖‖‖‖‖‖‖‖‖‖‖‖‖ 554
South Africa	‖‖‖‖‖‖‖‖‖ 211
Economic Aid	‖‖‖‖‖‖‖‖‖‖‖‖‖‖‖‖‖‖‖‖‖‖‖‖‖‖‖‖‖ 543
Congo	‖‖‖ 62
Human Rights	‖‖‖‖‖‖‖‖‖‖‖ 259
Rep. in UN Organs	‖‖‖‖‖‖‖‖ 185
Disarmament	‖‖‖‖‖‖‖‖‖ 201
Refugees	‖‖‖ 74
China	‖‖ 43
International Law	‖‖‖‖ 93
	Nineteenth Assembly
Decolonization	‖‖‖‖‖‖‖ 153
South Africa	‖‖‖ 65
Economic Aid	‖‖‖‖‖‖‖ 152
Congo	‖‖ 30
Human Rights	‖ 14
Rep. in UN Organs	‖ 37
Disarmament	‖‖‖‖‖‖ 135
Refugees	‖ 18
China	‖‖ 30
International Law	‖ 5

[a] Speech count includes all plenary and main committee meetings. See Appendix A for the speech count by State.

in determining the future trend of demands is that whereas speeches on decolonization declined by 28.2 percent at the seventeenth session from the level at the sixteenth session, speeches on economic aid and development increased by 128.1 percent during this same period. As the liquidation of the colonial empires reaches its conclusion, concern over economic developments clearly appears to be destined to assume the role of the dominant demand made by the new nations on the Organization.

On no issues other than decolonization and economic development did the new nations in general place strong and consistent demands

TABLE III.3

Analysis of the Number of Speeches by the New Nations on Ten Key Issues at Two Sessions of the General Assembly[a]

Topic	Number of Speeches										
	0	100	200	300	400	500	600	700	800	900	1000

Twentieth Assembly

Topic	
Decolonization	||||||||||||||||||||||||||||||||||||||||||||||||||| 624
South Africa	|||||||||||||||||| 204
Economic Aid	|||||||||||||||||||||||||||||||||||||||||||||||||||||| 663
Congo		2
Human Rights	||||||||||||||||||||||||||||||||| 404
Rep. in UN Organs	|||||54
Disarmament	||||||||||||||||||||| 251
Refugees	||||||| 74
China	||||||||||| 116
International Law	|||||||||||| 131

Twenty-First Assembly

Topic	
Decolonization	||||||||||||||||||||||||||||||||||||||||||||||||||||||||||||||||||||||||||| 896
South Africa	||||||||||||||||||| 207
Economic Aid	|||||||||||||||||||||||||||||||||||||||||||||||||||||||||||||| 723
Congo		3
Human Rights	||||||||||||||||||||||||||||||||||||||| 459
Rep. in UN Organs	|||||56
Disarmament	||||||||||||||||| 195
Refugees	|||||||| 87
China	||||||| 70
International Law	||||||||||| 122

[a] Speech count includes all plenary and main committee meetings. See Appendix A for the speech count by State.

on the Organization. For example, at the fifteenth session 54.4 percent of the new nations did not deliver a single speech on disarmament, and as late as the twenty-first session 20 percent of these nations failed to speak on disarmament.[8] Similarly, 69.7 percent of the new nations did not speak on any of the international law topics before the fifteenth Assembly, and at the twenty-first session 32.6 percent of these nations did not speak on this subject. Whereas only one new nation did not speak on decolonization and economic development at the seventeenth session, 39.6 percent avoided the Congo,

[8] These figures are derived from the speech count contained in Appendix A.

51.2 percent the question of representation in United Nations organs, 37.2 percent the question of Chinese representation, and 32.6 percent avoided refugee questions.

This method of analysis yields a distinct picture of a very intense but limited range of concern on the part of the new nations. During the period under consideration, the new nations have concentrated their attention in the United Nations almost exclusively upon questions of decolonization and economic development. This pattern of concern was placed with great forcefulness before the Organization. In a series of twenty interviews conducted in 1967 and 1968 split equally between the delegates of new nations and non-new nations, the author found that the pattern of concerns revealed by the analysis of speeches was the same pattern perceived by these delegates. Each when asked to rank the top three concerns of those states that have gained independence and entered the Organization since 1945 ranked either decolonization or South Africa first or second, followed closely by economic and social development. Interestingly, in over half the cases the immediate comment following this ranking was an unsolicited description of the rising importance of economic development questions and the belief that the wave of the future lies in this area.

With regard to the primacy of the necessity to eradicate colonialism, the Ghanian representative articulated a view at the sixteenth session that would be subscribed to by almost all of the new nations.

In our view, colonialism is the greatest evil of the modern world, the source of all the troubles which presently afflict mankind. It is the root-cause of the arms race and the problem of disarmament. Colonialism and neo-colonialism are a perpetual threat to the peace and security of the world. Colonialism is the cause of war and conflict among nations and is, therefore, the greatest danger to world peace.[9]

Economic development was also viewed as being related to larger world perspectives. The Pakistani delegate, Zulfiqar Ali Bhutto, underlined this connection when he told the Assembly:

There are two aspects of this difference in the standards of living which are of crucial importance to the world today: first, that the disparity is not

[9] Mr. Ado-Adjei (Ghana), United Nations General Assembly *Official Records*, 16th Session, 1015th meeting (Sept. 20, 1961), para. 54.

only great but growing; and, secondly, that the peoples of the under-developed countries, living so long at levels of bare survival, are no longer prepared to accept such conditions of life as immutable. A revolution of rising expectations is sweeping through these countries. Fatalism and resignation have given way to expectation and demand.[10]

It is with this translation of the pattern of concern revealed in this chapter into specific demands for action that the next chapters concern themselves.

[10] United Nations General Assembly *Official Records*, 15th Session, 878th meeting (Sept. 29, 1960), para. 27.

Chapter IV

THE EXTENT OF INFLUENCE—I

The United Nations is a multipurpose organization called to consider and act on a broad range of problems. It is now a common occurrence for the agenda of the annual session of the General Assembly to contain over 100 items. On the other hand, political influence is a highly discrete quality that cannot be expected to remain uniform over as broad a range of issues as that dealt with by the United Nations. These two factors—the multipurpose nature of the Organization and the discrete nature of political influence—ensure that the extent of the political influence of the new nations cannot be determined from a study of two or three major issues. While the case study in Chapter VI will demonstrate the methods and means of exercising influence, it does not go very far in demonstrating either the scope of this influence or the consistency with which it is exercised. To obtain this depth and perspective, another type of analysis is needed. For this purpose the multitude of issues dealt with by the United Nations has been separated into five categories: decolonization, economic aid and development, East-West issues, the human rights area, and organizational questions.

Two of these issue categories, decolonization and human rights, will be considered individually in this chapter with attention focused upon major questions in the period 1960–1967, the positions of the new nations, and the development of these questions in relation to the alternatives advocated by the new nations.

Decolonization

In the hierarchy of priorities of the new nations, no issue exceeds in importance their commitment to securing a speedy and complete end of Western colonialism. While their drive in the United Nations to advance this goal is certainly less important to its achievement than the underlying surge of nationalism in Africa and Asia, it has been the central focus of the diplomacy of the new nations in the United Nations. It is with this topic, therefore, that one expects to find the most intense and consistent exercise of political influence by the new nations.

The Declaration and the Special Committee   The systematic decolonization campaign of the new nations can be dated from their efforts in 1960 to secure Assembly adoption of their draft Declaration on Colonialism. The campaign succeeded at the following session of the Assembly in securing the establishment of a Special Committee to examine the implementation of the Declaration. Since both of these efforts will be extensively analyzed in Chapter VI, attention here will focus upon the later activities of the new nations in the Special Committee.

The first task faced by the Special Committee was to decide exactly what its broad Assembly mandate meant in terms of operational procedures.[1] In the context of parliamentary diplomacy the Committee's operation would be governed by rules of procedure "subject to tactical manipulation to advance or oppose a point of view"; hence the determination of the rules of procedure could decisively affect the future role of the Special Committee.[2] During the Committee's discussion of the procedures to be followed, which lasted from February 20 until March 5, 1962, two alternative positions emerged. The administering powers endeavored to model the Special Committee's rules of procedure on those of the Committee on Information from Non-Self-Governing Territories.[3] These states

[1] General Assembly Resolution 1654(XVI), Nov. 27, 1961, para. 5. "Directs the committee to carry out out its task by employment of all means which it will have at its disposal within the framework of the procedures and modalities which it shall adopt for the proper discharge of its functions."

[2] Dean Rusk, "Parliamentary Diplomacy—Debate vs. Negotiation," *World Affairs Interpreter,* 26, No. 2 (Summer 1955), 121–22.

[3] The 17 members named to the Special Committee in 1961 were Austrialia, Cambodia, Ethiopia, India, Italy, Madagascar, Mali, Poland, Syria, Tanganyika, Tunisia, U.S.S.R., United Kingdom, United States, Uruguay, Venezuela, and Yugoslavia. When its membership was increased to its present strength of 24, the following additional members were named: Bulgaria, Chile, Denmark, Iran, Iraq, Ivory Coast, and Sierra Leone.

wished to see the committee develop as another center for the collection and discussion of information about the colonial areas. Particular objection was lodged by the administering powers to all proposals that the Special Committee design its rules of procedure to accommodate country-by-country studies followed by specific recommendations to the responsible administering power. Sir Hugh Foot, in placing before the Special Committee the particularly strong British rejection of all proposals for investigations of individual countries, said: "The United Kingdom did not agree with the proposal to take up countries one-by-one. They should be considered category by category or according to the area in which they are situated."[4] The United States supported the British on the point that "the Committee's main task should be to discuss what measures were appropriate in particular types of situations."[5] Also objectionable to the administering powers were all proposals that the Special Committee should be able to adopt resolutions by formal voting; they vehemently opposed the idea that the Special Committee might be able to dispatch visiting missions or receive petitions without the approval of the administering power concerned.[6] On the other hand, the new nations recognized the importance of this initial decision and were not disposed to yield the victory gained in the Assembly.

The new nations on the Special Committee—particularly Madagascar, Mali, Tanganyika, and Tunisia—sought the adoption of rules of procedure which would allow the Special Committee to become an active force in increasing the tempo of decolonization and provide it with the means for directly pressuring any recalcitrant administering power. To this end they sought procedures that would allow the Special Committee to pass resolutions addressed to specific administering powers, to send visiting missions to colonial areas and to receive petitioners.

This important procedural battle was finally won by the new nations. It was agreed among the committee's members that the chairman, C. S. Jha of India, should summarize what he felt to be

---

[4] United Nations Document A/AC. 109/SR. 8, Apr. 5, 1962, 4.
[5] United Nations Document A/AC. 109/SR. 2, Apr. 5, 1962, 4.
[6] *Ibid.*; United Nations Document A/AC. 109/SR. 5, Apr. 5, 1962, 16; Taieb Slim, "The Work of the Committee of 24" *Annual Review of United Nations Affairs 1963–1964.* Edited by Richard N. Swift. (New York: Oceana by arrangement with New York University Press, 1965), 1–12.

the consensus of the Special Committee as to the rules of procedure
to be followed; this statement, with any reservations and explana-
tions that members might wish to add, would form the basis of the
committee's future work.[7] Mr. Jha noted that, while it was the hope
of all members that agreement could be reached without voting, "it
was understood, however, that voting procedures would be resorted
to whenever any member felt that the procedure was necessary in
any particular case."[8] Most members agreed that the Special Committee should immediately proceed to the study of three or four
countries and that priority should be given to the territories of
Africa. "It was understood that petitioners would be heard at the
discretion of the Committee and not as a matter of course and that
the Committee would have the discretion to screen petitions."[9] On
the delicate question of visiting missions, the Committee recognized
"the need for securing the cooperation of the Administering Powers
concerned."[10] This victory of the new nations was formalized at the
sixteenth session of the Assembly when in the course of enlarging
the Special Committee considerable attention was devoted to its
procedural difficulties. The Assembly concluded by accepting the
Committee's methods and inviting it "to continue to seek the most
suitable ways and means for the speedy and total application of the
Declaration to all territories which have not yet attained independence."[11]

Southern Rhodesia Rather than attempt to cover the Special
Committee's activities with regard to the approximately 70 territories that it considered between its first meeting on February 10,
1962 and the end of 1967, Southern Rhodesia will be used to illustrate the use to which the new nations have put the Special Committee in their drive to abolish colonialism. As the first territory
considered by the Special Committee and the one that has received
the most sustained attention of this body, Southern Rhodesia is
particularly suited to this purpose.

Situated in south central Africa, Southern Rhodesia is the northern

[7] United Nations Document A/AC. 109/SR. 6, Apr. 4, 1962, 5–6.
[8] United Nations Document A/5238, Oct. 8, 1962, 18.
[9] *Ibid.*
[10] *Ibid.*
[11] General Assembly Resolution 1810 (XVII), Dec. 17, 1962.

bastion of the white-dominated third of Africa. With the Zambezi River as its northern frontier, it sprawls over 150,000 square miles of rich agricultural country populated by 3,610,000 Africans and only 221,500 Europeans. Although first seized as a private venture by Cecil Rhodes in the late nineteenth century, Southern Rhodesia passed in 1923 to the United Kingdom as a self-governing territory with control of the territory's foreign relations resting with Britain. From 1953 until 1963 white-dominated Southern Rhodesia was part of an uneasy federation with Northern Rhodesia and Nyasaland, two territories having significant African control of their governments. This British-sponsored federation broke up in 1963 largely over the antagonistic racial policies of the Southern Rhodesian government. With the dissolution of the federation, Northern Rhodesia and Nyasaland quickly gained independence as Zambia and Malawi, while Southern Rhodesia continued as a self-governing but nonindependent British territory. The Southern Rhodesia Constitution of December 6, 1961, which had eliminated most of the residual powers formerly held by the United Kingdom while holding only the most tenuous promises for any meaningful African participation in the government, served as the constituent document of the territory until its unilateral declaration of independence in 1965.

The Special Committee initially turned its attention to Southern Rhodesia at the request of the General Assembly. At its sixteenth session the Assembly, in spite of strong Western and Latin American resistance, requested that the newly formed Special Committee "consider whether the territory of Southern Rhodesia has attained a full measure of self-government."[12] After devoting 15 of its first 26 meetings to Southern Rhodesia, the Special Committee established, with Western acquiescence, a Subcommittee on Southern Rhodesia. This subcommittee, composed of India, Mali, Syria, Tanganyika, Tunisia, and Venezuela, immediately undertook to establish contact with the British Government to discuss the future of the territory. After holding talks with the British Government in London between April 7 and April 14, 1962, the Subcommittee recommended that "the situation in Southern Rhodesia should be considered by the General Assembly at its resumed sixteenth session

---

[12] United Nations General Assembly Resolution 1745 (XVI), Feb. 23, 1962. The vote on this resolution was 57 in favor and 21 opposed with 24 abstentions.

or at a special session, as a matter of urgency."[13] The Special Committee, over the objections of Australia, Italy, the United Kingdom, and the United States, endorsed this recommendation and further recommended Assembly consideration of a draft resolution placed before the Special Committee by Ethiopia, Mali, and Tunisia. This draft resolution recommended by the Special Committee declared that Southern Rhodesia was a non-self-governing territory within the meaning of Chapter XI of the Charter and requested Britain to take immediate steps to set aside the 1961 Constitution, to restore civil liberties, to immediately apply the 1960 Declaration on Colonialism, and to repeal all laws that sanctioned racial discrimination.[14]

Over sustained Western objection, the Assembly in June 1962 took up the Special Committee's recommendations. The British position, which had been placed previously before the Subcommittee and the Special Committee, was reiterated before the Assembly. Resting on the nuances of British constitutional practices, the British contended that they had no power to annul the Rhodesian Constitution and that because it was a self-governing territory neither the United Kingdom nor the United Nations had a right to discuss its internal affairs. A 39-power Afro-Asian draft was offered to the Assembly as a moderate alternative to the more sweeping draft recommended by the Special Committee. While the 39-power draft affirmed that Southern Rhodesia was a non-self-governing territory within the meaning of Chapter XI of the Charter, it avoided calling directly upon Britain to annul the Rhodesian Constitution. However, the 39-power draft did request Britain "to undertake urgently the convening of a constitutional conference . . . which would ensure the rights of the majority of the people in conformity with the principles of the Charter of the United Nations and the Declaration on the granting of independence to colonial countries and peoples . . ."[15] The Assembly debate revealed that a clear majority of the membership felt that Britain had a moral obligation, which should transcend any constitutional limitations, to protect the African majority from the white-dominated government of Southern Rhodesia. The compromise draft was overwhelmingly approved by a vote of 73 in favor

---

[13] United Nations Document A/5124, May 21, 1962, Annex I, para. 45.
[14] Ibid., Annex III.
[15] United Nations Document A/L.386/Rev. 1 and Add. 1–4, June 18, 1962, June 19, 1962.

to one against, with 27 abstaining and Portugal and Britain present but not voting.[16] Only South Africa voted no in the face of this overwhelming Afro-Asian, Soviet, and Latin American coalition.

Neither the British nor the Southern Rhodesian whites were moved to change their previously announced positions by the Assembly's action. Faced with this intransigence, the new nations decided upon seeking another Assembly resolution before the first elections could be held at the end of 1962 under the 1961 Constitution. In a display of power that both angered and awed many delegates, the Afro-Asian nations forced a closure of Fourth Committee debate on their draft on October 31, 1962, only one day after its introduction, before all states had an opportunity to speak and brought the draft before plenary that night. This draft called upon Britain to secure "the immediate suspension of the enforcement" of the 1961 Constitution, "the immediate convening of a constitutional convention," and "the immediate extension to the whole population, without discrimination, of the full and unconditional exercise of their basic political rights . . ."[17] In both its tone and substance this draft went further than the resolution on the same subject approved by the Assembly four months earlier, but the Assembly approved it on the same evening it was brought before the plenary session. In fact, the vote this time was even more lopsided, with 81 in favor, two opposed, 19 abstaining, and the United Kingdom not participating.[18] Again there was no response from the United Kingdom other than the familiar reply that Southern Rhodesia had been self-governing since 1923 and neither Britain nor the United Nations had a right to intervene in its internal affairs.

In March 1963 the Special Committee returned to the question of Southern Rhodesia and again dispatched a Subcommittee to London for talks with the British. On the basis of its London visit this Subcommittee, composed of Mali, Uruguay, Syria, Sierra Leone, Tanganyika, and Tunisia, recommended consideration of the question of Southern Rhodesia at a special session of the Assembly, drew the attention of the Security Council to the deteriorating situation

[16] United Nations General Assembly *Official Records*, 16th Session, 1121st meeting (June 28, 1962), para. 17. United Nations General Assembly Resolution 1747(XVI), June 28, 1962.

[17] United Nations Document A/C.4/L.753, Oct. 31, 1962.

[18] United Nations General Assembly Resolution 1760(XVII), Oct. 31, 1962.

in Southern Rhodesia, and requested the Secretary-General to draw the attention of the United Kingdom to the seriousness of the situation.[19] On June 23, 1963, the Special Committee, with Australia, Denmark, Italy, and the United States abstaining and Britain not participating, approved its Subcommittee's report and recommendations and also requested Britain to abrogate the 1961 Constitution.[20] The Chairman of the Special Committee transmitted its report to the Security Council, and this was quickly followed by the request of 32 African states for an urgent meeting of the Security Council on the grave threat posed to the peace and security of the African continent by Southern Rhodesia.[21] When the Security Council convened on September 9, 1963, three new nations submitted a draft resolution which requested the United Kingdom not to grant independence to Southern Rhodesia until a fully representative government had been established.[22] This draft was vetoed by the United Kingdom—France and the United States abstaining—and the Security Council was forced to adjourn without adopting any resolution.

Having failed to obtain Security Council approval of their demands, the new nations brought them before the eighteenth session of the Assembly and quickly obtained their adoption.[23]

On March 23, 1964, with the Assembly decisions in hand, the Special Committee—minus the Western States—drew the Security Council's attention to "the explosive situation" in Southern Rhodesia.[24] At the same time, the Special Committee asked the United Kingdom to declare that independence would not be granted to Southern Rhodesia except on the basis of universal adult suffrage. The Special Committee also requested all states to refrain voluntarily from supplying arms and ammunition to Southern Rhodesia. In May 1964 the Special Committee decided to send to London a third Subcommittee, composed of Ethiopia, Mali, Sierra Leone, and Yugoslavia, to discuss the implementation of the previously adopted

[19] United Nations Document A/5446/Add.3, July 30, 1963, Appendix, para. 52.
[20] Ibid., 88–91.
[21] United Nations Document S/5409, Aug. 30, 1963.
[22] United Nations Document S/5425, Sept. 11, 1963. The sponsors were Ghana, Morocco, and the Philippines.
[23] United Nations General Assembly Resolution 1883(XVIII), Oct. 14, 1963; United Nations General Assembly Resolution 1889(XVIII), Nov. 6, 1963.
[24] United Nations Document A/AC.109/61, Mar. 23, 1964.

United Nations resolutions. In its report of June 17, 1964, this Subcommittee called for the repeal of all repressive and discriminatory legislation, the removal of all restrictions on African political activity and the holding of a constitutional conference on the basis of universal adult suffrage.[25] The Subcommittee concluded that further discussions with the United Kingdom were "unlikely to yield fruitful results" and called upon the Security Council to consider again the question of Southern Rhodesia "as a matter of urgency.[26] After considering its Subcommittee's report, the majority of the Special Committee adopted a resolution on June 26, 1964, deploring "the persistent refusal" of Britain to cooperate in the implementation of the United Nations resolutions on Southern Rhodesia.[27] This resolution also endorsed the conclusions and recommendations of the Subcommittee and reiterated the call for Security Council action. On October 27, 1964, the Special Committee drew "once again . . . the attention of the Security Council to the question of Southern Rhodesia."[28] The Special Committee on November 17, 1964, authorized its Subcommittee to keep the situation under review and to maintain close contact with the United Kingdom with a view to achieving the implementation of the United Nations resolutions.[29]

The Rhodesian case illustrates vividly the circuitous policy that the new nations have followed in attempting to influence the course of events in the remaining colonial areas. Secure in their control over the Special Committee, the new nations have used it and its subcommittees as originating points for new initiatives and as organs of constant surveillance of these colonial areas.[30] Subcommittees, which lack even the token Western representation of the parent body, have borne the main burden of conducting initial investigations and formulating recommendations. Usually over Western opposition, the Special Committee endorses the reports of its Subcommittees, although sometimes toning down their draft resolutions. Next, the Special Committee's recommendations are forwarded to

[25] United Nations Document A/AC.109/L.128, June 17, 1964.
[26] Ibid., paras. 63 and 64.
[27] United Nations Document A/AC.109/88, June 26, 1964.
[28] United Nations Document A/5800/Add.1, part II, Dec. 22, 1964.
[29] United Nations Document A/AS.109/SR.315, Nov. 19, 1964.
[30] For example, during the period 1962–1964 Southern Rhodesia was considered at the following meetings of the Special Committee: 9, 11, 13–26, 37, 44, 45, 47–49, 53, 71, 107, 130–40, 143, 144, 146, 168, 171–77, 223–33, 245–49, 252, 254, 255, 258, 259, 262, 263, 268, 269, 271–73, 277, 278, 286, 294–96, 315.

the General Assembly, Within the Assembly, as the case of Southern Rhodesia illustrates, the dominant anticolonial majority ensures a sympathetic hearing for the Special Committee's recommendations, although some modification is usually introduced in order to obtain the largest possible majority. Simultaneously, the Special Committee has called for Security Council action on its reports. In 1964 three separate pleas were addressed to the Security Council for action on Southern Rhodesia.

The Special Committee has not been altogether successful in obtaining even a hearing, much less action, from the Council on its proposals. However, it appears that since the enlargement of the Council on January 1, 1966, to include a larger Afro-Asian representation this tactic has a greater chance of success. This circuitous policy has been most successful in maintaining continuous United Nations involvement with the colonial areas and increasing the verbal intensity of the resolutions adopted. It had been successful by the end of 1964 in obtaining broad and repeated censure of the remaining recalcitrant colonial regimes. However, by the end of 1964 this circuitous policy had yet to produce any change in the policy of these hard core regimes or any operational role for the Organization in bringing about some change in this area. This failure demonstrates vividly the two dimensions of political influence exercised by the new nations. With regard to the first dimension, that is, influence directed at shaping the policy outputs of the Organization, the new nations in the Southern Rhodesian case as of the end of 1964 were successful in maintaining the involvement of the Organization and in escalating its verbal assaults on the regime, but they were not successful in their attempts to have the Security Council apply mandatory sanctions to the Smith regime. However with regard to the second dimension, influence directed at shaping the policy of states in the environment external to the Organization, the influence of the new nations had as of the end of 1964 produced no substantial policy alterations.

Ironically, through their threats of a unilateral declaration of independence from Britain and finally with such a declaration on November 11, 1965, the Southern Rhodesian Government brought about the direct involvement of the United Nations that the new nations had been unable to achieve. In the early autumn of 1965 as the signs of an early unilateral declaration of independence multiplied, 40 states, 37 of them new nations, rushed a draft resolution through the Fourth Committee and Assembly condemning any attempt by the Southern Rhodesians to seize independence and calling upon the United Kingdom to use all possible means to prevent a unilateral declaration of independence.[31] In the event of such a declaration, the resolution called upon the United Kingdom to take all necessary steps to put an end to the rebellion. Only Portugal and South Africa voted against this resolution, while France abstained and the United Kingdom did not participate in the voting. The Assembly again appealed on November 5, 1965, for British action to prevent a Rhodesian declaration of independence.[32] This resolution, sponsored by 56 states, 45 of which were new nations, was in stronger terms than the October resolution and, in fact, called upon the United Kingdom "to employ all necessary measures, including military force" to prevent a unilateral declaration of independence. The severity of this resolution alienated some states, particularly Western European and Latin American Members that had supported the earlier resolution, but it was still adopted by the overwhelming vote of 82 in favor, 9 opposed, and 18 abstaining. In reaction to the Rhodesian declaration of independence on November 11, the Assembly in near unanimity adopted a resolution that condemned "the unilateral declaration of independence made by the racialist minority in Southern Rhodesia" and recommended that the Security Council consider the situation as a matter of urgency.[33] This resolution, sponsored by 36 African states, was adopted by 107 in favor, 2 against, and 1 abstaining. As was the case with the October resolution, only Portugal and South Africa voted against this resolution, while France abstained.

At the behest of the United Kingdom the Security Council met on November 12, 1965, to consider the Rhodesian situation. With this meeting the principal locus of United Nations concern with Rhodesia shifted from the General Assembly to the Security Council where it remains at the time of this writing, late 1969. In requesting a Security Council meeting on Southern Rhodesia, the British were

[31] United Nations General Assembly Resolution 2012(XX), Oct. 12, 1965.
[32] United Nations General Assembly Resolution 2022(XX), Nov. 5, 1965.
[33] United Nations General Assembly Resolution 2024(XX), Nov. 11, 1965.

finally abandoning their position that neither the United Kingdom nor the United Nations had the right to interfere in the territory's internal affairs. During November 1965 the Security Council passed resolutions that condemned the unilateral declaration of independence, called upon all states to refrain from recognizing or assisting the regime, requested all states to break economic relations with Southern Rhodesia, and requested the establishment of an embargo on oil and petroleum products to Southern Rhodesia.[34]

In defiance of the Security Council's request for an embargo on the shipment of oil and petroleum products to Southern Rhodesia, two oil tankers were discovered in April 1966 to be nearing the port of Beira in Portuguese Mozambique with cargoes rumored for transshipment to Rhodesia. At the request of the British government the Security Council met, declared that the "situation constitutes a threat to the peace," and authorized the British to prevent "by the use of force if necessary" oil from reaching Rhodesia through the port of Beira.[35] This marked the first time that a specific state had been authorized to carry out a mandatory decision of the Security Council.

The tempo of United Nations action against Rhodesia was again increased in December 1966 after the collapse of renewed negotiations between London and the Ian Smith regime. Under strong African pressure the United Kingdom asked the Security Council to approve for the first time since its founding selective, mandatory sanctions against a regime.[36] During a week of discussion the African states made a concerted attempt to alter drastically the British draft to include more commodities and to provide enforcement provisions to ensure that the Council's edict was carried out. The African states also sought to have the Security Council deplore the British refusal to use force against Rhodesia and to call upon the United Kingdom to withdraw all previous offers to the Rhodesian regime and to declare flatly that it would grant independence to Rhodesia only under majority rule.[37]

In this attempt the African states largely failed, although the final resolution contained eight African amendments, including a ban on

[34] Security Council Resolutions 216 (1965), Nov. 12, 1965; and 217 (1965), Nov. 20, 1965.
[35] Security Council Resolution 221 (1966), Apr. 9, 1966.
[36] The New York Times, Dec. 9, 1966, p. 22.
[37] The New York Times, Dec. 17, 1966, p. 9.

the supply of oil and oil products to Rhodesia.[38] On December 16, by a vote of 11 to 0 with Bulgaria, France, Mali, and the Soviet Union abstaining, the Security Council approved a ban on the purchase of twelve of Rhodesia's chief exports and the supply to Rhodesia of oil and oil products. Not only did this mark the first use of mandatory sanctions by the Security Council, but the Council itself emerged as a new instrument in the politics of decolonization. The success or failure of these developments will, moreover, have a profound effect upon the Organization's relations with the remainder of southern Africa.

Thus, by the beginning of 1967 the Rhodesians by their own actions had provided the occasion for the United Nations to initiate mandatory sanctions against the regime. This was an action long desired by the new nations but one which even their adroit use of political influence within the Organization had been unable to obtain prior to the Rhodesian unilateral declaration of independence.

The Special Committee—Its Future   In the eight years since its first meeting, the Special Committee on Colonialism has been the principal tool of the new nations for engaging the United Nations in the process of decolonization. The new nations showed a remarkable amount of political sophistication in quickly seeking an institutionalized focus—and one that they could clearly control—for their principal goal in the United Nations. This Committee rapidly fulfilled the hopes of its sponsors in becoming a ceaseless channel through which their demands for the immediate dismantling of the colonial empire could be repeatedly brought before the Organization. Its success and limitations in expanding the circle of condemnation for colonialism was set out above with regard to Southern Rhodesia.

However, there is another aspect of the Special Committee's operation that is little remarked upon outside of the immediate circle of the United Nations. The habit of the Committee from its very beginning of relying on small subcommittees that lack even the token Western representation of the full Committee has been remarked upon earlier. During the last three years this habit has been coupled with a radicalization of an articulate segment of the Committee centered on the representative of Tanzania. This segment of the Com-

[38] Security Council Resolution 232 (1966), Dec. 16, 1966.

mittee has avoided communication and negotiation with the representatives of the Western members and has relied upon the automatic voting majority to turn out Committee recommendations that the Western members have had only the briefest of opportunities to comment upon and no real opportunity to shape.

Seemingly without realizing it, the new nations on the Special Committee have abandoned during the last three years, on an increasing number of issues, their earlier tactic of expanding the circle of condemnation by engaging the Western members, however reluctantly, in the Committee's operation. The reaction of the Western members has not been long in coming. As the United States told the Committee early in 1968,

The United States has been giving careful and searching thought in recent months to the question whether any purpose would be achieved by continued United States membership on the Committee. It was questionable in our eyes, and indeed it remains questionable, whether the pattern which has characterized the work of this Committee leaves room for effective and worthwhile participation by the United States. We accordingly engaged in broad consultations with other delegations to explain our views about the serious difficulties which have existed in this Committee, our doubts as to whether any purpose would be achieved by further United States participation, and our consequent assessment that the time had come for us to withdraw, while continuing to cooperate during consideration of United States territories. As a result of their responses, we have decided to express our views in this full and frank fashion at this meeting, and to defer a decision on continued membership, reserving for ourselves the right to review the situation at any time.[39]

That the United States could seriously explore the possibility of its pulling out of the Special Committee in the face of the predictable heavily negative reaction of the African states and the unfavorable parallels that inevitably would be drawn between this action and the actions of the United States in Vietnam is an indication of the extent of its disillusionment with the Committee's operation. And certainly the United States is not alone among Western States in this disillusionment, nor would it be alone, in all probability, if it were to decide to withdraw.

At least of late, the leading segment of new nations in the Special

[39] Seymour M. Finger, Statement in the Committee of 24, on the Work of the Committee of 24, Feb. 8, 1968, Press Release USUN-17 (68).

Committee has failed to remember that the Special Committee does not have the resources to reorder the remaining colonial areas. If these resources are to be marshalled to the task of restructuring these areas, they must come voluntarily from the Western nations. This failure to make any attempt to engage these states in the operations of the Special Committee is rapidly depriving the Committee of its chief resource for attaining its stated aims. Unless this process is reversed at an early date, it can be confidently predicted that most of the Western States will soon leave the Committee and that it will then have lost any real relevance to the dismantling of the remaining bastions of colonialism.

South Africa United Nations concern with the racial policies of the South African Government is of long standing, the General Assembly having first dealt in 1946 with complaints of racial discrimination against peoples of Indian origin in South Africa. With the new nations in the vanguard, the Organization since 1960 has applied increasing pressure to force South Africa to change its policy of apartheid. In the period from 1946 until 1960 the General Assembly was content to censure by repeated resolutions the policy of apartheid. Since 1960 the Assembly has moved from general to specific resolutions requesting Member States to take separate and collective actions against South Africa.

The new nations, particularly the new nations of Africa, have made extremely clear the direction in which they think the United Nations policy toward the problems of apartheid should evolve. At the fifteenth session of the Assembly the delegate of Ghana clearly pointed to the desire of the African states for United Nations sanctions against South Africa:

All here have agreed that *apartheid* is a menace, that it is a disease, that it is a cankerworm which must be uprooted. We in all the 25 African States, the independent African States, and if I may say so, the 200 million Africans, are all with one voice appealing to the Assembly to consider sanctions. To us the sanctions would serve as a sword of Damocles over the head of the Union of South Africa, that is, over the heads of probably two million or one and a half million whites in the Union who are recalcitrant.[40]

[40] Mr. Quaison-Sackey (Ghana), United Nations General Assembly *Official Records*, 15th Session, 981st meeting (Apr. 18, 1961), para. 39.

Less than a year later the Nigerian delegate in pointing to the possibility of expelling South Africa from the Organization said,

I want to warn South Africa once more. We have managed to get it out of the Commonwealth. If South Africa persists in this behavior we may have to get it outside this world. Those who are interested in South Africa because of investments in the mineral resources of Africa should begin to think twice. South Africa cannot continue to behave as it is doing. . . . We are opposed to everything that the present South African Government stands for in respect of the treatment of the black man in Africa.[41]

The thrust of the proposals advocated by the new nations with regard to South Africa is directed at the elimination of South African control over South-West Africa and the enactment of mandatory economic and military sanctions against South Africa as a means of forcing it to abandon apartheid.

In 1960 the significant increase in African representation in the Organization coincided with the Sharpeville riots in South Africa to produce a significant development in the United Nations concern with the apartheid policies of South Africa. In the aftermath of these riots, 29 Afro-Asian states combined to press the Security Council to undertake collective measures to force the abandonment of the policy of apartheid.[42] The Security Council found little difficulty in denouncing the policy of apartheid but only with the greatest of difficulty succeeded in categorizing the situation in South Africa "as one that has led to international friction and if continued might endanger international peace and security."[43] While the Security Council had certainly not met the demands of the new nations, this resolution of April 1960 marked the opening ploy in what was to become a continuing effort of the new nations to obtain Security Council sanction for mandatory collective measures against South Africa.

By 1961 South Africa found itself increasingly isolated in the United Nations. In April the British joined most of the rest of the Assembly in agreeing that apartheid was "now so exceptional as to be *sui generis*" and thus no longer shielded from United Nations concern by the provisions of Article 2(7) regarding domestic juris-

[41] Mr. Wachuku (Nigeria), United Nations General Assembly *Official Records*, 16th Session, 1031st meeting (Oct. 10, 1961), para. 34.
[42] United Nations Document S/4279, Mar. 25, 1960.
[43] United Nations Document S/4300, Apr. 1, 1960, para. 1.

diction.[44] The new nations of the Commonwealth had succeeded in forcing South Africa to withdraw from that grouping, and thus another tie was severed. When the resumed session of the fifteenth Assembly turned to consideration of apartheid, the new nations were ready with a draft that continued their new emphasis on collective measures. This resolution, adopted by a lopsided vote of 88 in favor and one opposed, with eight abstentions, requested all states "to consider taking such separate and collective action as is open to them in conformity with the Charter of the United Nations, to bring about the abandonment of these policies."[45] At the sixteenth session of the Assembly the new nations succeeded in obtaining an endorsement of the previous resolution and a request calling the Security Council's attention to a situation that "seriously endangers international peace and security."[46] Indicative of both the changing mood of the Assembly and the shifting balance of power in it was the Assembly's censure of the South African Foreign Minister for his speech during the General Debate of the sixteenth session. This speech of Eric H. Louw on October 11, 1961, did not differ in tone or content from past apologies for apartheid, but it was met by immediate demands from the new African delegates for its censure. In an exercise of voting power and impetuousness which alarmed many Western and even some Asian nations, these new nations pushed through this censure on the same day by a vote of 67 in favor to one opposed, with 20 abstaining, 3 absent, and 9 present but not participating.[47] It was the view of the African new nations that South Africa by its racial policies had voluntarily placed itself outside the community of nations envisaged in the Charter and hence had no grounds to ask for the normal respect of divergent opinions that usually marked United Nations proceedings. For these nations racial segregation, like colonialism, was a defined evil. On these two issues they were determined to impose their own views and were understandably ill-disposed to permit the open advocacy of apartheid.

[44] United Nations General Assembly *Official Records*, 17th Session, Special Political Committee, 242d meeting (Apr. 5, 1961), 77.
[45] General Assembly Resolution 1598(XV), Apr. 13, 1961.
[46] General Assembly Resolution 1663(XVI), Nov. 28, 1961, para. 7.
[47] United Nations General Assembly *Official Records*, 16th Session, 1034th meeting (Oct. 11, 1961), para. 83.

However, it was at the seventeenth session of the Assembly that the new nations achieved their most important victory up to that time in their drive toward imposing collective measures on South Africa. For the first time the resolution adopted on apartheid, sponsored by 33 Afro-Asian nations, included a specific list of diplomatic and economic measures that Members were requested to take in order "to bring about the abandonment of those policies." The measures requested were:

    (a) Breaking of diplomatic relations with the Government of the Republic of South Africa or refraining from establishing such relations;

    (b) Closing their ports to all vessels flying the South African flag;

    (c) Enacting legislation prohibiting their ships from entering South African ports;

    (d) Boycotting all South African goods and refraining from exporting goods, including all arms and ammunition, to South Africa;

    (e) Refusing landing and passage facilities to all aircraft belonging to the Government of South Africa and companies registered under the laws of South Africa.[48]

This resolution, which marked an important advance in the campaign of the new nations to obtain a United Nations program of sanctions against South Africa, was adopted by a roll-call vote of 67 in favor, 16 opposed, and 23 abstentions.

In addition to requesting Member States to take the above measures against South Africa, the resolution established a Special Committee on *Apartheid*, composed of Algeria, Costa Rica, the Federation of Malaya, Ghana, Guinea, Haiti, Hungary, Nepal, Nigeria, the Philippines, and Somalia, all but three of whom were new nations. Finally, the resolution requested the Security Council to "take appropriate measures, including sanctions, to secure South Africa's compliance with the resolutions of the General Assembly and of the Security Council . . ."

During 1963 and 1964 the new nations followed a three-pronged approach in their efforts to pressure the Security Council into some form of mandatory action against South Africa's apartheid policies. First, the General Assembly provided a forum for directing requests to the Security Council for action. The seventeenth session was particularly marked by repeated demands from the rostrum for the Security Council to recognize "the threat to the peace" existing in

[48] General Assembly Resolution 1761(XVII), Nov. 6, 1962.

South Africa and to undertake mandatory sanctions. Secondly, the newly established Special Committee on *Apartheid*, whose chairman was Guinea, began in 1963 to direct a steady stream of requests and reports to both the Assembly and the Council.[49] Finally, the new nations joined together to request Security Council action against South Africa.

Although it has refused to emulate the Assembly's zeal for adopting sanctions against South Africa, the Security Council under the continuous pressure of the African nations has moved in that direction. It was a joint request by the African nations in July 1963 that opened the latest phase of Council involvement in the affairs of South Africa. While the new nations' request for a boycott of all South African goods and an embargo on the export of all strategic goods to South Africa was rejected, an important breach was made at this time in the formerly implacable Western attitude against Security Council involvement with the problem of apartheid. During the Council's debate the new nations drew heavily upon the report of the Special Committee on *Apartheid* in an effort to characterize the situation in South Africa as a "threat to the peace" in the meaning of Article 39 of the Charter, hence making the provisions of Chapter VII with regard to mandatory collective measures applicable. This was further than the West was prepared to go. However, an alternative proposal, judiciously worded so as to avoid a determination that the situation came under Article 39, was adopted by the Council. This resolution, on which France and the United Kingdom abstained, described the situation in South Africa as "one that has led to international friction and if continued might endanger international peace and security."[50] It called for South Africa to abandon apartheid and requested all states to halt "the sale and shipment of arms, ammunition . . . and military vehicles" to South Africa. While the debate in the Security Council clearly reveals that the West did not believe that the situation in South Africa was such as to fall under the provisions of Chapter VII,[51] the resolution finally adopted was a reversal of previous

---

[49] United Nations Document A/5497, Dec. 16, 1963; United Nations Document A/5692, Mar. 25, 1964, and United Nations Document A/5707, May 25, 1964.

[50] United Nations Document S/5386, Aug. 7, 1963.

[51] See, for example, the statement of Ambassador Stevenson for the United States. United Nations Document S/PV. 1052, Aug. 2, 1963, 31–37.

Council inertia on apartheid and an important opening for the new nations.

As a result of continued South African unresponsiveness to the earlier appeal, the Security Council returned to the problem of apartheid in late November 1963. Although again refusing to accept the African states' demand for collective measures against South Africa, the Council did adopt unanimously a Norwegian proposal that a group of experts be established "to examine the methods of resolving the present situation in South Africa . . ."[52] In its report in April 1964 the expert group, which had worked under the chairmanship of Mrs. Alva Myrdal of Sweden, urged the immediate convening in South Africa of a national convention, representing all elements of the population, to set a new course for the future. Although expressing a belief in the effectiveness of universally applied economic sanctions, this group recommended an expert examination of the "economic and strategic aspects of sanctions."[53] If South Africa failed to reply within a stipulated period to the Security Council's proposal to discuss the establishment of a national convention, the expert group recommended that the Council "apply economic sanctions in the light of the results of the examination recommended . . ."[54] The reception of this report was marked by expressions of joy from the new nations and extreme caution from the West. A Norwegian proposal that the Security Council establish a governmental Committee of Experts to make a technical study of sanctions was finally agreed to by the United Kingdom and the United States on the condition that their votes be understood as implying no prior commitment to accept the recommendations of this Committee of Experts.[55] On this resolution the Soviet Union and Czechoslovakia abstained as a protest because they felt it to be too weak, and France abstained because it was too strong.

With the Security Council establishment of this Committee of Experts, United Nations action, except for the continuing investigations of the Special Committee on *Apartheid*, was held in abeyance

[52] United Nations Document S/5471, Dec. 4, 1963. This group of experts, composed of individuals serving in their private capacity, consisted of Mrs. Alva Myrdal, Sir Edward Asfu-Adjaye, Sir Hugh Foot, and Mr. Dey Ould Sidi Baba.
[53] United Nations Document S/5658, Apr. 20, 1964, para. 110.
[54] *Ibid.*, para. 121.
[55] United Nations Document S/5773, June 18, 1964.

while awaiting the Committee of Experts' report in early 1965.[56] What did the new nations accomplish from 1960 to 1964 in their steady assault on South Africa's racial policies? Largely through their pressure the United Nations had produced a steady stream of reports, recommendations, regrets, and denunciations of the recalcitrant attitude of the South African Government. However, in spite of this deluge of condemnation, apartheid during this period grew even more repressive. Although the new nations had been unable by the end of 1964 to convince the Security Council to emulate the Assembly's zeal for sanctions, they had steadily moved it in that direction. While still refusing to categorize the situation in South Africa as falling under the provisions of Chapter VII of the Charter, the Security Council had been persuaded by the new nations to go through a host of preliminary motions that have increasingly incorporated the principle, already endorsed by the Assembly, of collective measures against South Africa.

Despite the general condemnation of the apartheid policies of South Africa on the part of virtually all Members of the Organization and increased pressure from the new nations, the Organization has not moved beyond its 1964 position in its confrontation with South Africa. The impotence of the new nations so far in this respect is best typified in the unexpected fate of General Assembly Resolution 2054 of December 15, 1965. A guiding stratagem—often chronicled in this work—of the new nations for moving the West toward a position that the West wished to avoid is to have a Committee appointed by the Assembly to "investigate," "examine," or "analyze" the problem. The membership of such a Committee—the Special Committee on Colonialism is the best-known example—is artfully composed to have a preponderant anticolonial majority but with sufficient Western membership to associate the West with the always heavily anticolonial recommendations of the Committee.

At the Twentieth Assembly the new nations again resorted to this stratagem in successfully guiding through the Assembly Resolution 2054, which *inter alia* requested that to the Special Committee on *Apartheid*'s present membership be added six new members chosen according to: (a) primary responsibility in world trade, (b) primary

---

[56] The report of the Expert Committee was issued on Mar. 2, 1965. United Nations Document S/6210, Mar. 2, 1965.

responsibility under the Charter for the maintenance of international peace and security, and (c) equitable geographical distribution.[57] Altogether 19 States were asked to consider membership on the Special Committee but 15 States, including the United States, the United Kingdom, and France, declined membership.[58] Only the Soviet Union expressed an unconditional willingness to serve on the Special Committee with the result that the entire expansion was dropped. This unprecedented refusal to be mousetrapped in this hitherto successful stratagem led to sharp recriminations from the new nations and also sharply delineated the limits of their influence on the problem of South Africa. Accounting for only a small amount of the trade with South Africa and lacking a credible military potential vis-a-vis South Africa, the new nations have to marshall the power and influence of the developed states of the West if they are to stand a chance of inducing South Africa to abandon its antagonistic racial policies. Yet in this episode we find the West for the first time saying, in effect, "We see where you are going; and we are not willing to take even the first step." This is a significant departure from the conduct of the West only two years before in the case of the Committee of Experts and can be explained largely in terms of an increasing awareness on the part of the United States as to where this procedure was leading and a critical judgment of the politically most opportune place to stop. The reaction of the new states to this decision did not hide the fact that it was an effective counter to the new nations' use of this particular stratagem. This decision demonstrated that the influence of the new nations has its limits even when it is confined to attempts at shaping the policy of the United Nations. The limitation of their influence in attempting to shape the external political environment with respect to South Africa is even more apparent.

As of late 1969 the new nations have been unable to energize the power of the United Nations into a frontal assault backed by mandatory collective measures on South Africa. In fact, the voluntary arms embargo and voluntary economic sanctions called for by the Security

[57] The members of the Special Committee were then Algeria, Costa Rica, Ghana, Guinea, Haiti, Hungary, Malaysia, Nepal, Nigeria, Philippines, and Somalia.

[58] United Nations Document A/6356, June 29, 1966. Also declining membership were Argentina, Australia, Austria, Belgium, Brazil, Ceylon, Japan, Mexico, Netherlands, Norway, Spain, and Sweden. Canada did not reply, and Denmark and Italy replied conditionally.

Council and the General Assembly have been publicly flaunted by France and quietly circumvented by other states. Stopped in their drive to obtain mandatory sanctions against South Africa, the new nations have focused their efforts recently upon directing public attention to the evils of apartheid. It was in this effort that a United Nations Seminar on *Apartheid* was held in Brazil from 1966, and an International Seminar on *Apartheid*, Racial Discrimination, and Colonialism in Southern Africa was held in Zambia in 1967.

South Africa presents two different problems to the Organization, although in practice the new nations have often blurred this distinction. One problem concerns the application by the Republic within South Africa of a constellation of racial policies going under the rubric of apartheid designed to maintain separation of the races and also to preserve white domination of the government, economy, and the society of South Africa. This is the problem discussed above. However, there is a second problem which concerns the administration and future of the Mandated Territory of South-West Africa. First seized from the Germans in 1915 and then placed under a League Mandate in 1920, South-West Africa has been administered by South Africa for approximately 50 years as an integral part of its territory, although South Africa grudgingly admits an international responsibility for its administration. After having its 1946 proposal for the annexation of the territory rejected by the General Assembly, South Africa has rebuffed all suggestions that it follow the lead of the other administering powers of League Mandates and conclude a Trusteeship Agreement with the United Nations. Acting on the basis of a 1950 Advisory Opinion of the International Court of Justice, the General Assembly has attempted to exercise the supervisory functions of the League with respect to the Mandate in spite of a total lack of cooperation on the part of South Africa.

Whereas between 1946 and 1960 the main scene of United Nations concern with South-West Africa had been the General Assembly and its committees—they had passed more than 60 resolutions on South-West Africa in this period—an important new scene was added in 1960. During the second conference of independent African states at Addis Ababa in June 1960, agreement was reached to sponsor a submission to the International Court of Justice for adjudication of South Africa's responsibilities under the Mandate to South-

West Africa. As the only two African members of the League, Ethiopia and Liberia initiated this proceeding against South Africa in November 1960. The Court was asked by Ethiopia and Liberia to find that South Africa violated the Mandate by its extension of apartheid into South-West Africa, its unilateral changes in the legal status of the territory and its failure to submit reports on the territory to the Assembly.[59]

The legal proceedings surrounding this case have been extremely long and complex and the final decision was not delivered until July 18, 1966. However, the new nations refused to accept the argument made by Western delegations that, since the matter was *sub judice*, the Assembly should hold in abeyance action on the question. Within a month of the initial Ethiopian-Liberian submission the Assembly adopted a resolution declaring that the situation in South-West Africa was a "serious threat to international peace and security" and decided to dispatch a visiting mission to the territory.[60] South Africa's refusal to permit such a visit provoked the new nations into obtaining the adoption of an Assembly resolution which called the Security Council's attention to the situation as one likely to "endanger international peace and security."[61] At the sixteenth session the new nations expressed their dissatisfaction with the limited role played by the Committee on South-West Africa, which was modeled after the League's Permanent Mandates Commission. Over considerable behind-the-scenes opposition to dealing with a matter so intimately bound up with issues before the Court, they obtained Assembly approval of a more powerful new Committee by a vote of 90 in favor to one opposed, with four abstentions.[62] This resolution instructed the newly established Committee, the Special Committee on South-West Africa to make arrangements for the evacuation of all South African military forces from the territory, the release of political prisoners, the repeal of all apartheid legislation in the territory, preparations for general elections on the basis of universal adult suffrage under United Nations supervision, assistance to the resulting government with a view to preparing the Territory for

[59] The issues raised by Ethiopia and Liberia are set forth in "South West Africa Cases, Preliminary Objections, Judgment of Dec. 21, 1962," *International Court of Justice Reports* 1962, 7–11.
[60] United Nations General Assembly Resolution 1568(XV), Dec. 18, 1960.
[61] United Nations General Assembly Resolution 1596(XV), Apr. 7, 1961.
[62] United Nations General Assembly Resolution 1702(XVI), Dec. 19, 1961.

full independence, and the coordination of specialized agency assistance.

At its seventeenth session the Assembly reiterated its opinion that the people of South-West Africa had a right to independence and condemned the recalcitrant attitude of South Africa on this matter.[63] These sentiments were again expressed by the Assembly in substantially the same form at its eighteenth session.[64] While refraining from any new action on South-West Africa during 1963 and 1964, the new nations through the Special Committee on Colonialism attempted to keep the spotlight of public attention on the problem while waiting for the Court's decision.[65] As with the related problem of apartheid, the intensive concern of the new nations with the question of South-West Africa has produced no concession on the part of the Government of South Africa. In fact, if the information of the Special Committee on Colonialism is accurate, South Africa is rapidly implementing the recommendations of the Odendaal Commission for the closer integration of the territory on an ethnic basis.[66] On the other hand, the new nations succeeded in laying a firm basis for future action if South Africa were to be faced—as everyone expected—with an unfavorable International Court of Justice opinion and chose to flout the opinion. It is in this respect that the seemingly redundant Assembly resolutions of 1960–1964 have played an important role. Through a none too subtle use of their voting power and appeals to widely held moral beliefs, the new nations transformed race relations in South Africa into international relations, while at the same time repeatedly censuring the policies of South Africa. Their efforts have produced a broad moral consensus with regard to the inequity of South Africa's position. The hope among the new nations at the end of 1964 was that the long-delayed International Court of Justice opinion would provide the opportunity to use this moral consensus as the foundation for enacting a program of mandatory sanctions against the regime of South Africa.

However, to the great surprise of almost all observers—and espe-

[63] United Nations General Assembly Resolution 1805(XVII), Dec. 14, 1962.

[64] United Nations General Assembly Resolution 1899(XVIII), Nov. 13, 1963.

[65] As part of a reorganization designed to eliminate duplication of effort, the 17th Session of the Assembly abolished the Special Committee on South-West Africa and assigned its duties to the enlarged Special Committee on Colonialism. United Nations General Assembly Resolution 1805(XVII), Dec. 14, 1962.

[66] United Nations Document A/5800/Add.2, Dec. 18, 1964.

cially the new nations—the World Court in July 1966 dismissed the claims of Liberia and Ethiopia without ruling on the merits of the case.[67] In an eight to seven decision, the Court ruled that the applicants had no legal right or interest in the subject matter of their claim and this, hence, made it unnecessary for the Court to rule on the merits of the case, although the Court had taken 336 hours of oral testimony, 3756 pages of evidence and in six years had held 112 court sessions devoted largely to the merits of the case.

This decision came as a particular shock to the new states of Africa. Their strategy from 1960 until 1966 had been premised upon an eventual World Court condemnation of South Africa which would provide the needed leverage to gain some form of direct United Nations presence in South-West Africa. A sense of profound bitterness at this decision was directed by the new nations both at the Court and at the Western states which had supported six long years of Court proceedings as the reasonable procedure to obtain a redress of grievances.

As could be expected, the Twenty-First Assembly was marked by a venting of much of this bitterness and by a search for a new strategy of asserting United Nations authority over South-West Africa. The device decided upon was a draft resolution, sponsored by a large group of new nations, that terminated South Africa's mandate and called for the General Assembly to "assume direct responsibility for administration of the Mandated Territory."[68] For an interim period before independence, a United Nations Administering Authority would govern the territory, and the Security Council would be requested "to take the necessary effective measures to enable the Administering Authority to discharge its functions in accordance with the present resolution."

This draft in its clear call for enforcement measures and in its establishment of a United Nations regime to administer the territory went further than a large number of Western and Latin American

---

[67] For a discussion of the legal issues and reasoning surrounding this strange decision, see John R. Stevenson, "Judicial Decisions," *American Journal of International Law*, 61, No. 1 (Jan. 1967), 116–210; Richard A. Falk, "The South West Africa Cases: An Appraisal," *International Organization*, 21, No. 1 (Winter 1967), 1–23; Rosalyn Higgins, "The International Court and South West Africa: The Implications of the Judgment," *International Affairs* (London), 42, No. 4 (Oct. 1966), 573–99; Ernest A. Gross, "The South West Africa Case: What Happened?," *Foreign Affairs*, 45, No. 1 (Oct. 1966), 36–48.

[68] United Nations Document A/L.483, Sept. 26, 1966.

states were prepared to go. In an attempt to find a common ground the Latin American group advanced amendments which instead of calling for enforcement measures merely called the Security Council's attention to the resolution and postponed any United Nations acquisition of the territory until an *Ad Hoc* Committee for South-West Africa recommended to a special session of the Assembly in April 1967 practical measures of administering the territories.[69] Again the Latin Americans in searching for an acceptable compromise had performed a significant service for the new nations. Even as amended, the draft would terminate the mandate and assure a special session of the Assembly, with only a three-month delay, that would concentrate attention on administrative arrangements for the territory. And, of course, the most significant service that the Latin Americans had performed was in assuring that, if their amendments were accepted, the resolution would be approved by such an overwhelming majority that Western States, particularly the United States, would be severely embarrassed if they did not support the resolution.

As expected, the amended draft was accepted on a vote of 114 in favor, Portugal and South Africa opposed, with France, Malawi and the United Kingdom abstaining.[70]

When this newly created *Ad Hoc* Committee turned to its work in January 1967, it found that the Committee divided among four positions.[71] Ethiopia, Nigeria, Pakistan, Senegal, and the United Arab Republic wanted a special United Nations Council to administer the territory until it could be granted independence, which was to take place no later than June 1968.[72] Chile and Mexico advanced a proposal which, although calling for a United Nations Council to administer the territory, provided for prior contact between the Council and the South African Government to establish procedures for transferring the territory.[73] Canada, Italy, and the United States, while reaffirming the United Nations commitment to self-determination and independence for South-West Africa, recommended that the

---

[69] United Nations Document A/L.488, Oct. 25, 1966.

[70] General Assembly Resolution 2145(XXI), Oct. 27, 1966.

[71] The members of this committee were Canada, Chile, Czechoslovakia, Ethiopia, Finland, Italy, Japan, Mexico, Nigeria, Pakistan, Senegal, U.S.S.R., United Arab Republic, and the United States.

[72] United Nations Document A/AC.129/L.5, Mar. 7, 1967.

[73] United Nations Document A/AC.129/L.7, Mar. 15, 1967.

only immediate action should be the establishment of a Special Representative to collect information, establish contacts in the territory, and make recommendations to the Assembly.[74] The Soviets opposed all the other proposals and demanded immediate independence for South-West Africa under the supervision of the Organization for African Unity supported by enforcement action by the Security Council.[75]

It is not surprising that these positions could not be bridged and that the Fifth Special Session of the Assembly in April 1967 was but another forum for the same proposals and disagreements to be repeated. However, rather than admit the impossibility of action the new nations showed considerable sophistication in seeking out the Latin Americans to see if a compromise could not be reached that would have such overwhelming numerical support that the West would have no choice but to go along. The result of these negotiations was a draft that avoided reference to the possibility of enforcement action under Chapter VII and provided that a Council for South-West Africa should enter into contact with South Africa to establish procedures for a transfer of territory. While this resolution was approved by the Assembly, the vote was far from decisive.[76] The 85 states supporting the resolution were from the expected quarters of Africa, Asia, the Caribbean, and Latin America plus Cyprus, Greece, Israel, Spain, and Yugoslavia. While no one should have been surprised at the negative votes of Portugal and South Africa, the large number of abstentions, 30, was a disappointment to the sponsors.[77] This was particularly so in the case of the United States, and to a lesser extent France and the United Kingdom. In the case of the United States the final decision rested on a judgment that the course which the resolution set if really followed would lead either to chaos and bloodshed in southern Africa or more likely to complete frustration of the efforts of the United Nations. It was the belief of the United States that, if it supported a resolution with these likely

---

[74] United Nations Document A/AC.129/L.6, Mar. 15, 1967.

[75] United Nations Document A/AC.129/SR.8, Mar. 20, 1967.

[76] General Assembly Resolution 2248(S-V), May 19, 1967.

[77] The states abstaining were Luxembourg, Malawi, Malta, Mongolia, Netherlands, New Zealand, Norway, Poland, Romania, Sweden, Ukrainian S.S.R., U.S.S.R., United Kingdom, United States, Australia, Austria, Belgium, Botswana, Bulgaria, Byelorussian S.S.R., Canada, Cuba, Czechoslovakia, Denmark, Finland, France, Hungary, Iceland, Ireland, and Italy.

outcomes, it would be held responsible for the results. The Soviet abstention was more palatable for the new nations as it was claimed to rest on the fact that the resolution did not go far enough toward immediate independence for South-West Africa and enforcement measures against South Africa.

As called for in the resolution, the Assembly elected an eleven-member Council for South-West Africa, and the Secretary-General appointed the Legal Counsel of the United Nations, Constantin Stavropoulos, to serve as acting Commissioner for South-West Africa.[78] As of early 1968 the Council has not yet agreed upon the procedure to be followed in implementing its mandate.

It appears that with regard to South-West Africa, as in the case of South Africa, the new nations have reached the limits of their ability to move the United Nations or its Members to take effective action to transform the situation in southern Africa. They have the influence to secure in the Assembly repeated resolutions castigating South Africa, calls for voluntary economic sanctions, and requests for Security Council consideration of the problem; there will probably be numerous such resolutions in the future. However, what the new nations have lacked in the past and will probably continue to lack in the immediate future is the power or influence to move France, the United Kingdom, or the United States to commit their prestige and resources to a forceful attempt to change the South African social and political system. The likely result of this inability of the new nations to secure desired action will be increasing frustration and a search for revolutionary solutions outside the Organization by the more radical African states. The moderate African states, while feeling the same frustration at the inability of the United Nations to find an acceptable solution, will undoubtedly find their ideological flank exposed to their more radical neighbors. This is a mixture that if fed by East-West conflict or Chinese intervention could destroy the Organization as well as threaten international peace. The potential that this issue has for halting United Nations activities in other areas was well illustrated at the Second United Nations Conference on Trade and Development in February 1968. An attempt by a group of Afro-Asian states to have South Africa

---

[78] The members of the Council are Chile, Colombia, Guyana, India, Indonesia, Nigeria, Pakistan, Turkey, the United Arab Republic, Yugoslavia, and Zambia.

expelled from the Conference almost led to a breakup of the Conference. It was only in the face of the strongest of legal opinions by the United Nations Legal Counsel that such an action would be contrary to the United Nations Charter and the rules of procedures of the Organization and a threat that the Secretary-General would be forced to withdraw all United Nations Secretariat services from the Conference that the move was thwarted. As it was, the maneuvering wasted valuable time and distracted attention from the vital economic problems of the less developed countries. Many delegates expect that the future will be marked by an increased generalization of the South African problem to every aspect and organ of the Organization.

The Voting Perspective   A systematic analysis of the Assembly's voting record is a significant tool in measuring the success with which the new nations have wielded political influence in shaping the policy of the Organization on colonial issues. Such an analysis is particularly well suited to determining publicly acknowledged shifts in positions and the number of battles won or lost.[79] For the purpose of this study 70 roll-call votes on colonial issues taken during the sixteenth, seventeenth, eighteenth, twentieth, and twenty-first plenary sessions of the General Assembly have been selected for analysis. Selection was based on the importance of the issues

---

[79] However, a caveat is owed the reader as to the shortcomings of voting analysis in elucidating the workings of the political process of the United Nations. First the number of votes taken in the Organization each year has soared to such an extent that it even has become onerous using modern high speed computers to encompass every vote taken. In their recent study Alker and Russett, in fact, found that it was no longer practical to include every main committee and plenary roll-call when concerned with only one session, the sixteenth, of the Assembly. Alker and Russett, *World Politics in the General Assembly*, p. 27. While there are guide lines, there are no hard and fast rules as to which votes should be selected for analysis and which ones rejected. This is a hazardous process; but to pretend that any guarantee exists as to proper selection other than the skill of the observer would be misleading. Although it does not lessen the subjective content of the selection process, the guide lines used in determining which votes to include in this study are set forth later. Another important limitation on the use of voting analysis in a study of the United Nations derives from the nature of its political process in which so much negotiation takes place behind the scenes. If voting analysis is coupled with extensive qualitative analysis of the political system, the limitation is not so acute. Voting analysis, properly undertaken, is only one tool among many available to the political scientist in probing the nature of a given political system. When used in conjunction with the other tools of the profession, it is a valuable aid in examining those decisions in which states are forced to publicly take sides. Like any of the other tools of the profession, when used alone voting analysis all too often presents at best a limited and somewhat facile picture of the system and at worst a picture of another system entirely.

involved and with the aim of providing as representative a grouping as possible.[80] Where multiple votes, that is, paragraph-by-paragraph votes, were taken on a draft, an attempt was made to select the vote that best represented the issue involved.[81] In general, the plenary vote was used in this analysis. However, in cases where the only roll-call vote on a resolution was in committee or where the committee vote reflected an element not present in the plenary vote, the committee vote was selected.

One indication of the extent of influence exercised by the new nations on colonial issues in the United Nations can be provided by determining the extent of their concurrence with the United Nations majority on these issues. While it is true that frequent concurrence with the majority cannot prove that effective influence was exercised —it may only indicate a slavish following of the majority—lack of such agreement would demonstrate the absence of effectively applied influence.[82] The certainty with which a high degree of concurrence with the majority can be used as one index of effectively applied political influence increases when the states concerned are found to have actively engaged in initiating and pushing the proposals voted upon. Such intimate involvement with the issues of parliamentary diplomacy is largely incompatible with a blind desire to be always on the winning side regardless of the merits of the question at stake. As the central focus of the diplomacy of the new nations in the United Nations, colonialism certainly qualifies as an area in which they have been actively engaged. Thus, if it is found that the new nations have a high majority agreement voting score on the colonial questions analyzed, it would be at least presumptive evidence of the effective exercise of political influence on their part.[83]

On the 70 colonial votes analyzed in which 50 percent or more of

---

[80] Of course, one important criterion in the selection of votes was the availability of the voting records in a form usable for analysis. If one considered all the votes taken in any one session of the Assembly, in both plenary and main Committee, it is found that the great majority are not recorded on a country-by-country breakdown as they are not roll-call votes. This inherent limitation in selection is somewhat mitigated by the general rule-of-thumb that the most important votes are those taken on a roll call.

[81] The issues selected, as well as the country-by-country vote tally, are set forth in Appendices D, E, and F.

[82] Riggs, *Politics in the United Nations*, p. 170.

[83] A majority in plenary sessions of the General Assembly is actually a two-thirds majority on "important questions." United Nations Charter, Article 18.

the new nations voted together, they were in agreement with the Assembly majority on 97 per cent of the votes.[84] This majority agreement score is particularly impressive as an index of the effective exercise of political influence, when it is noted that 97 percent of

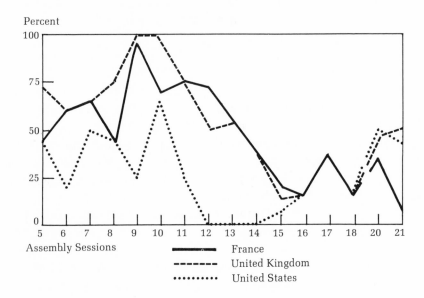

CHART IV.1   Percentage of "no" votes cast by France, the United Kingdom, and the United States on selected decolonization issues, Fifth to Twenty-first Sessions of the General Assembly. The issues selected and vote totals are presented in Appendices B and C.

the votes were on items initiated and sponsored in the whole or in major part by the new nations. The possibility of servile followship yielding a specious index is considerably reduced by this intimate involvement with the issues.

A telling demonstration of the effectiveness of the new nations' influence on colonial issues is provided in Chart IV.1. This chart presents an analysis of the number of negative votes cast by France, the United Kingdom, and the United States on 145 decolonization

[84] By comparison, the majority agreement scores of the U.S.S.R., the United States, and the United Kingdom were as follows: U.S.S.R., 92.8 percent; United States, 20.0 percent; United Kingdom, 14.2 percent. The data for these and all other calculations in this section is contained in Appendices D, E, and F.

issues between the fifth and twenty-first sessions of the General Assembly.[85] The chart shows a steady, though somewhat irregular, decline in the percentage of negative votes cast by these three states commencing with the eleventh session in 1956. This decline in negative voting coincides with the accelerated entry of new nations into the Organization and their opening of an intensive campaign against colonialism. More significant as evidence of the effective influence of the new nations than the decline of negative voting by these three states is that it occurred during a steady escalation in severity of the resolutions being voted upon. For example, at the seventh session of the Assembly France and the United Kingdom voted against and the United States abstained on the question of establishing a commission to study the question of race conflict in South Africa, but at the eighteenth session all three states voted in favor of a resolution condemning the Government of South Africa for its policy of apartheid. At the seventh session of the Assembly France, the United Kingdom and the United States voted against a resolution upholding the right of all peoples and nations to self-determination, yet at the fifteenth session these states failed to vote against a much more far-reaching resolution designed to secure the immediate granting of independence to colonial countries and peoples. The records are replete with many similar cases in which France, the United Kingdom, and the United States have since 1956 either acquiesced in or supported anticolonial resolutions far stronger than these three states voted against in earlier years.

Also of significance in measuring the effectiveness of the political influence wielded by the new nations is the extent to which the other Assembly groupings have supported or opposed the new nations. Chart IV.2 clearly shows the extent to which the new nations have gained the support of the other nations on colonial issues. As might be expected, the non-new nation members of the Afro-Asian group have been the most consistent in their support, while the Western European nations have failed to support the new nations most consistently. However, the most striking fact revealed in this analysis is the extent to which it has become exceedingly unpopular to oppose the anticolonial thrust of the new nations. While the majority

[85] Appendices A, B, and C contain the 145 decolonization issues upon which this chart is based.

of the Latin American nations supported the new nations on 76.2 percent of 23 analyzed colonial votes, not once did a majority of the Latin American Members oppose the new nations on these issues. Even the Western European states have found the sanctuary of abstention more alluring than outright opposition to the new nations on colonial issues. On only 22.7 percent of the analyzed roll-call votes did a majority of the Western European states vote in opposi-

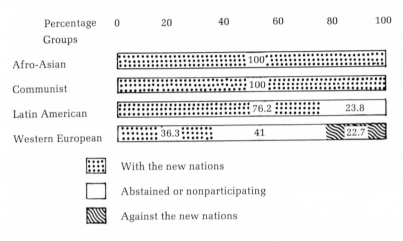

CHART IV.2 Comparison of votes on colonial issues of the majority of other assembly groups in relation to the New Nations, Sixteenth to Eighteenth Sessions of the General Assembly. This analysis is based on the vote tally   in Appendix D. All groups are exclusive of any new nations that might normally be considered members of them.

tion to the new nations. The extent to which states are unwilling to record publicly through the medium of a roll-call vote their opposition to the anticolonial measures advanced by the new nations in the United Nations is a convincing demonstration that at least with respect to this issue category the new nations have sucessfully used their political influence to delegitimize colonialism. It is no longer respectable or politic to vote against such measures, and the only prudent means of registering opposition in the Assembly has become abstention.[86]

[86] Of course, this says nothing about the types of measures adopted, the compromises made or the ultimate goals sought, but these are questions most suitable for descriptive techniques and are so handled in other sections of this study.

Certainly one element of the success of the new nations in regard to colonial issues is the cohesion of the group on this issue. Of the 23 votes analyzed for the sixteenth through the eighteenth sessions of the Assembly, there are only six instances in which states voted in an opposite direction from that of the majority of the group and all six of these instances were on the two roll calls in which a majority of the group abstained.[87] On the other 21 votes there was not a single case of a state voting in the opposite direction from that of a majority. Even more impressive as an index of cohesion is the failure of any of the new nations to resort to abstention on any of the 12 votes from the seventeenth and eighteenth sessions.[88] At least on colonial issues the new nations form a cohesive group that has an impressive record for initiating and obtaining the adoption of a wide range of anticolonial measures.

Decolonization—A Summary One must view as an outstanding achievement of the new nations their successful forging between 1960 and 1964 of an international moral consensus against the continuation of Western colonialism. By 1964 the impropriety of any defense of the continued existence of colonialism was apparent to all except the retrograde regimes of southern Africa. Within the United Nations itself the new nations succeeded during this period in making their own uppermost concern, colonialism, the uppermost concern of the Organization. At the behest of the new nations the Assembly has moved from general pronouncements of moral and legal rights, such as the 1960 Declaration on Colonialism, to condemnations of specific nations accompanied by requests for diplomatic and economic sanctions and threats of military sanctions. The Special Committee on Colonialism has maintained a constant surveillance of the remaining colonial areas, while its new nation directorate has kept up a steady stream of reports and recommendations to other organs of the United Nations.

As frustration grew over the recalcitrant attitude of the remaining colonial powers, the new nations sought Security Council endorse-

[87] The states that voted in opposition to the majority of the new nations on the 23 votes analyzed were Tunisia, Malaysia, Pakistan, Philippines, and Israel.

[88] As can be seen from the vote tally in Appendix B, there were scattered instances of absences by new nations, but as noted earlier, many of these cases are probably the product of understaffed missions rather than any opposition to the issue at hand.

ment of mandatory enforcement programs designed to eliminate these regimes. By the end of 1969 the new nations had not been able to obtain such Security Council actions. However, in the case of South Africa under the impact of repeated appeals of the new nations, the Security Council had gone through a host of preliminary actions which, if the attitude of the South African Government remains unchanged, may ultimately lead to the desired enforcement action. The greatest success of the new nations' wielding of political influence during these years remained the success in shifting their concern and outlook on colonialism over to the United Nations. This same degree of influence, however, was not manifested with respect to the international political environment outside the United Nations. In the cases of both Southern Rhodesia and South Africa, the success of the new nations in obtaining favorable resolutions was not matched by comparable success in obtaining favorable modifications of the international political environment in regard to Southern Rhodesia and South Africa.

Human Rights

For the new nations the traditional concern of the United Nations with human rights has been but another vehicle for advancing their attack on colonialism and associated forms of racial discrimination. Traditionally, the promotion of human rights has been viewed from the perspective of protecting the citizen in the fullest possible exercise, compatible with organized society, of those rights that flow from the dignity and worth of the individual. For this perspective, centered as it is on the individual, the new nations have substituted a perspective centered on the evils of Western colonialism with its domination of black by white. As Louis Henkin has aptly noted,

. . . the struggle to end colonialism, also swallowed up the original purpose of cooperation for promotion of human rights. The gradual elimination of dependent areas and their admission to the UN meant an ever increasing Assembly majority with some agreed attitudes, particularly a determination to extirpate the remnants of white colonialism and white discrimination. These attitudes impinged on the human rights program as well. Of course, they assured the sharpest scrutiny of human rights in dependent areas. . . . But it was a championship of anticolonialism, designed to accelerate "self-determination." It was not an assertion of general standards which other nations, including the champions, were prepared to accept in their own countries.[89]

The extent to which the new nations' concern with eliminating all vestiges of colonialism dominated the perspective from which they viewed the human rights activity of the Organization was pointedly demonstrated at the Assembly's seventeenth session. In preparation for the fifteenth anniversary in 1963 of the adoption of the Universal Declaration of Human Rights, the United States joined with six other states at the seventeenth Assembly in requesting the Secretary-General to appoint a Special Committee to draft plans for the anniversary.[90] During the Third Committee's consideration of this draft, three new nations, Guinea, Mali, and Mauritania, joined in offering an amendment expressing the hope "that all States will implement General Assembly resolution 1514 (XV) [Declaration on the Granting of Independence to Colonial Countries and Peoples] so that the Fifteenth Anniversary of the Universal Declaration of Human Rights may be celebrated in an atmosphere of independence and freedom."[91] For the new nations self-determination and national independence, rights of political groupings and not of individuals, head the list of human rights that the Organization should promote. This redefinition of the traditional individual-centered concept of human rights has gained acceptance with the entry of the new nations into the Organization, and both the Committee and the Assembly accepted this amended version of the draft.

At the seventeenth session the Assembly approved a draft sponsored by 34 states, 24 of whom were new nations, requesting the Commission on Human Rights to prepare a draft declaration and a draft convention on the elimination of all forms of racial discrimination.[92] Using the draft declaration prepared by the commission as a basis for discussion, the eighteenth Assembly proceeded to draft the final text of the Declaration on Elimination of All Forms of Racial Discrimination.[93] During the course of the Third Committee's

[89] Louis Henkin, "The United Nations and Human Rights," *International Organization*, 19, No. 3 (Summer 1965), 512.
[90] United Nations Document A/C.3/L.991/Rev. 1, Oct. 15, 1962.
[91] United Nations Document A/C.3/L.1002/Rev. 1, Oct. 25, 1962.
[92] United Nations Document A/C.3/L.1006/Rev. 6/Add.1, Nov. 1, 1962 and Nov. 5, 1962. United Nations General Assembly Resolution 1780(XVII), Dec. 7, 1962.
[93] The draft prepared by the Commission on Humah Rights is annexed to Economic and Social Council Resolution 958E(XXXVI), July 12, 1963.

consideration of the draft declaration, three of the nine paragraphs of the preamble and eight out of the ten operative paragraphs were successfully amended by various new nations. One new paragraph each was added to the preamble and the operative paragraphs. The net effect of these successful maneuvers of the new nations was to impose a sense of urgency on the draft and to sharpen its application to the remaining white colonial regimes of Africa and particularly South Africa. The draft expressed alarm at racial discrimination and specifically singled out apartheid for condemnation. Citing the Declaration on Colonialism as its authority, the draft proclaimed the "necessity of bringing colonialism to a speedy and unconditional end." It declared that "an end shall be put without delay to governmental and other public policies of apartheid, as well as all forms of racial discrimination and separation resulting from such policies." And finally, every state "shall fully and faithfully observe the provisions of the present Declaration, the Universal Declaration of Human Rights, and the Declaration on the granting of independence to colonial countries and peoples."[94] With 17 states abstaining, the Third Committee approved the amended draft which the Assembly adopted unanimously.[95]

Of course, the major thrust of the political interest of the new nations in human rights has been directed against South Africa. The problem of apartheid is "ugly in its present reality and uglier still in its violent and destructive potentiality."[96] Because of its close relationship to the problems of colonialism the new nations' course of action against South Africa was considered earlier as one aspect of their general attack on the remnants of colonialism.

In assessing the role played by the new nations on human rights questions, Henkin's appraisal seems sound.

The anticolonial atmosphere of the Assembly and the increasing and

[94] United Nations Document A/5603, Nov. 12, 1963.

[95] United Nations General Assembly *Official Records,* 18th Session, Third Committee, 1245th meeting (Oct. 28, 1963), para. 2. The 17 states abstaining in Committee were Australia, Belgium, Canada, Denmark, Finland, France, Greece, Iceland, Ireland, Italy, Luxembourg, Netherlands, New Zealand, Norway, Sweden, United Kingdom, and United States. South Africa remained absent from both the committee and plenary because of the specific mention of apartheid. United Nations General Assembly Resolution 1904 (XVIII), Nov. 20, 1963.

[96] Waldemar A. Nielsen, *African Battleline: American Policy Choices in Southern Africa* (New York: Published for the Council on Foreign Relations by Harper & Row, 1965), p. 59.

confident majorities of "new nations" led to the injection of anticolonial issues into the human rights covenants. Self-determination was added to the roster of human rights as an additional weapon against colonialism although there was no suggestion that this was a right of the individual that the individual could claim it against an unrepresentative government, or that minorities could invoke it to support secession. . . . Human rights was being used as a political weapon against colonialism or economic imperialism, not to enhance the rights of all persons against all governments.[97]

[97] Henkin, "The United Nations and Human Rights," *International Organization*, 19, No. 3 (Summer 1965), 513.

Chapter V

THE EXTENT OF INFLUENCE—II

In the preceding chapter, attention was focused on decolonization and human rights from the perspective of the new nations. This chapter will be concerned with the remainder of the issue spectrum, specifically, the topics of economic aid and development, East-West questions and organizational questions. The framework of analysis remains as in the preceding chapter directed at the major questions in each issue category during the period 1960–1967, the positions of the new nations, and the development of these questions in relation to the alternatives advocated by the new nations.

Economic Aid and Development

The efforts of the United Nations in advancing economic development have been greatly accelerated in the post-1960 period.[1] As the new nations are to a large extent both the initiators and the objects of United Nations development policies, their views on the proper role of the Organization in the development process are of considerable importance. All indicators point to the fact that economic development ranks next to colonialism as the topic of greatest concern in the hierarchy of values of the new nations. What policies have they advocated and how successful have they been in exercising the political influence necessary to obtain adoption of these policies?

The United Nations Capital Development Fund For a number of years prior to 1960 the developing countries advocated the creation

---

[1] Article 55 of the Charter is the only article in which economic development is directly referred to as an objective of the Organization: ". . . the United Nations shall promote: a. higher standards of living, full employment, and conditions of economic and social progress and development."

of a special United Nations fund to be used solely for capital invest-ment in their countries. However, this idea found little favor among the developed countries, who were willing to agree only to weak substitutes such as the Special Fund and the International Develop-ment Association. The stalemate that existed up to 1960 is accurately reflected in the Secretary-General's report on the replies of Members to a request for their views on the early establishment of a United Nations capital development fund. On the basis of the responses by Member States the Secretary-General was forced to conclude that "the replies do not indicate any significant new developments in connection with the establishment of a United Nations capital devel-opment fund."[2] The United States response, which was but a repeti-tion of its earlier views, was typical of the replies received from the developed nations.

. . . . We should not waste resources available for financing by multiply-ing machinery for distributing it. . . . We would see no merit in creating or even discussing additional machinery, when the real problem is to use effectively the machinery already in the process of being established.[3]

However, by the start of the 1960 Assembly session, the political climate had changed considerably. At the fifteenth session 45 devel-oping nations, 20 of whom were new nations, introduced into the Second Committee a draft resolution calling for the Assembly to decide "that a United Nations capital development fund shall be established."[4] During committee consideration of the draft, the spon-sors agreed to accept an amendment proposed by Denmark, Greece, and the Netherlands which would have the Assembly decide "in principle that a United Nations capital development fund shall be established."[5] The Second Committee then proceeded to adopt the amended draft by a vote of 68 in favor, 4 against, with 8 abstentions.[6] By a simple show of hands, the plenary agreed on a vote of 71 in favor, 4 against, with 10 abstaining, to the establishment "in princi-

---

[2] United Nations Document E/3393, June 2, 1960, para. 5.
[3] Ibid., Annex, p. 5.
[4] United Nations Document A/C.2/L.472/Rev.1 and Add.1, Dec. 1, 1960 and Dec. 6, 1960.
[5] United Nations Document A/C.2/L.535, Dec. 2, 1960.
[6] United Nations General Assembly Official Records, 15th Session, Second Committee, 705th meeting (Dec. 6, 1960), para. 33. Those voting against were Australia, Union of South Africa, United Kingdom, United States. Those abstaining were Belgium, Canada, Finland, France, Ireland, Japan, New Zealand, and Sweden.

ple" of a United Nations capital development fund.[7] This resolution, which failed to gain the support of the developed nations, called for the creation of a twenty-five member committee appointed by the Assembly's President to consider all preparatory measures.[8] This committee did not meet until May 15, 1961, and was able to accomplish very little before its June deadline for reporting to the Economic and Social Council. With France, South Africa, the United Kingdom, and the United States dissenting, the Second Committee recommended that the Assembly renew the committee's mandate for another year, and the sixteenth Assembly approved this recommendation without a roll-call vote.[9] At the committee's resumed meeting in the spring of 1962 the unwillingness of the capital-exporting nations to become associated with any new United Nations machinery in this field was dramatized. Seven delegations, representing Canada, Denmark, France, Japan, the Netherlands, the United Kingdom, and the United States, refused to participate in preparing a draft statute for the United Nations Capital Development Fund.[10] The representative of the United Kingdom stated that

in view of the fact that his delegation felt that the establishment of the Fund was not a practical proposition, it could not in good faith take part in the discussion or drafting of the Statute which was, in its view, an exercise which was at least premature, and which could only arouse unfounded expectations.[11]

In a similar vein the United States representative noted that

the United States Government prided itself on never entering into a commitment either expressed or implied that it could not properly fulfill. Since, in the present instance, the United States was resolved not to contribute to or be a part of a United Nations Capital Development Fund, it would not be proper for it to participate in drafting a statute for such a

[7] United Nations General Assembly *Official Records,* 15th Session, 948th meeting (Dec. 15, 1960), para. 16. United Nations General Assembly Resolution 1521(XV), Dec. 15, 1960.
    [8] United Nations General Assembly *Official Records,* 15th Session, 968th meeting (Mar. 27, 1961), para. 1, The members of the Committee on a United Nations Capital Development Fund were Argentina, Brazil, Burma, Canada, Chile, Czechoslovakia, Denmark, France, Ghana, India, Indonesia, Iraq, Italy, Ivory Coast, Japan, Netherlands, Nigeria, Pakistan, Peru, Sudan, U.S.S.R., United Arab Republic, United Kingdom, United States, and Yugoslavia.
    [9] United Nations General Assembly Resolution 1706(XVI), Dec. 19, 1961.
    [10] United Nations Document E/3654, June 14, 1962, para. 18–20.
    [11] *Ibid.,* para. 18.

body . . . it felt the time had come to strengthen the existing machinery and not to be deluded into believing that problems could be solved by the establishment of a new body.[12]

A majority of the committee decided to proceed with the drafting of a statute and finally approved such a draft statute, which was then transmitted to the Economic and Social Council. The lack of enthusiasm of the capital-exporting nations for the creation of a capital development fund was apparent during the Economic and Social Council's discussion of the draft statute. The Council finally approved, with the capital-exporting states abstaining, a resolution to forward the draft statute to the General Assembly along with a request that the economically advanced countries reconsider the possibility of establishing such a fund.[13] Faced with this same division of opinion, the seventeenth Assembly was content to request the Secretary-General to inquire of the Member States as to their views on the draft statute and to extend again the mandate of the Committee on a United Nations Capital Development Fund.[14] Meetings of this committee during 1963, as well as discussions at the eighteenth session of the Assembly, revealed no change in the positions of Member States. Again with the major capital-exporting states abstaining, the less developed nations had to be content with extending the mandate of the Committee on a United Nations Capital Development Fund for another year.[15]

In 1964 the developing countries used the United Nations Conference on Trade and Development (UNCTAD) to continue their campaign for the establishment of a capital development fund. Here they were able to secure the passage, although without the support of the principal capital-exporting countries, of a resolution calling for the Capital Development Fund to "start its operations at an early date."[16] UNCTAD also adopted a resolution, again without the support of the principal capital exporters, which called for the gradual

[12] *Ibid.*
[13] United Nations, Economic and Social Council Resolution 921(XXXIV), Aug. 3, 1962.
[14] United Nations General Assembly Resolution 1826(XVII), Dec. 18, 1962. Even on this relatively innocuous resolution nine states, Australia, Belgium, Canada, France, Ireland, Japan, New Zealand, United Kingdom, and the United States, abstained during the vote in the Second Committee. United Nations General Assembly *Official Records,* 17th Session, Second Committee, 860th meeting (Dec. 4, 1962). The plenary vote, which was by a show of hands, was 85 votes for to none against, with 12 abstentions.
[15] United Nations General Assembly Resolution 1936(XVIII), Dec. 11, 1963.
[16] United Nations Conference on Trade and Development, *Final Act,* Annexes A.IV.7.

transformation of the Special Fund into a Capital Development Fund.[17]

Finally in 1966, six years after the Assembly had decided on the establishment "in principle" of a United Nations capital development fund, the twenty-first Assembly established a United Nations Capital Development Fund.[18] During this prolonged gestation period the aim of the fund remained "to assist developing countries in the development of their economies by supplementing existing sources of capital assistance by means of grants and loans, particularly long-term loans made free of interest or at low interest rates." But while the 1966 resolution spoke of bringing into operation the Capital Development Fund and provided that the first annual pledging conference should be held in the fall of 1967, that a Board should be elected by the twenty-second Assembly, and that the Secretary-General should appoint a Managing Director to assume office on January 1, 1968, in actuality the Fund was not much closer to a meaningful role than in 1960. The pledging conference in October 1967 was such a failure that it again revealed the impotence of its sponsors for all to see. Only the miniscule amount of $1,298,654 was collected and less than $500,000 of this was in convertible currency, the only kind that has any real meaning in an international undertaking to transfer resources. The pledging conference was boycotted by all of the developed Western states except the Netherlands and all of the Eastern European states except Yugoslavia. And, in fact, as of the spring of 1968 the Secretary-General had made no decision on whether this pauper's fund justified the cost of a Managing Director.

Despite the persistent efforts of the new nations operating in conjunction with the other developing nations, the industrialized nations were able to prevent during this period the effective establishment of the United Nations Capital Development Fund. Their campaign has had two high-water marks: the 1960 Assembly decision to establish the Fund "in principle" and the 1966 Assembly decision to move ahead and implement this earlier decision. However, neither of these decisions has yet resulted in the creation of a fund endowed with sufficient resources even to commence meaningful operations.

There were several reasons for the inability of the new nations to

---

[17] *Ibid.*, Annexes A.IV.8.
[18] United Nations General Assembly Resolution 2186(XXI), Dec. 13, 1966.

exercise sufficient political influence to operationalize the Capital Development Fund. Any development fund to be successful requires more than the acquiescence of the industrialized nations; it requires their active support in terms of large financial commitments. In sharp contrast to their disarray on colonial issues, the developed nations of the West were able to maintain a united front on this issue. The new nations also realized that Soviet voting support on these issues was an asset of dubious value because of the Soviet's unwillingness to match this voting support with requisite amounts of financial support. This significant factor deprived the new nations of the maneuvering room that they used to such advantage on colonial issues. But much of the inability of the developing nations to muster sufficient political influence to carry this project to fruition can be traced to the nature of the issue. First, the drive to establish a development fund did not have the same dynamism behind it as did the drive to end colonialism. Self-determination and racial equality are forces that transcend boundaries and move men of all nations to action, but the same cannot be said of a United Nations Capital Development Fund. The developing nations also lacked an economic doctrine that universalized their claim to economic development, while unifying them in the struggle to achieve the means for such development. It was just such a political doctrine, nationalism and self-determination, that had given the decolonization drive its main impetus.

The Drive to UNCTAD The calling under United Nations auspices of an international trade conference to try to improve on the record of the unsuccessful Havana Conference of 1948 was an established idea long before the new nations swelled the membership of the Organization. During the 1950's it was a stock proposal in the Soviet repertory,[19] but the Western fear that in the cold war of the 1950's such a conference would only provide a forum for Soviet attacks on GATT and on the strategic trade controls of the West prevented such a conference.

However, with the sudden surge to membership of the new nations in 1960, a metamorphosis took place in the sponsorship and aims of the proposed international trade conference. Now it was the developing nations, with the new nations in the forefront, that were

[19] See, for example, United Nations Document A/C.2/L.282, Nov. 26, 1956.

pressing for the convening of the conference. At the Assembly's sixteenth session 18 African, three Asian and six Latin American Members combined to produce a draft that recognized "the maximum expansion" of trade as being essential to economic development and requested the Secretary-General to consult member governments as to their views on holding an international trade conference and possible topics for a provisional agenda.[20] Although the major trading nations had opposed the draft at the time of the Second Committee's vote, the plenary adopted the draft unanimously.[21]

It became apparent when the Secretary-General consulted the Members that the major trading nations had not significantly altered their opposition to the trade conference. Of the 66 replies received, 45 were favorable to the holding of such a conference, 18 were opposed, and 3 states were noncommittal.[22] Typical of the replies of the major trading powers is that of the United Kingdom, which while "fully aware of the extent of the problems of international trade . . . considers that an international trade conference would not at present contribute to the solution of the problems of world trade."[23]

Soon after the opening of the thirty-fourth session of the Economic and Social Council in July 1962, it became apparent that the major trading nations had altered their course. Although unprepared to emulate the enthusiasm of the new nations for the conference, the trading nations indicated that they were prepared to acquiesce in its calling, provided that satisfactory terms of reference could be obtained. Five developing nations submitted a draft resolution to the Economic Committee of the Economic and Social Council which, inter alia, provided for (a) the calling by the Economic and Social Council of a United Nations Conference on Trade and Development (UNCTAD); (b) a preparatory committee of governmental experts to meet in the early spring of 1963 "to consider the agenda and docu-

[20] United Nations Documents A/C.2/L.550/Rev.2/Add.1, Nov. 7, 1961; A/C.2/L.556/Add.1/Rev.1, Nov. 7, 1961; A/5056, Dec. 18, 1961; A/L.379, Dec. 18, 1961.

[21] United Nations General Assembly Resolution 1707(XVI), Dec. 19, 1961.

[22] United Nations Document E/3631 and Add.1-4, May 10, 1962. Those opposing the conference were Australia, Austria, Belgium, Canada, Colombia, Federal Republic of Germany, France, Ireland, Italy, New Zealand, Netherlands, Nicaragua, Norway, South Africa, Spain, Switzerland, United Kingdom, and the United States. The responses of Greece, Japan, and Sweden were noncommittal.

[23] United Nations Document E/3631/Add.1, June 12, 1962, 18.

mentation for the Conference with particular reference to the problems of the developing countries"; and (c) the preparatory committee to report back to the Economic and Social Council at its summer session in 1963.[24] The new attitude of the major trading states was apparent in the statement of the United States representative, Mr. Klutznick, before the Economic Committee. The United States "had been impressed by the constructive attitude adopted by the sponsors of the draft resolution." The United States was also in agreement with the draft's sponsors that the conference should be focused on the trade problems of the developing countries. Mr. Klutznick concluded with the announcement that the United States would support the draft "with a fair degree of optimism."[25] On the next day the Economic Committee voted unanimously in favor of the draft, and it was similarly adopted by the Economic and Social Council on August 3, 1962.[26]

While the decision to hold UNCTAD had been formally made, much remained unsettled. As of the time of the convening of the seventeenth session of the General Assembly, no decision had been reached on when the conference would take place, who would attend it, what it would discuss, or how it would be organized. In what must rank among the most complex of any negotiations ever conducted within the confines of the Assembly, the seventeenth session made substantial progress on all of these questions.[27] Negotiations were centered on a thirty-five Power draft introduced in the Second Committee by the developing nations.[28] This draft, which maintained the initiative of the developing nations, provided for the convening of the conference by June 1963, the appointment of a Secretary-General, a series of "fundamental points" to be taken into account in the preparation of the draft agenda and the enlargement of the Preparatory Committee to 30 members. The Second Committee vote which approved an amended version of this draft by a vote

[24] United Nations Document E/L.958/Rev.2, July 30, 1962. The sponsors of this draft were Brazil, Ethiopia, India, Senegal, and Yugoslavia.
[25] United Nations Document E/AC.6/SR.327, Oct. 24, 1962, 9.
[26] United Nations, Economic and Social Council, *Official Records*, 34th Session, 1236th meeting (Aug. 3, 1962), 209. Economic and Social Council Resolution 917(XXXIV), Aug. 3, 1962.
[27] As the purpose of this section is to examine the scope and consistency with which the new nations have exercised political influence in five broad issue categories, no attempt will be made here to present a detailed account of these complex negotiations.
[28] United Nations Document A/C.2/L.648/Rev.2/Corr.1, Nov. 14, 1962.

of 75 to 10, with 23 abstentions, found the major trading states in opposition.[29] However, when the draft came before the plenary the developing nations by accepting a joint Canadian-Peruvian amendment, which postponed the conference until early 1964 and somewhat softened the language regarding the Common Market, were able to re-establish their basis of wide political support. This amended version of the draft was approved by a vote of 91 to 0, with one abstention.[30]

The detailed planning for the conference now fell on the expanded Preparatory Committee, which consisted of the representatives of 30 governments.[31] Of the 30 members of the Preparatory Committee, 17 were developing nations and 6 of these new nations. At its April 1963 session the Economic and Social Council increased the size of the Preparatory Committee by two with the addition of the Federation of Malaysia and Indonesia to the group.[32] This brought the number of developing nations on the Preparatory Committee to 19, 8 of which were new nations. It was during the three sessions of the Preparatory Committee held between January 1963 and February 1964 that the conference moved from an idea to a reality. The Preparatory Committee considered matters ranging from the provisional agenda to the seating in the committee rooms.[33] The Economic and Social Council at its July-August 1963 meeting unanimously approved the holding of the United Nations Conference on Trade and Development from March 15 to June 15, 1964.

In terms of the political influence exercised, the convening of UNCTAD represented a substantial success for the new nations. One indicator of the dimensions of this success was the shift of the major trading nations from an attitude as late as May 1962 of public

[29] United Nations General Assembly *Official Records,* Second Committee, 17th Session, 839th meeting (Nov. 15, 1962), para. 31. The ten states voting against the draft were Belgium, France, Ireland, Italy, Luxembourg, Rwanda, South Africa, Spain, the United Kingdom, and the United States.

[30] United Nations General Assembly Resolution 1758(XVII), Dec. 8, 1962.

[31] The 30 members of the Preparatory Committee consisted of the 18 members of the Economic and Social Council in 1962 and 12 other members elected by the Economic and Social Council. The 30 members were Argentina, Australia, Austria, Brazil, Canada, Colombia, Czechoslovakia, Denmark, El Salvador, Ethiopia, France, India, Italy, Japan, Jordan, Lebanon, Madagascar, New Zealand, Nigeria, Pakistan, Peru, Poland, Senegal, Tunisia, United Arab Republic, U.S.S.R., United Kingdom, United States, Uruguay, and Yugoslavia. *United Nations Yearbook 1962* (New York: Published by Columbia University Press in cooperation with the United Nations, 1964), 693.

[32] United Nations, Economic and Social Council Resolution 943(XXXV), Apr. 18, 1963.

[33] For a summary of the Preparatory Committee's work, see its three reports: United Nations Documents E/3720, Feb. 6, 1963; E/3799, July 5, 1963; and E/Conf. 46/65, Feb. 18, 1964.

opposition to such a conference to an attitude in July 1962 of "fair optimism" toward it. With the sudden increase in the number of less developed Members of the Organization in the post-1960 period, the industrialized nations found their own refusal to enter into multilateral talks over trade problems increasingly untenable. It seems safe to say that without this change in the composition of the Organization the industrialized countries would have had little reason for altering their opposition to the conference.

Of great portent for the future of the Organization was the emergence during the struggle to convene UNCTAD of a common view of the problem of economic development, with which not only the new nations but all of the less developed nations could agree. On the colonial issue the new nations had been able to ask and obtain broad support because self-determination and racial equality had transnational appeal. The new nations were able to claim for themselves the sole right of interpretation of the meaning of these moral doctrines because the only remaining colonial areas lay within their cultural and geographical sphere. But economic underdevelopment was another story entirely. Economic development as a right owed by the industrialized countries to the underdeveloped ones was at best an inchoate right and certainly lacked the emotive overtones of self-determination and racial equality. Furthermore, underdevelopment was so widespread as to deny any one grouping the exclusive right to define the problem and its solution. The problems of development were immediate and severe for over 70 countries, each with its own special interests. However, during the campaign to convene UNCTAD a common view of the problems of international trade and development began to emerge. This view, which was enshrined in a resolution of the eighteenth Assembly as the Joint Declaration of the Seventy-Five Developing Nations, has significant operational importance because it provides two-thirds of the Organization's Members with a common basis from which to advance claims against the industrialized minority.[34] If this proves to be an enduring basis of collaboration among the underdeveloped

[34] United Nations General Assembly Resolution 1897(XVIII), Nov. 11, 1963. In commenting on this new attitude, the delegate of Mali said. "A new outlook had . . . emerged at Geneva at the same time that a new strategy developed whereby the developing countries had been able to submerge their own special interests and come to an understanding on underdevelopment, which was their most important denominator." United Nations Document TC/B/SR.6, Apr. 14, 1965, 16 as cited in "Issues before the 20th General Assembly," International Conciliation, No. 554 (Summer 1965), 113.

Members of the United Nations, it will provide an important means in the future for amplifying the political influence within the Organization of the new nations.[35]

Economic Development—The Uncontroversial Perspective The consistency with which the new nations have influenced United Nations development policies cannot be gleaned solely from an analysis of controversial issues, such as the Capital Development Fund and UNCTAD. While over 85 percent of the personnel and funds of the United Nations system are engaged in development-related activities, most of it is in programs that generate little open controversy and few roll-call votes.[36] The United Nations is to a considerable extent a major battleground in what has been described as a "curious war in which everyone professes to be on the same side, marching under the same banner, toward the same goal."[37] However, valid indications of the extent of the influence exercised by the new nations can be obtained by analyzing the development of this large sector of uncontroversial development programs.

In the immediate post-war period the United Nations system, to the extent that it was concerned with economic problems at all, centered its attention on the twin problems of the relief and reconstruction of war-torn Europe, Asia, and after 1948, Palestine. Accompanying the Organization's concern with reconstruction was a broader desire to ensure through international economic collaboration the harmonizing of various national fiscal and monetary policies.[38] It was only in the early 1950's, when the principal tasks of relief and reconstruction had been completed, that the problems of the underdeveloped countries received widespread attention from the Organization. As Asher has noted, "At about midpoint in the first decade of United Nations history, the special problems of the

[35] For an excellent description of how the politics of UNCTAD-I looked to an American participant, see Richard N. Gardner, "The United Nations Conference on Trade and Development," *International Organization,* 22, No. 1 (Winter 1968), 99–130.

[36] In analyzing all the votes taken on economic questions in the 16th through the 22d sessions of the General Assembly in both main committee and plenary meetings, it was found that over 95 percent of the votes were either unanimous or simply by show of hands. In United Nations practice a show-of-hands vote is not recorded on a country-by-country basis. For example, there were only six roll-call votes during 1962–1963, so that a sufficient statistical base did not exist for meaningful voting analysis.

[37] Isador Lubin and Robert E. Asher, "The Struggle for a Better Life," Chapter IV of *The U.S. Stake in the U.N.,* The American Assembly (New York: Columbia University Press, 1954), p. 74. Cited in Robert Asher, et al. *The United Nations and Economic and Social Cooperation* (Washington, D.C.: The Brookings Institution, 1957), p. 491.

[38] Asher, *The United Nations and Economic and Social Cooperation,* pp. 56–86, 96–158.

underdeveloped countries ceased being special problems and became the stock in trade of United Nations economic and social programs."[39]

However, it was not until later that the United Nations system began to devote significant amounts of financial resources to the problems of development. The timing of this increased financial

TABLE V.1

Budget Levels for Selected Elements of the United Nations System (In Millions of Dollars)

	1950	1955	1960	1961	1962	1963	1964	1965	1966	1967
Expanded Program of Technical Assistance	–	25.1	34.4	38.1	49.0	53.6	53.0			
Special Fund	–	–	39.0	47.0	62.8	75.7	85.7			
UNDP [a]								156.1	175.9	187
FAO	5.0	6.6	9.2	9.2	14.3	14.3	17.8	17.8	23.8	23.8
UNESCO	8.0	10.3	13.0	15.1	15.5	19.0	19.0	23.9	23.9	30.1
WHO	7.5	10.0	16.9	18.9	24.1	30.9	34.7	39.4	43.5	53.3
Total Budget of All Specialized Agencies	31.0	36.3	55.5	61.6	74.2	88.6	99.3	120.5	134.7	151.7
Regular Budget Technical Aid Programs	1.3	1.8	2.4	5.6	6.4	6.4	6.4	6.4	6.4	6.4
United Nations Regular Budget	44.5	46.9	58.3	73.0	82.1	92.9	91.9	99.8	114.9	118.1

[a] Expanded Program of Technical Assistance and the Special Fund were merged in 1965 to form the United Nations Development Program.

Source: *U.S. Participation in the U.N.*, Report by the President to the Congress for the Years 1950, 1955, 1960–1966. *Yearbook of the United Nations* (New York: United Nations), 1950, 1955, 1960–1966.

contribution is of more than passing interest as an indicator of the role played by the new nations as both the initiators and the objects of United Nations development policy. As is shown in Table V.1, a marked acceleration took place in the rate of growth of the budgets of the components of the United Nations system within one year of the peak influx of new nations into the Organization. Whereas

[39] *Ibid.*, 435.

the budget of the Expanded Program of Technical Assistance (EPTA) increased 37 percent in the period 1955–1960, between 1960 and 1963 it increased by 57.1 percent, and the United Nations Development Program which resulted from a merger of EPTA and the Special Fund had a budget of $187 million for 1967 or 155 percent more resources than it had in 1960. The most striking example is provided by the World Health Organization, the budget of which increased by about 70 percent between 1955 and 1960 but increased by 215 percent in the period 1960–1967. Specialized Agencies, as a group, enjoyed a 173-percent increase in their budgets for the period 1960–1967. In absolute amounts the increases were even more impressive. Whereas the budgets of the specialized agencies totaled 31 million dollars in 1950 and 55.5 million in 1960, these combined budgets were in excess of 150 million dollars by 1967. This same acceleration can be found in the technical assistance portion of the regular budget of the United Nations during this period. Regular budget assessments for technical assistance programs, which in the period 1950–1960 had gradually increased from 1.3 to 2.4 million dollars, suddenly shot up to 5.6 million in 1961 and 6.4 million in 1962. Of course, the problems of the developing countries are immense and even these significant increases in financial assistance made only a small contribution to their solution. But these sharp accelerations in the resources devoted to the problems of the new nations occurring after their admission to the Organization point to the extent to which they used their political influence to gain significant benefits for themselves.[40]

East-West Issues

As the cold war has for twenty years been the most pervasive force affecting contemporary international relations, the new nations

[40] That many of these budgetary increases may have been supported, or even initiated, in the hope of gaining future support from the new nations on other issues is only a recognition of the fact that influence is, as Lasswell has noted, a "deference value." In fact, if there were cases where the new nations were catered to in the hope of gaining their future support, this is but another indicator of their influence potential within the Organization. Harold D. Lasswell and Abraham Kaplan, *Power and Society, A Framework for Political Inquiry* (New Haven, Conn.: Yale University Press, 1950), 55–73. Also see Walter M. Kotschnig, "The United Nations as an Instrument of Economic and Social Development," *International Organization*, 22, No. 1 (Winter 1968), 16–43.

could not have avoided dealing with its manifestations in the United Nations. U. Thant, speaking as a Burmese delegate, concisely summarized a view of the cold war to which most new nations would subscribe.

At the outset, let me reiterate Burma's firm conviction that the main obstacle to the settlement of international problems and the achievement of a genuine world peace is the unmitigated persistence of the so-called cold war, the chief feature of which is the sharp division of the world into two hostile ideological camps each one suspicious and fearful of the other, and both scrambling to entice new recruits into their respective ranks.[41]

The manner in which the new nations have exercised their political influence in the Organization when faced with questions arising from "the sharp division of the world" can be gleaned from an analysis of several perennial East-West issues. As a result of the large number of roll-call votes on East-West issues at each Assembly, voting analysis can make a useful contribution to determining the manner in which the new nations have exercised their influence on these issues.

The "New Recruits" Parliamentary diplomacy as practiced in the United Nations forces States to do more than propound general platitudes. On most issues—some claim far too many—public debate is followed by voting on "formal conclusions ordinarily expressed in resolutions," and this forces a State to publicly record its position in a manner that can be compared easily with that of other Members.[42] Pushed by the pressure of the cold war, both East and West have maneuvered to obtain the largest possible voting majorities for their positions. Sometimes this has meant that disputes are kept on the agenda long after the time any useful contribution can be made by the United Nations. On other issues, such as disarmament or the question of Chinese representation, the conflict is still very much alive and is manifested in highly charged efforts to advance and gain adoption of the most favorable resolution possible. Such issues, thoroughly permeated with the East-West conflict have come before every Assembly, and the determination with which they have

---

[41] United Nations General Assembly *Official Records*, 15th Session, 897th meeting (Oct. 10, 1960), para. 104.
[42] Rusk, "Parliamentary Diplomacy—Debate vs. Negotiation," *World Affairs Interpreter*, 26, No. 2 (Summer 1955), 122.

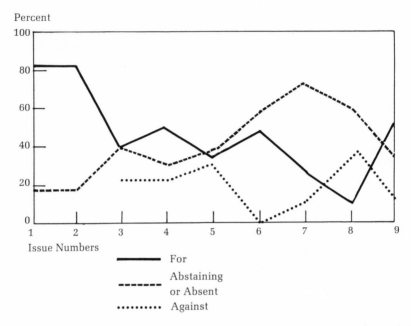

Percent

CHART V.1 Analysis of New Nations' voting behavior on selected East-West issues at the Fifteenth Assembly according to types of votes cast.

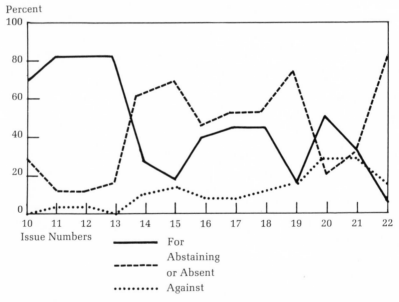

Percent

CHART V.2 Analysis of New Nations' voting behavior on selected East-West issues at the Sixteenth Assembly according to types of votes cast.

been pressed to a vote has insured that the new nations have been unable to escape the necessity of making repeated decisions on questions that both East and West viewed as questions of faith.

To analyze the manner in which the new nations reacted to this "sharp division of the world," 50 roll-call votes on East-West issues at the fifteenth through the twenty-second sessions of the Assembly have been selected for study.[43] One of the most notable features of the new nations' voting behavior on colonial issues was the extent to which they voted identically. As will be recalled, on 60 of the 70 colonial votes analyzed there was not a single case of a new nation voting in an opposite direction from that of the majority of new nations. In addition, there was not one abstention by a new nation on any of the 12 colonial votes selected from the seventeenth and eighteenth sessions of the Assembly.

A similar degree of cohesion among the new nations was not found on the 32 East-West votes analyzed. The dispersion of the new nations' voting behavior is graphically demonstrated in Charts V.1, V.2, V.3, and V.4. On only 12 of the 50 votes did 50 percent or more of the new nations vote as a group either in favor or against the question. Significantly, 6 of these 12 instances involved votes on disarmament drafts whose sponsors included substantial numbers of new nations. As can be seen from the charts, the typical voting pattern on these 50 roll calls found from 50 to 60 percent of the new nations split among the opponents and proponents, and roughly 40 to 50 percent of the new nations either abstaining or absent on the roll call. Forty percent or more of the new nations either abstained or were absent on 54 percent of the 50 selected votes.

The voting pattern of the new nations on the hardiest of the cold war perennials, the question of Chinese representation, is illustrative of their splintering. Since 1950 the United Nations has been faced with a difficult political and constitutional problem as to whether the Nationalist Chinese on Taiwan or the representatives of the Peking Government are the proper representatives of China, an original member of the Organization and a permanent member of the Security Council. This complex problem and various interpreta-

---

[43] See the caveat on voting analysis in footnotes 69 and 70 of this chapter. The 50 votes selected appear in Appendixes G, H, I, and J, along with a state-by-state vote tally for each of the 32 roll calls.

Percent

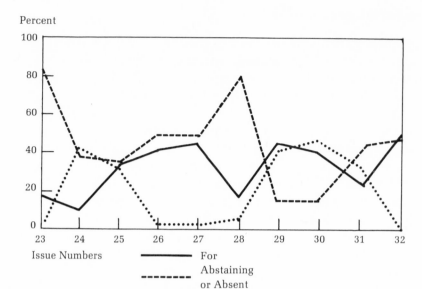

Issue Numbers

For
Abstaining
or Absent
Against

CHART V.3 Analysis of New Nations' voting behavior on selected East-West issues at the Seventeenth and Eighteenth Sessions of the General Assembly according to types of votes cast.

Percent

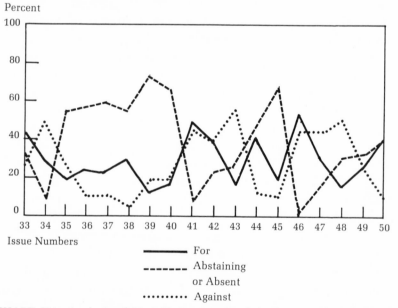

Issue Numbers

For
Abstaining
or Absent
Against

CHART V.4 Analysis of New Nations' voting behavior on selected East-West issues at the Twentieth, Twenty-first, and Twenty-second Sessions of the General Assembly according to types of votes cast.

tions of it pass in United Nations practice under the rubric of the question of Chinese representation. At the fifteenth session of the Assembly on the vote to reject the Soviet request for inclusion of an agenda item on Chinese representation, slightly more than 12 percent of the new nations favored the rejection, 33 percent of them opposed the rejection, and 58 percent either abstained or were absent on the roll call. Although the form of the issue placed before the Assembly changed at the sixteenth session, the dispersion of the new nations' votes did not.

For the first time since 1950, the Assembly decided in 1961 to consider the actual question of Chinese representation. The decision of the United States not to oppose this move was a significant indication of the influence of the new nations. The African members of this group, in particular, had been growing increasingly restless under the old procedural device of dodging the vexing question of Chinese representation. In a bid to prevent this resentment over a procedural stratagem from being transformed into votes for the seating of representatives from the Peking Government, the United States yielded to the desire of many new nations that this question be placed on the Assembly's agenda.[44] At the behest of the United States the Assembly was first asked to decide that the question of Chinese representation was an important question requiring a two-thirds majority of those present and voting. On this draft, which made the seating of the representatives of the Peking Government more difficult, 48.6 percent of the new nations voted in favor, 29.8 percent opposed, and 21.6 percent abstained or were absent. When the Assembly then proceeded to vote upon a Soviet draft calling for removal of the Nationalist Chinese and seating representatives of the Peking Government, 35.1 percent of the new nations favored this move, 29.8 percent opposed it, and 35.1 percent abstained or were absent. At the seventeenth session 44.5 percent of the new nations favored a Soviet draft again calling for the seating of Peking and the removal of the Nationalists, 41.9 percent opposed the draft, and 14.6 percent either abstained or were absent. The eighteenth session found 41.8 percent of the new nations favoring a joint Albanian-Cambodian draft calling for the seating of Peking, 46.5

[44] Arthur M. Schlesinger, Jr., *A Thousand Days: John F. Kennedy in the White House.* Boston, Mass.: Houghton Mifflin Company, 1965, pp. 479–81.

TABLE V.2

*Percentage of Abstentions and Absences of New Nations on
Selected East-West Votes at the Fifteenth, Seventeenth,
Twentieth, and Twenty-second Sessions of the General Assembly*

State	Fifteenth Session	Seventeenth Session	Twentieth Session	Twenty-Second Session
Algeria	–	66.7	0	0
Botswana	–	-	–	20.0
Burundi	–	57.2	87.5	0
Cameroon	77.7	28.6	87.5	60.0
Central African Republic	66.6	28.6	25.0	0
Chad	44.5	57.2	75.0	20.0
Congo (Brazzaville)	55.6	57.2	37.5	0
Congo (Leopoldville)	66.6	71.5	50.0	40.0
Dahomey	33.3	28.6	87.5	0
Gabon	33.3	42.9	25.0	20.0
Gambia	–	–	75.0	20.0
Ghana	22.2	57.2	37.5	80.0
Guinea	22.2	57.2	12.5	0
Ivory Coast	33.3	28.6	50.0	0
Kenya	–	–	75.0	40.0
Lesotho	–	–	–	20.0
Libya	44.5	53.9	87.5	60.0
Madagascar	44.5	28.6	12.5	20.0
Malawi	–	–	25.0	0
Mali	55.6	57.2	12.5	20.0
Mauritania	–	42.9	37.5	0
Morocco	22.2	71.5	50.0	60.0
Niger	33.3	28.6	37.5	0
Nigeria	44.5	100.0	62.5	40.0
Rwanda	–	42.9	87.5	0
Senegal	22.2	71.5	87.5	40.0
Sierra Leone	–	57.2	75.0	40.0
Somali Republic	44.5	57.2	62.5	40.0
Sudan	11.1	85.7	37.5	0
Tanzania	–	57.2	25.0	20.0
Togo	44.5	100.0	12.5	20.0
Tunisia	33.3	71.5	87.5	60.0
Uganda	–	83.4	37.5	40.0
Upper Volta	66.6	28.6	25.0	40.0
Zambia	–	–	75.0	20.0

Source: Appendices G, I, and J.

TABLE V.2 (continued)

State	Fifteenth Session	Seventeenth Session	Twentieth Session	Twenty-Second Session
Barbados	–	–	–	20.0
Guyana	–	–	–	20.0
Jamaica	–	33.4	100.0	40.0
Trinidad and Tobago	–	33.4	75.0	60.0
Burma	22.2	71.5	25.0	0
Cambodia	55.5	57.2	62.5	0
Ceylon	33.3	57.2	62.5	20.0
Indonesia	33.3	57.2	–	40.0
Laos	66.6	57.2	62.5	40.0
Malaysia	44.4	14.3	0	20.0
Maldive Islands	–	–	100.0	80.0
Mongolia	–	0	0	0
Pakistan	22.2	28.6	50.0	20.0
Philippines	33.3	0	0	0
Singapore	–	–	75.0	60.0
Cyprus	33.3	57.2	100.0	60.0
Malta	–	–	37.5	0
Israel	22.2	42.9	12.5	0
Jordan	33.3	42.9	62.5	40.0
Kuwait	–	–	87.5	80.0

percent opposing it, and 11.7 percent of the new nations either abstaining or absent. On this East-West perennial the new nations mirrored the sharp division of the rest of the Organization.

The extent to which individual new nations found it advantageous either to abstain or to be absent from East-West roll calls is apparent in Table V.2.[45] At the seventeenth session, for example, 63.2 percent of the new nations abstained on 40 percent or more of the votes. In stark contrast to their deep involvement with colonial questions, one manifestation of which was very few abstentions on their part, a majority of the new nations found abstaining to be a convenient

[45] It is true that some absences are entirely unpremeditated and result from the debilitating effects of the New York climate on seriously overworked staffs and the inability of small missions to cover every main committee. However, since 31 of the 32 roll calls took place in either plenary or the First Committee, the two bodies every mission covers first, it is not felt that the inability to separate the absences according to the motives behind them introduces a large possibility of error.

or necessary way to reconcile the demands of parliamentary diplomacy and East-West pressures. Not surprising is the fact that the
two states which abstained the least on the 50 cold war roll calls
were Mongolia and the Philippines, the two new nations with the
closest ties to the East and West, respectively.

While the extent to which the new nations divided their votes
and abstained on East-West questions is one of the analytically
significant keys in seeking to determine the amount of political influence wielded by the new nations on these issues, the cold war has
generated its own framework of analysis which cannot be ignored.
On these 50 votes the question ultimately faced by a new nation on
any given issue was whether to vote with the East or West or to
avoid the conflict entirely. On these issues the effects of the cold war
were so pervasive and the concern of each side so active that none
of the new nations could afford to disregard either view in arriving
at a decision on how to vote.

In Charts V.5, V.6, V.7, and V.8 the voting behavior of the new
nations on the 50 East-West votes is presented in relation to the
votes cast by the United States and the U.S.S.R. on these questions.
On 58 percent of the roll calls, more new nations voted with the
United States than with the Soviet Union, while on 34 percent of
the roll calls more new nations voted with the Soviet Union than
with the United States. Four of the roll calls found an equal number
of new nations voting with each of the bloc leaders. As the United
States possesses a larger initial voting base than the Soviet Union
and hence needs fewer outside votes to secure a voting majority on
East-West votes, this slightly less than two-to-one proclivity of the
new nations to vote with the United States than with the U.S.S.R.
is a considerable cold war success for the West. The unwillingness
of the new nations to become associated with either East or West
is demonstrated by the fact that on 54 percent of the roll calls more
new nations abstained or were absent than voted with either the
East or the West. However, in terms of cold-war politics this large
abstention factor worked to the advantage of the United States because of its larger initial voting base. When the new nations abstained, they deprived the Soviets of needed votes without offsetting
the United States-oriented votes of Latin America and Western
Europe.

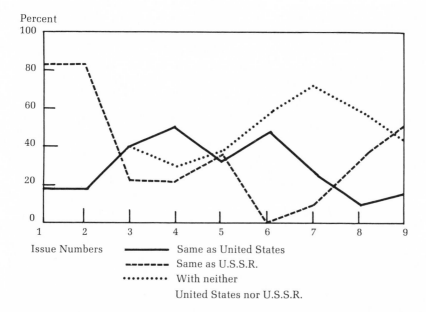

CHART V.5 Analysis of New Nations' voting behavior on selected East-West issues at the Fifteenth Assembly in relation to the United States and the U.S.S.R.

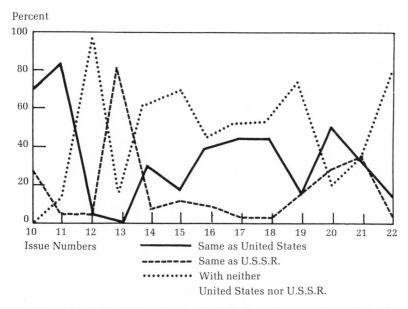

CHART V.6 Analysis of New Nations' voting behavior on selected East-West issues at the Sixteenth Assembly in relation to the United States and the U.S.S.R.

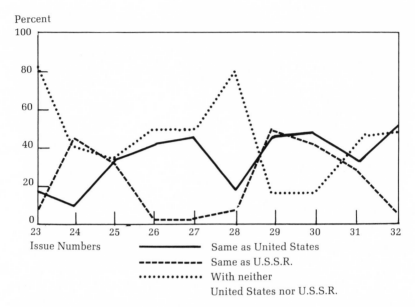

CHART V.7 Analysis of New Nations' voting behavior on selected East-West issues at the Seventeenth and Eighteenth Assemblies in relation to the United States and the U.S.S.R.

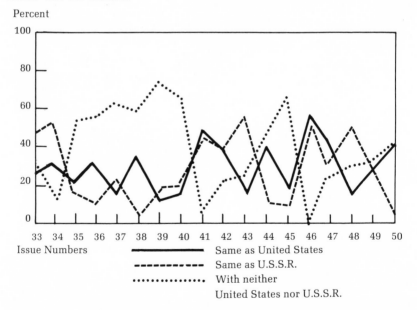

CHART V.8 Analysis of New Nations' voting behavior on selected East-West issues at the Twentieth to Twenty-second Assemblies in relation to the United States and the U.S.S.R.

Financing Peacekeeping—"The Congo Labyrinth" United Nations peacekeeping operations in the Congo precipitated a financial and political crisis which thrust the Organization into the midst of the East-West struggle. This largest and costliest of the United Nations peacekeeping operations confronted the new nations with probably the severest test to date of their ability to exert significant influence within the Organization on a question of direct concern to the United States and the Soviet Union. To examine the effectiveness of the new nations in exercising influence on this question, we must focus attention on the important financial resolutions adopted by the General Assembly in 1963.

In response to the internal chaos and civil war that threatened to consume the former Belgian Congo in July 1960, the United Nations dispatched a force that at its peak numbered approximately 20,000 men and cost $10 million a month to maintain.[46] More than 93,000 men from 35 states served in the United Nations Operation in the Congo (ONUC) during its four-year existence. However, during its entire operation the very existence of ONUC, and indeed of the United Nations itself, was repeatedly threatened by the problem of how to finance the operation.

While the form of the problem presented to the Organization by ONUC was predominantly financial, its substance was political and reflected the lack of political consensus behind ONUC.[47] Although the Soviet Union had initially agreed to the sending of a peacekeeping force to the Congo, by September 1960 it had reversed its position and launched vigorous attacks on both ONUC and the Secretary-General, Dag Hammarskjöld. As one manifestation of its extreme dissatisfaction with ONUC, the Soviet Union actively opposed the apportionment by the General Assembly of the expenses of the operation and refused to pay its share of these expenses. The Soviet position was that under the Charter the only body authorized to take action in the maintenance of international peace and security is the Security Council. They further asserted that the Security Council alone has the power to adopt decisions in all matters re-

[46] For a detailed account of the actual operations of the United Nations in the Congo, see King Gordon, *The United Nations in the Congo: A Quest for Peace* (New York: Carnegie Endowment for International Peace, 1962); and Ernest W. Lefever, *Crisis in the Congo: A United Nations Force in Action* (Washington, D.C.: Brookings Institution, 1965).
[47] Inis L. Claude, Jr., "The Political Framework of the United Nations' Financial Problems," *International Organization*, 17, No. 4 (Autumn 1963), 831–59.

lating to the establishment of United Nations armed forces, the definition of their duties, their composition and size, the direction of their operations, and the manner of financing the forces. Consequently, the U.S.S.R. repeatedly informed the United Nations that any attempt by the General Assembly to level assessments for ONUC would be illegal and not binding on the Member States.[48] France supported the Soviet Union in the contention that only the Security Council could impose binding obligations and that it is the duty of the Council to establish the mode of financing peacekeeping operations.[49] Along with a substantial number of other states, the United States contended that all Members share a collective responsibility for peacekeeping operations and it is the responsibility of the General Assembly under Article 17 of the Charter to make the assessments for such operations.[50]

Undisguised behind the thin veneer of opposing legal and financial arguments placed before the Assembly was the ominous fact that the major powers were at crossed swords over the continuation of ONUC and that neither side was likely to yield its position easily. A steady increase can be seen in the ambiguity of the Assembly's resolutions on the financing of ONUC adopted between 1960 and 1962. Paralleling this growing ambiguity was a rapidly worsening financial problem, resulting from the repeated failure to find a broadly based political consensus for the Congo operation. Whereas the initial Assembly resolution on the financing of ONUC had recognized that "the expenses involved in the United Nations operations in the Congo for 1960 constitute 'expenses of the Organization' . . . and that the assessment thereof against Member States creates binding legal obligations on such States to pay their assessed shares," the Assembly just four months later in a resolution to provide the financing for ONUC during 1961 failed to mention the binding nature of the assessment and in fact noted that "the extraordinary expenses for the United Nations operations in the Congo are essentially different in nature from the expenses of the Organization under the

---

[48] United Nations General Assembly *Official Records,* Fourth Special Session, Fifth Committee, 986th meeting (May 22, 1963), paras. 4–18. The U.S.S.R. also maintained the same position toward the United Nations Emergency Force (UNEF) in the Middle East.
[49] United Nations General Assembly *Official Records,* Fourth Special Session, Fifth Committee, 998th meeting (June 14, 1963), paras. 17–36.
[50] United Nations General Assembly *Official Records,* Fourth Special Session, Fifth Committee, 986th meeting (May 22, 1963), paras. 25–36.

regular budget . . ."[51] In 1962 the Assembly had failed to even appropriate the funds for ONUC and consequently had not been able to decide upon the shares of these expenses to be borne by each Member. Although the Assembly decided in December 1962 to accept the International Court of Justice's advisory opinion that the expenses of ONUC and UNEF were in fact "expenses of the Organization" within the meaning of Article 17(2) of the Charter and hence were to be apportioned by the Assembly as binding obligations, this action did not materially improve the financial status of the Organization.[52]

By the summer of 1963, when the Fourth Special Session of the Assembly met on the financial crisis, the accumulated arrears from United Nations peacekeeping forces stood at approximately $100 million. At the end of 1962 fully three-fourths of the Member States had failed to pay their full ONUC assessment. To survive in this precarious financial state, the Organization had been forced in 1962 to resort to the authorization of $200 million in bonds. However, the bond issue was an emergency measure, and it was clear to all that the Assembly in 1963 would be called upon to make crucial decisions on the financing of peacekeeping operations. If ONUC were to continue in 1963, it was necessary for the Assembly to discover some method of apportioning its expenses that could muster a two-thirds majority.

In line with their conduct on the majority of other East-West issues, the new nations were deeply divided on the question of financing peacekeeping operations, with a significant number of these states determined to avoid the conflict entirely by abstaining on roll-call votes. On the six roll-call votes on resolutions concerning the financing of ONUC taken at the fifteenth and sixteenth sessions of the Assembly, the average number of new nations voting in favor of the resolutions was only 16.6, while the average number of new nations abstaining or absent on these votes was 17.[53] The deep di-

[51] United Nations General Assembly Resolutions 1583(XV), Dec. 20, 1960; and 1619 (XV), Apr. 21, 1961.

[52] United Nations General Assembly Resolution 1854(XVII), Dec. 19, 1962.

[53] The six roll-call votes were on United Nations Documents A/C.5/L.638, Dec. 31, 1960; and A/C.5/L.677, Oct. 21, 1961 and United Nations General Assembly Resolutions 1590(XV), Dec. 20, 1960; 1619(XV), Apr. 21, 1961; 1620(XV), Apr. 21, 1961; 1732(XVI), Dec. 20, 1961. No roll-call votes were taken on resolutions concerning the financing of peacekeeping operations at the 17th Session.

visions among the new nations on the financing of ONUC underlined by their voting behavior in the previous sessions of the Assembly augered ill for their active and effective participation in the shaping of the financial decisions of 1963. However, when the Fourth Special Session of the Assembly convened on May 14, 1963, important changes were afoot in Africa that were destined to have an immediate, although temporary, effect on the cohesion of this significant group of new nations. Earlier in the month at Addis Ababa the independent African states had formed the Organization of African Unity (OAU), one purpose of which was to further a united front of the African states in the United Nations. Coinciding with the limited-unity movement of Addis Ababa was a moderating of internal dissension in the Congo. By the summer of 1963 the Katanga secession movement had ended. The Congolese Premier, Cyrille Adoula, appeared to have the ability to bring the degree of internal stability to the Congo necessary to allow within a short period the removal of ONUC, a move ardently desired by both moderate and radical African states. Thus one of the major causes of dissension among the new nations, the existence of opposing views among the African states on the internal events in the Congo,[54] was at a record low in the summer of 1963. The result of these events was that the new nations played a largely unanticipated role at the Fourth Special Session in the negotiating of resolutions designed to finance United Nations peacekeeping operations.

As the Assembly went through the ritual of opening the session and the general debate on the financial crisis began in the Fifth Committee, a select negotiating group was meeting behind the scenes to attempt to reach a solution acceptable to a majority of the Members. This negotiating group consisted of representatives of three African and Asian states, headed by Chief S.O. Adebo of Nigeria, two Latin American states, and five economically advanced states of the West.[55] It is significant that the new nations were prepared

[54] Robert C. Good, "Congo Crisis: The Role of the New States," in *Neutralism*. Edited by Lawrence W. Martin. (Washington, D.C.: The Washington Center of Foreign Policy Research, School of Advanced International Studies, The Johns Hopkins University, 1961), 1–46.

[55] Thomas J. Hamilton, "Gain Made in U.N. on Peace Forces," *New York Times*, June 18, 1963, p. 3. Hamilton on this occasion provided the *Times'* readers with detailed reporting of the negotiations in progress at the Fourth Special Session and his account has been relied on to a large extent for many of the details of these negotiations.

to enter into extensive private negotiations over a highly contentious East-West issue with a group that contained no representatives of the Soviet bloc. During these negotiations the new nations joined forces with the Latin Americans to press for the acceptance of three points.[56] The first point involved the acceptance of at least a 65-percent reduction in the assessments of underdeveloped countries for peacekeeping operations and a recognition of the general principle that the economically less developed Members had a limited capacity to pay. A second point most adamantly advanced by the Latin American representatives, but with considerable support from the Afro-Asian representatives, was the general principle that the five permanent members of the Security Council by virtue of the special privileges granted them bore a special responsibility for the financing of peacekeeping operations. Finally, the African-Asian negotiators on behalf of the Arab states pressed for the acceptance of the principle that the victims of aggression should be exempted from assessments for the cost of United Nations peacekeeping operations.

In these negotiations the representatives of the developed Western states pressed for recognition of the principle of collective responsibility of all Members for the financing of peacekeeping operations. The United States reiterated its position that it would pay no more than 32.02 percent of the cost of any peacekeeping operation. As this percentage represented the United States assessment under the regular scale of assessments, it means in effect that the United States was rejecting any special scale for the assessment of ONUC.

By May 31 the negotiating group had reached a compromise. The United States would pledge $2 million as a voluntary contribution to peacekeeping expenses, thus raising its total contributions to 37 percent of these expenses. In addition to the United States pledge, the other developed countries agreed to a voluntary contribution of $1.7 million.[57] In return Afro-Asian and Latin American representatives agreed to accept a 55-percent reduction in the assessment of underdeveloped countries for peacekeeping expenses rather than the 65-percent reduction for which they had been pressing. Instead

---

[56] Stoessinger, *Financing the, United Nations System*, pp. 133–38.
[57] Thomas J. Hamilton, "U.S. Will Give U.N. Extra $2 Million," *New York Times*, June 4, 1963, 3.

of the Arab demand for recognition of the principle that the victims of aggression be given reduced assessments for peacekeeping operations, the negotiating group had agreed on the purposely vague phrase that "where circumstances warrant, special consideration might be given to the situation of any Member State which suffers consequences from the events which led to a peacekeeping operation."[58] During these negotiations it was agreed that, while the drafts being prepared would affirm the collective responsibility of all Members for the financing of peacekeeping operations, they would also affirm "the special responsibilities" of the permanent members of the Security Council in connection with their contribution to the financing of peace and security operations.

When this compromise proposal was presented to the Afro-Asian group on June 3, its principal advocate, Chief S. O. Adebo of Nigeria, found the reception to be less than enthusiastic. Many states were unhappy with the size of the reduction granted the underdeveloped nations and felt they were being called upon to divert desperately needed resources from internal needs. The Arab delegates demanded in the caucus that a specific reference to the "victims" of aggression be made in the drafts. The resistence to the compromises encountered during the meetings of the Afro-Asian caucus on June 3, June 6, and June 12 was so severe that the negotiating group was reconstituted with four additional Afro-Asian representatives, bringing their total to seven.[59] In slightly less than a week this new negotiating group agreed that the underdeveloped countries would accept a 55-percent reduction in their assessments for peacekeeping in exchange for concessions regarding the Arab demand that the "victim" be exempted from assessments. It was agreed that the Assembly should affirm that where circumstances warrant "special consideration" would be given "to the situation of any Member States which are victims of, and those which are otherwise involved in, the events or actions leading to a peacekeeping operation."[60] This phraseology did not mollify the Arab states who retaliated by refusing to cosponsor the drafts, but the compromise as a whole was

[58] Thomas J. Hamilton, "Arabs in U.N. Call for Cost Changes," New York Times, June 7, 1963, p. 3.
[59] Thomas J. Hamilton, "Bloc in U.N. Asks Assessment Cut," New York Times, June 14, 1963, p. 4; Hamilton, "Gain Made in U.N. on Peace Forces," New York Times, June 14, 1963, p. 3.
[60] United Nations Document A/C.5/L.782, June 20, 1963.

accepted by the Afro-Asian group. The four drafts covered by the compromise, each sponsored by over 30 African, Asian, Latin American, and Western European states, were introduced in the Fifth Committee by Chief S. O. Adebo on June 20.[61]

An interesting sidelight to these negotiations is that they resulted in the Assembly's adopting the first official list of the "economically less developed countries." The two resolutions containing the financing arrangements for ONUC and UNEF note that the Assembly

Decides that, for the purpose of the present resolution, the term "economically less developed countries" shall mean all Member States except Australia, Austria, Belgium, Byelorussian S.S.R., Canada, Czechoslovakia, Denmark, Finland, France, Hungary, Iceland, Ireland, Italy, Japan, Luxembourg, Netherlands, New Zealand, Norway, Poland, Romania, South Africa, Sweden, Ukrainian S.S.R., U.S.S.R., United Kingdom of Great Britian and Northern Ireland, and the United States of America.[62]

The Assembly's purpose in determining which countries were "economically less developed" was to identify those countries that were eligible for the 55-percent reduction in peacekeeping assessments. The only clue to the intriguing question of how the negotiators agreed on the 85 states that were "economically less developed" is provided by the Mexican delegate, Cuevas Cancino, who was intimately involved in the private negotiations leading to these resolutions. On May 20, just as these private negotiations were getting underway, Cuevas Cancino told the Fifth Committee that

. . . if the Assembly wished to establish a more equitable scale than the one prescribed in the Charter for the regular budget, it should adopt a proportional system favoring the poorer members of the international community.

It would not seem necessary for the Secretariat to undertake a very broad inquiry to determine which countries were underdeveloped today. It could probably provide that answer immediately.[63]

In contrast to the Assembly resolutions adopted on financing at the three previous sessions, the four draft resolutions presented to

[61] United Nations Documents A/C.5/L.782, June 20, 1963; A/C.5/L.783, June 20, 1963; A/C.5/L.784, June 20, 1963; A/C.5/L.785, June 20, 1963.
[62] United Nations General Assembly Resolutions 1875(S-IV), June 27, 1963, para. 5; 1876(S-IV), June 27, 1963, para. 5.
[63] United Nations General Assembly *Official Records,* Fourth Special Session. Fifth Committee, 985th meeting (May 20, 1963), para. 26.

the Assembly as a result of private negotiations led by the Nigerian delegate, Chief S. O. Adebo, were passed with resounding majorities and a high degree of cohesion among the new nations. The resolution setting forth general principles for sharing the cost of future peace-keeping operations was adopted by a vote of 92 to 11, with 3 abstentions.[64] On the resolution providing for the financing of UNEF and ONUC the votes were 80 to 11 with 16 abstentions, and 80 to 12, with 15 abstentions, respectively.[65] The fourth resolution, which contained an appeal for those Members in arrears without prejudice to their political or juridical objections, was adopted by a vote of 79 to 12, with 17 abstentions.[66] The Soviet bloc opposed all of these resolutions. Only 6.5 percent of the new nations opposed or abstained on these four resolutions.

Six months later, at the eighteenth session, 16 African states joined in requesting a final appropriation for ONUC, which would terminate on June 30, 1964. The apportionment of assessments in this draft followed the pattern set at the Fourth Special Session, and it was easily adopted by a vote of 76 to 11, with 20 abstentions.[67]

During 1963 the new nations reversed three years of dissension and in the face of strong East-West pressures played a leading role in the drafting and adoption of resolutions to finance ONUC and to provide guide lines for the financing of future peacekeeping operations. Their influence and votes were instrumental in securing recognition of the principles that the economically underdeveloped states had a limited capacity to pay for such operations and that the permanent members of the Security Council bore a "special responsibility" toward the financing of these operations.

The success and unity of 1963, however, were short-lived. With the approach of the nineteenth session it became clear that the Soviet Union and France were not going to retreat on the question of financing peacekeeping operations. This confronted the Organization with the awesome question of whether the provisions of Article 19 of the Charter regarding the loss of a Member's vote in the Assembly for the failure to pay its assessments should be applied to

---

[64] United Nations General Assembly Resolution 1874(S-IV), June 27, 1963.
[65] United Nations General Assembly Resolutions 1875(S-IV), June 27, 1963; 1876(S-IV), June 27, 1963.
[66] United Nations General Assembly Resolution 1877(S-IV), June 27, 1963.
[67] United Nations General Assembly Resolution 1885(XVIII), Oct. 18, 1963.

these major powers.[68] Regardless of its substantive content, the question of the application of Article 19 was transformed into a direct United States-U.S.S.R. confrontation, with the very existence of the Organization at stake.[69] Primarily responsible for this transformation of the constitutional question of the applicability of the provisions of Article 19 into a highly charged political question concerning the future of the Organization was the Soviet threat to leave the United Nations if Article 19 were invoked against it. In the face of this great power clash, the unity the new nations had demonstrated in 1963 dissolved, and these nations failed to take any decisive action designed to resolve the conflict. Faced with dissension within their ranks and a pervasive feeling of impotency over their own ability to affect the outcome of a direct great power collision, inaction and a willingness to agree to any subterfuge as long as it avoided this collision became the dominant themes of the political activity of the new nations at the abortive nineteenth session of the Assembly.

The political crisis of the Organization over the application of Article 19 was resolved during the summer of 1965 when the United States agreed not to press for the application of Article 19 to those Members in arrears because of peacekeeping expenses. Quite probably, the limits of effective new-nation action with regard to a direct East-West conflict were defined during the course of the Organization's handling of the financial quagmire created by ONUC. The diversity and dissension that is so rife among the new nations when compounded by conflicting pressures from the great powers tends to engender a hasty retreat to the sidelines of the arena. Common initiative and action were possible in 1963 only because the euphoria from the creation of the Organization of African Unity and a return to near "normalcy" for the Congo created a fragile bond of unity among these nations. However, by 1964 the euphoria was gone and the Soviets had effectively transformed a legal and financial ques-

[68] United Nations Charter, Article 19, reads as follows: "A Member of the United Nations which is in arrears in the payment of its financial contributions to the Organization shall have no vote in the General Assembly if the amount of its arrears equals or exceeds the amount of the contributions due from it for the preceding two full years. The General Assembly may, nevertheless, permit such a Member to vote if it is satisfied that the failure to pay is due to conditions beyond the control of the Member."
[69] For an analysis of the Article 19 controversy, see Robert Owen Keohane, "Political Influence in the General Assembly," *International Conciliation*, No. 557 (Mar. 1966), 42–64.

tion into the fundamental political question of whether the United Nations should continue. Under such conditions of intensive East-West combat, purposeful initiatives by the new nations have proven impossible.

Disarmament As was noted earlier, only on the disarmament questions included in the 50 East-West votes analyzed was there a consistent tendency of the new nations to vote together. Since 1946 the United Nations has struggled with the complex problems of disarmament. While all Members have recognized the gravity of the problems, the amount of progress has been slight. The major powers and their allies have tended to view disarmament strictly as a problem of preventing the outbreak of a nuclear war, while at the same time preserving the ability of each state to maintain its own independence. The new nations presented a different view of disarmament to the United Nations. Just as the major powers viewed disarmament from the perspective of their own problems of security, the new nations viewed it from the perspective of their problems of economic underdevelopment. Prince Hassan of Morocco cogently placed the new nations' assessment of the disarmament problem before the fifteenth Assembly when he stated:

Indeed, is there a single new country which has not felt it an affront to its own poverty that such vast sums should be swallowed up by armaments, which are particularly costly in view of their rapid obsolescence? Besides constituting a permanent threat to life itself on our planet, the manufacture of these weapons ties up productive forces and thus jeopardizes the prospect of a better life for us all.[70]

This linking of economic development and disarmament is a constant refrain found in every discussion by new nations of the problems of disarmament, and the linkage is inevitably given the preponderant place economic development has in their hierarchy of values.[71]

[70] Prince Moulay Hassan (Morocco), United Nations General Assembly *Official Records*, 15th Session, 886th meeting (Oct. 4, 1960), para. 143.

[71] The United Nations Charter in Article 26 also recognizes that "the regulation of armaments" is an element in preventing "the diversion for armaments of the world's human and economic resources." However, the Charter's linkage of these two concerns rests on a preatomic conception of the nature of the international security problem and a limited realization of the actual size of the economic underdevelopment problem. At the time of the Charter's drafting, disarmament was seen as a distinctly subsidiary method for maintaining international peace and security. The new nations, on the other hand, view disarmament in the atomic era as the principal hope for avoiding global incineration and, equally important to them, as the chief source of capital development funds.

Of the sixteen draft resolutions on disarmament introduced at the Assembly's fifteenth session, significant numbers of new nations were among the sponsors of only four of the drafts. However, only one of these drafts was adopted by the Assembly. Significantly, the three drafts not adopted were not even voted upon the First Committee as a result of a bilateral United States-U.S.S.R. agreement to postpone all consideration on these items to the sixteenth session.[72] The fourth draft—14 of its 26 sponsors were new nations—urged that every effort be made to reach agreement "on the cessation of tests of nuclear and thermonuclear weapons, under appropriate international control" and that the voluntary suspension of testing be continued.[73] Although 11 Western nations, including the United States, abstained, this draft was adopted by a vote of 83 to 0, with 11 abstentions.[74]

At the sixteenth session, as at the fifteenth, the great majority of draft resolutions continued to be sponsored by the delegations of the older nations. Disarmament, the new nations discovered, was a very complex question, the subtleties of which required a large amount of staff work; since their main efforts were then being devoted to colonialism and economic assistance questions, the severely overtaxed missions simply did not have adequate time or resources to devote to disarmament questions. However, the new nations were able to obtain the adoption at the sixteenth session of two of their drafts tabled the previous year. Fourteen African states, 11 of them new nations, joined in reiterating their request that Africa be declared a "denuclearized zone."[75] The West, primarily out of a fear that this would establish a precedent for uninspected and uncon-

[72] These three drafts were: (1) United Nations Document A/C.1/L.259 and Add. 1 and 2, Nov. 15, 1960 and Nov. 16, 1960, which contained seven directives designed to serve as "the basis for an agreement on general and complete disarmament; (2) United Nations Document A/C.1/L.254 and Add. 1–3, Nov. 1, 1960, Nov. 2, 1960, Nov. 11, 1960 and Nov. 16, 1960, which would have declared the use of nuclear and thermonuclear weapons to be "a direct violation of the United Nations Charter" and "contrary to the rules of international law and to the laws of humanity"; (3) United Nations Document A/C.1/L.264/Rev. 1, Dec. 5, 1960, which would have declared the African continent to to be a nuclear-free zone.

[73] United Nations Document A/C.1/L.258/Rev. 1, Nov. 25, 1960. The sponsors were Afghanistan, Burma, Cambodia, Ceylon, Cyprus, Ethiopia, Federation of Malaya, Ghana, Guinea, India, Indonesia, Iraq, Japan, Jordan, Lebanon, Liberia, Libya, Morocco, Nepal, Nigeria, Sudan, Tunisia, United Arab Republic, Venezuela, Yemen, and Yugoslavia.

[74] United Nations General Assembly Resolution 1578(XV), Dec. 20, 1960.

[75] United Nations Document A/C.1/L.291/Rev. 1 and Add. 1–3, Nov. 7, 1961, Nov. 8, 1961, Nov. 9, 1961 and Nov. 10, 1961. Sponsored by Ethiopia, Ghana, Guinea, Liberia, Mali, Morocco, Nigeria, Sierra Leone, Somalia, Sudan, Togo, Tunisia, and the United Arab Republic.

trolled moratoriums, refused to support this initiative but decided to abstain rather than to vote against the draft. The draft was thus adopted by the Assembly on a vote of 55 to 0, with 44 abstentions.[76]

Much stiffer opposition met the proposal by 12 states, 10 of whom were new nations, that the Assembly adopt a resolution on banning the use of nuclear weapons.[77] The draft requested the Assembly to declare, inter alia that (a) the use of nuclear weapons was a direct violation of the United Nations Charter; (b) the use of nuclear weapons was contrary to the rules of international law and to the laws of humanity; (c) the use of nuclear weapons was directed against mankind in general; (d) any state using nuclear weapons was committing a crime against mankind and civilization. Contending that such a resolution would create a false sense of security and thus heighten the prospect of nuclear war, the United States and the United Kingdom strenuously opposed this draft. The West reiterated its contention that a ban on nuclear weapons could not be separated from complete and controlled disarmament. On this draft the new nations received the complete support of the Soviet bloc, and this support plus their own numbers proved more than sufficient to hand the West a considerable defeat. The Assembly adopted the draft by a vote of 55 to 20, with 26 abstentions.[78] As an example of the effective exercise of political influence, this victory of the new nations was of even greater importance because it occurred on a subject that had long been presumed in Assembly practice to be a preserve of the major powers.

It was the general view of many new nations that, if the major powers were left to themselves to devise an acceptable disarmament scheme, no such scheme would ever be found. From this view they drew the conclusion that only by discarding the old idea of leaving disarmament to those with the arms could a solution be reached. As Sukarno said at the fifteenth session,

. . . this problem is of such vital importance for the whole of mankind that all of mankind should be involved in its solution. In fact, I think we

[76] United Nations General Assembly Resolution 1652(XVI), Nov. 24, 1961.
[77] United Nations Document A/C.1/L.292 and Add. 1–3, Oct. 24, 1961, Oct. 30, 1961, Nov. 8, 1961 and Nov. 9, 1961. Sponsored by Ceylon, Ethiopia, Ghana, Guinea, Indonesia, Liberia, Libya, Nigeria, Somalia, Sudan, Togo, and Tunisia.
[78] United Nations General Assembly Resolution 1653(XVI), Nov. 24, 1961.

may say now that only pressure and effort from the nonaligned nations will produce the results which the whole world needs.[79]

The major forums for disarmament negotiations up to 1961 had been the Ten-Nation Committee on Disarmament, composed of five Warsaw Pact states and five NATO states, and *ad hoc* summit meetings of the nuclear powers. During 1961, however, the uncommitted Members of the Organization, the majority of whom were new nations, succeeded in overcoming Western objection to enlarging these discussions to include a contingent of small, uncommitted states. The hope of these uncommitted states was that they could exercise the decisive pressure necessary to bring the nuclear goliaths to their senses. Thus, at the end of 1961 the Assembly approved the establishment of the Eighteenth-Nation Committee on Disarmament (ENDC) to be composed of Brazil, Bulgaria, Burma, Canada, Czechoslovakia, Ethiopia, France, India, Italy, Mexico, Nigeria, Poland, Romania, Sweden, the U.S.S.R., the United Arab Republic, the United Kingdom, and the United States.[80] Experience with the reconstituted body, which began meeting in Geneva in March 1962, soon disillusioned many of the new nations as to the ease with which they could accelerate progress among the major powers.[81] At the seventeenth Assembly the Burmese delegate emphasized the climate of distrust in Geneva that made the efforts of the nonaligned powers seem so futile:

. . . The very magnitude of the problem and the complexities involved make it impossible for agreement to be reached quickly, and where, as we found in Geneva, the essential element of mutual trust is not only completely absent but is replaced by complete mistrust, the stage has been set for a complete deadlock. . . . The joint memorandum of 16 April 1962 tabled by the eight nations at the Geneva Conference which belong to neither of the military blocs was designed to bring the two sides closer together and to provide them with a basis for further negotiations. Unfortunately, it was not so used by the two parties, both of which declared that they accepted it neither as the basis, nor a basis, for negotiations. In prolonged discussions, each side insisted that its interpretation of the

[79] United Nations General Assembly *Official Records*, 14th Session, 880th meeting (Sept. 30, 1960), para. 85.

[80] United Nations General Assembly Resolution 1722(XVI), Dec. 20, 1961.

[81] France immediately declined to participate because the talks were not restricted to those powers which could contribute effectively to an agreement.

memorandum was the only correct interpretation, with the result that there was no serious negotiation on the basis of the memorandum. . . .[82]

In a similar vein the Nigerian delegate in bemoaning the fact that the major powers had prevented the nonaligned states from finding a solution to the disarmament problem asserted that

. . . while the big Powers and the various factions into which the world has been divided talk of disarmament, one has the impression that there is no serious and genuine desire to disarm. The big Powers are playing hide and seek with us. If they would only be sincere with us we could find solutions. But there is always the element of suspicion and fear of each other, and that makes the problem rather difficult. . . .[83]

In the Assembly the new nations generally continued their practice of leaving the initiation and negotiation of disarmament resolutions to the small group of nonaligned states that had traditionally interested itself in these matters. Thus India, Mexico, and Sweden continued to play leading roles in the drafting of disarmament resolutions sponsored by the nonaligned states. And while many new nations co-sponsored these resolutions and the great majority voted for them, these resolutions were not active goals of the new nations' influence.

A nuclear test ban treaty covering all but underground tests was signed in August 1963; however, the impetus for its conclusion arose not from the Assembly's resolutions but from the private bilateral negotiations of the United States and the U.S.S.R.[84] Even the forum for its signing was not the Eighteen-Nation Committee on Disarmament with its contingent of new nations but bilateral East-West talks in Moscow.

Beginning with the summer of 1965 the United States and the Soviet Union began with a renewed earnestness the arduous process of negotiating a nonproliferation treaty. While the locus of this activity was nominally the ENDC, in actual fact the real bargaining took place in private discussions of the co-chairmen, the United States and the Soviet Union. Unable to participate effectively in these

[82] Mr. U Thi Han (Burma), United Nations General Assembly *Official Records,* 17th Session, 1131st meeting (Sept. 25, 1962), paras. 17–18.

[83] Mr. Wachuku (Nigeria), United Nations General Assembly *Official Records,* 17th Session, 1153rd meeting (Oct. 15, 1962), para. 112.

[84] Schlesinger, *A Thousand Days: John F. Kennedy in the White House,* 893–909. Schlesinger's insightful account of these discussions clearly indicates the important impact the Cuban missile crisis and the Chinese enigma had on motivating both sides to conclude this treaty.

discussions and feeling that the two super powers were neither motivated by a proper sense of urgency nor, more importantly, a concern for the interest of the nonnuclear states, the new nations became increasingly frustrated and hostile to these proceedings. In this context a Pakistani proposal at the twenty-first Assembly to call a conference of the nonnuclear powers gained wide support among the new nations. This conference was to explore the questions of security guarantees for nonnuclear states, the relationship between nonproliferation and other disarmament measures and the effect of nonproliferation treaty on the development of peaceful nuclear technology. This conference, which was to meet by July 1968, was opposed in Assembly negotiations by both the United States and the Soviet Union, which objected to the intrusion of the nonnuclear states and the possible disruption of their methodical negotiations. This attitude of the two super powers was not lost on the new nations when the Assembly finally adopted the proposal for a conference of the nonnuclear weapons states by a vote of 48 in favor, one opposed and 59 abstaining, including both the United States and the Soviet Union.[85] As the prospect of super power agreement became greater in 1967, the frustration of the new nations became more vocal. Adding to this frustration was the take-it-or-else attitude of the United States and the Soviet negotiating team at Geneva. In fact it appeared to many United Nations delegates that the Geneva teams of both super powers had become so addicted to the club-like atmosphere of their private negotiations that they had forgotten the political arts of multilateral United Nations diplomacy. An incipient rebellion at the twenty-second Assembly of these nations was prevented only by quick and sensitive actions taken by those United States delegates most familiar with United Nations politics. However, this frustration was not removed but only temporarily diverted. The Conference of Nonnuclear Weapons States in the summer of 1968 was the scene of a vocal demonstration of this frustration over an inability of the "have-nots" to influence effectively the super powers on arms policy.

Perhaps the most favorable evaluation that can be made of the

[85] United Nations General Assembly Resolution 2153B(XXI), Nov. 17, 1966. Interestingly, 8 of the 11 members of the preparatory committee for the conference were new nations. The committee's members were Chile, Dahomey, Kenya, Kuwait, Malaysia, Malta, Nigeria, Pakistan, Peru, Spain, and Tanzania.

influence of the new nations on the conclusion of both the test-ban treaty and the nonproliferation agreement is that repeated Assembly resolutions passed with the large majorities supplied by the votes of the new nations encouraged the major powers to continue negotiations that might otherwise have lapsed. On the other hand, the major powers seem to have found sufficient incentives in their own interests to keep the negotiations going without this additional prod.

The new nations have been more successful at affecting the tone than the substance of the disarmament debate. They can justly claim credit for supplying the votes necessary to gain Western acceptance of the principle that militarily insignificant, nonaligned nations have a right to be represented in certain of the disarmament negotiations. It was not until after the sudden influx of new nations that this principle, long advocated by India, was accepted insofar as the Geneva negotiations were concerned. Once at Geneva, however, the nonaligned contingent found their efforts hindered by the mutual distrust and competing security concerns of the major powers. To a large extent the repeated United Nations appeals for immediate conclusion of a test-ban treaty and continuation of the interim voluntary moratorium owe their adoption to the voting majority supplied the traditional supporters of such measures by the new nations. But there are few grounds for seeing a facile causative connection between these appeals and the eventual conclusion of the limited test-ban agreement or the nonproliferation agreement. Most evidence points to the sobering effects of the trip to the brink during the Cuban missile crisis as the immediate causative agent for the 1963 agreement and the fear of regional conflicts fought with nuclear weapons for the nonproliferation agreement. The pace and substance of disarmament negotiations during the period under study was primarily determined by the nuclear powers, and the new nations found that even with the additional votes that their numbers gave to those favoring more rapid progress, the United Nations had only a limited impact on the actual negotiations.

Organizational Questions

In an environment as politically saturated as the United Nations, organizational questions are fitting targets for political influence and, indeed, are judged primarily on their political merits. The new nations' own massive influx into the United Nations, coupled with a period of intensive changes in its tasks, brought a new importance to organizational questions during the period under study. One problem involved the role and composition of the Secretariat when the United Nations is wrenched by sharp ideological and policy cleavages. A second problem involved adapting the limited membership organs of the United Nations to the sudden expansion in membership. Both of these problems actively concerned the new nations and were subjects of intense political bargaining.

"Troikas" Are for Riding   Provoked by the realization, made all too apparent for them in the Congo during August and September 1960, that the Secretary-General had developed under Hammarskjöld into an independent center of initiative and action, the Soviets launched a truculent campaign at the fifteenth session against both the man and the office. Khrushchev clearly indicated the extent of the Soviet dissatisfaction with both Hammarskjöld and the office itself when he told the Assembly,

We do not, and cannot, place confidence in Mr. Hammarskjöld. If he himself cannot muster the courage to resign, in, let us say, a chivalrous way, we shall draw the inevitable conclusions from the situation. There is no room for a man who has violated the elementary principles of justice in such an important post as that of Secretary-General. . . . We cannot expect any Secretary-General to be the impartial representative of three different groups of States.[86]

Instead of a single Secretary-General, who as they saw it was the sole interpreter and executor of the decisions of the Security Council and the General Assembly, the Soviets proposed the creation of "a collective organ of the United Nations consisting of three persons, each of whom represent a certain group of States." This troika arrangement of the Secretary-General's office would provide, the Soviets claimed, "a definite guarantee that the work of the United Nations executive organ would not be carried on to the detriment of any one of these groups of States."[87]

[86] Nikita S. Khrushchev, United Nations General Assembly *Official Records*, 15th Session, 882d meeting (Oct. 3, 1960), paras. 24, 30, and 31.
[87] Nikita S. Khrushchev, United Nations General Assembly *Official Records,* 15th Session, 869th meeting (Sept. 23, 1960), paras. 283 and 285.

Hammarskjöld carefully limited both the tone and content of his reply to the vitriolic *ad hominem* attack of Khrushchev. "Let me say only this: that you, all of you are the judges. No single party can claim that authority. I am sure that you will be guided by truth and justice."[88] In the same measured tone, Hammarskjöld devoted most of his reply to the "issue which . . . in my view is not a question of a man but of an institution."[89]

The man does not count; the institution does. A weak or non-existent executive would mean that the United Nations would no longer be able to serve as an effective instrument for active protection of the interests of those many Members who need such protection. The man holding the responsibility as Chief Executive should leave if he weakens the executive. He should stay if this is necessary for its maintenance. This and only this seems to me to be the substantive criterion that has to be applied. . . . It is not the Soviet Union or indeed any other big Powers which need the United Nations for their protection. It is all the others. In this sense, the Organization is first of all their Organization and I deeply believe in the wisdom with which they will be able to use it and guide it. I shall remain in my post during the term of office as a servant of the Organization in the interests of all those other nations as long as they wish me to do so.[90]

Khrushchev's proposal that a single Secretary-General be replaced by a troika produced no great clamor of support from the new nations. Generally, these nations accepted Hammarskjöld's own analysis that the nonaligned world would only suffer from a such a development. As Prince Sihanouk of Cambodia, hardly a Western lackey, said,

We believe that we must avoid the splitting-up of our Organization into rival clans—a process which increasingly prevents the United Nations from playing its proper role, particularly as sole guarantor of the survival and independence of the small nations. This division, if extended to the Office of the Secretary-General might well paralyze it.

It seems to us on the contrary that the Secretariat with its present structure, headed by a strictly neutral person standing above all disputes of interest or compromise, offers the best possible guarantee of impartiality for the uncommitted nations. We would certainly not say of any man, no matter how neutral he may be, that he will never err; but what we are convinced of is that a directorate would be able to act only with the unanimous consent of its three members, which in the present state of

[88] United Nations General Assembly *Official Records*, 15th Session, 883d meeting (Oct. 3, 1960), para. 8.
[89] *Ibid.*, para. 9.   [90] *Ibid.*, paras. 9 and 11.

the world is out of question, and that its action could only be the result of wrangling or of shabby compromise.[91]

No formal move was made by the U.S.S.R. to initiate the Charter amendment which would have been required to establish the troika. While the East-European delegates continued to refer to the necessity of reorganizing the Secretariat to reflect the changed conditions of the world, no real sense of haste accompanied these remarks. The best guess is that the unreceptiveness of the new nations to the troika stood in such sharp contrast to their willingness to hound the colonial powers that the Soviets decided on the politically expedient course of putting the troika temporarily out to pasture.

However, the Soviet attack on Hammarskjöld personally was not long deterred by these manifestations of support for the Secretary-General. In fact, the *ad hominem* attacks rapidly grew in rancor in early 1961. Hammarskjöld was accused by the Soviets of having plotted the murder of Patrice Lumumba in the Congo and of having acted in the interest of the colonialists from the beginning of the United Nations operation on the Congo. Not only did the Soviets accuse Hammarskjöld of being a "murderer," but he was also accused of attempting to supplant the other United Nations organs "by his own person." The Soviet foreign minister told the Assembly that "If he [Hammarskjöld] is allowed to go on as he is going, he will probably soon fancy that he is Prime Minister of the World Government and, given half the chance, will assert, 'L'Organization, c'est moi!' "[92]

Hammarskjöld's response to the stepped-up attacks was to reiterate his view that the decision as to whether he should resign before the expiration of his term rested not with the major powers but "with that vast majority of Members who have an overriding interest in the proper functioning of this Organization and who cannot be suspected of reflecting any bloc interests."[93] Whenever a majority of the Assembly determined that it would be in the best interests of the United Nations for him to leave, Hammarskjöld declared, they

[91] United Nations General Assembly *Official Records,* 15th Session, 877th meeting (Sept. 29, 1960), paras. 39–40.

[92] Mr. Gromyko (U.S.S.R.), United Nations General Assembly *Official Records,* 15th Session, 965th meeting (Mar. 21, 1961), paras. 39 and 77.

[93] United Nations General Assembly *Official Records,* 15th Session, 977th meeting (Apr. 5, 1961), para. 42.

could consider themselves as having a standing offer of his resignation.[94]

But the personal barbarity of the Soviets had been too much for most new nations which, even though not agreeing in every respect with the conduct of the Congo operation, did not see malice or conspiracy on Hammarskjöld's part as likely causes for the problems in the Congo. More importantly, the new nations had reacted favorably to Hammarskjöld's analysis of the balance of forces within the Organization and their own dependency on a unified Secretariat for some measure of protection from the major cold-war protagonists. A tangible expression of the Assembly's support of Secretary-General Hammarskjöld's position was the approval on April 21, 1961, one month after Gromyko's diatribe, of a $100 million appropriation for the Congo operation.[95] In passing this resolution 54 Members voted in favor, 15 against, and 23 abstained. This total included 21 new nations in favor, only 2 opposed, and 6 abstaining.

If Hammarskjöld had not met his tragic death at Ndola on September 17, 1961, it is possible that the Soviets would have followed the precedent they had set in refusing to recognize the existence of Trygve Lie in his last year and a half in office. While his death prevented the full use of these harassing tactics, it did reopen for six weeks the question of the future organization of the Secretariat. The Soviets unrelentingly pressed for changes in the direction of a troika as their price for agreeing to the appointment of a successor for the unexpired portion of Hammarskjöld's term. Neither the new nations nor the West were willing to pay this ransom, and finally the Soviets agreed in late October to the naming of the chief representative of Burma, U Thant, as Acting Secretary-General. The new nations' influence had been an important element in preventing a radical rearrangement of the Secretary-General's office and in securing the appointment to that office of a representative of a new nation.

Significantly, throughout their year and a half of attack on the person and the institution of the Secretary-General, the Soviet Union was unable to gain the support of any sizable segment of the new nations. Faced with this inability to rally external support, the Soviets could only fall back on their old tactic of incessant attacks upon the Secretary-General. Hammarskjöld demonstrated that with

[94] Ibid., para. 39.
[95] United Nations General Assembly Resolution 1619(XV), Apr. 21, 1961.

the support of the small and medium powers a Secretary-General could at least temporarily weather such attacks. With his death the Soviets discovered that, while they were fully capable of preventing the appointment of a successor, they lacked the necessary support to obtain the changes they desired. Their procrastination, in fact, brought them under increasing pressure from the powers that had served as Hammarskjöld's main support.

Geographical Distribution There was another aspect of the organization of the Secretariat in which the new nations and the U.S.S.R. were in closer agreement. Their common concern was the geographical distribution of the approximately 1500 middle- and upper-level personnel of the Secretariat. Both the Charter and logic dictate that the international Secretariat should be drawn from all geographic regions to maintain its international character. Between the ideal of a widely recruited staff and practice in 1960 several problems intervened. The Secretariat had, of course, been initially staffed from the original Members of the Organization. In keeping with the concept inherited from the League of Nations of a career service, these officials recruited in the late 1940's had remained with the Secretariat, accumulating experience and tenure. Thus, 59.5 percent of the professional staff of the Organization in 1959 was drawn from Western Europe and North America.[96]

Many of the new nations found this situation inequitable and were quite frank in asserting that this "reflects the world of 1945, not the world of today."[97] In their view, the Charter in Article 101(3) placed the importance of achieving a wide geographical distribution on the same level as recruiting competent personnel. At the fifteenth Assembly 11 meetings of the Fifth Committee were devoted to the demands of the new Members of the Organization that more of their nations be appointed to the Secretariat.

One Latin American and 8 Afro-Asian states, 5 of which were new nations, joined in sponsoring a draft requesting the Secretary-General to intensify his efforts to achieve a better geographical distribution.[98] It also requested the Committee of Experts, established in 1959 for

---

[96] United Nations Document A/C.5/784, Oct. 1, 1959, Annex II.
[97] Sukarno, United Nations General Assembly *Official Records*, 15th Session, 880th meeting (Sept. 30, 1960), para. 186.
[98] United Nations Document A/C.5/L.628 and Add. 1, Nov. 23, 1960 and Nov. 24, 1960. The sponsors were Ceylon, Ethiopia, Ghana, India, Sudan, Tunisia, United Arab Republic, Venezuela, and Pakistan.

the purpose of examining how the United Nations might economize through greater administrative efficiency, to undertake a study of

the categories of posts subject to geographical distribution and the criteria for determining the range of posts for each Member State with a view to securing a wide geographical distribution of the staff of the Secretariat, taking into account, *inter alia*, the relative importance of various posts, and to report to the Assembly at its sixteenth session.[99]

This draft was adopted without dissent in the committee and plenary.

As might be expected in such a highly charged political atmosphere, the report of the Committee of Experts was found wanting.[100] In fact, the disagreement over what "equitable geographical distribution" entailed in terms of action was so intense during the Fifth Committee's consideration of the report at the sixteenth session that a Canadian proposal to postpone voting on any resolution on the subject for a year and then to ask the Secretary-General to present his views was accepted.[101] When the battle was renewed at the seventeenth session, the Fifth Committee had before it the Secretary-General's report recommending that (a) a minimum range of one to five posts be assigned each state on the basis of its membership; (b) 100 posts be reserved to take account of variations in size of population which would not otherwise receive sufficient weight; and (c) the remaining posts be assigned on the basis of ratios of assessed contributions.[102] Much of the heat was gone from the battle in 1962. In the first place, the Secretary-General formally met many of the demands of the new nations. Also, the formula appeared so complicated as to leave many delegates too confused to ask detailed questions as to how it would operate in practice. But more important in moderating the discussion than either of these factors was the fact that the new nations had only to look at the latest figures on geographic distribution, or more graphically, just to examine the cafeteria lines in the third floor Secretariat dining room to see that rapid progress was being made to meet their demands. As Sir Susanta De Fonseka of Ceylon noted,

[99] *Ibid.*, para. 1.
[100] United Nations Document A/4776, June 14, 1961.
[101] United Nations General Assembly *Official Records*, 16th Session, Fifth Committee, 890th meeting (Nov. 27, 1961), para. 31.
[102] United Nations Document A/5270, Oct. 24, 1962.

TABLE V.3

Regional Distribution of United Nations Staff Subject
to Geographical Distribution, 1959–1967

Region	Number of Staff as of 31 August								
	1959	*1960*	*1961*	*1962*	*1963*	*1964*	*1965*	*1966*	*1967*
Africa	36	43	61	81	105	117	124	159	179
Asia and Far East	204	211	214	215	241	243	236	263	296
Eastern Europe	68	84	107	144	164	157	167	201	221
Western Europe	364	360	363	341	349	341	343	367	404
Latin America	101	108	112	117	140	152	159	178	175
Middle East	41	41	42	51	60	65	67	72	78
North America and the Caribbean	295	294	294	283	299	330	352	374	403
Total	1109	1141	1193	1232	1358	1405	1448	1614	1756

Source: United Nations Document A/C.5/987, 11 October 1963, A/6487, 26 October 1966, A/6860, 16 October 1967.

There could be no doubt that the situation had very much improved during the past year, as was clear from the Secretary-General's report. Important changes had been made in the top-level posts and more than half of the appointments to such posts had been made from countries of Eastern Europe and Africa. In addition, almost 70 percent of Member States were already well within or above the median of the desirable range of posts, and a further improvement could be expected in the future.[103]

The committee approved with only ten dissenting votes, those of the Communist bloc, a draft approving the Secretary-General's formula, with the added provisos that no state should be considered "over-represented" if it had no more than five of its nationals in the Secretariat by virtue of its membership and that in striving for an equitable geographical distribution consideration should be given to "the relative importance of posts at different levels." The Assembly approved the draft without a roll call.[104]

The extent to which the new nations achieved their desire for increased representation in the Secretariat is illustrated in Table V.3.

[103] United Nations General Assembly *Official Records*, 16th Session, Fifth Committee, 956th meeting (Nov. 23, 1962), para. 1.
[104] United Nations General Assembly Resolution 1852(XVII). Dec. 19, 1962.

Whereas in 1959 the staff subject to geographical distribution included only 36 Africans, by 1963 there were 105 Secretariat members from Africa, and by 1967 there were 179 from Africa. During a period when the total size of the staff subject to geographical distribution increased by only 58.5 percent, the number of Secretariat members from Africa increased by almost 400 percent. While even in 1967 the percentage of Africans in the Secretariat, 10.2 percent, still fell short of their percentage of membership in the Organization, the magnitude of the progress made since 1960 was sufficient to create a favorable horizon of future expectations. A great deal of credit for this progress toward a broader geographical distribution of the staff belongs to the conscious and extremely active effort made by the Secretariat in reaction to the pressure from the new nations to secure as many competent personnel as possible from these countries.[105] The speed and extent of the change in the geographical distribution of the Secretariat were a result of the effective application by the new nations of large measures of political influence.

Charter Revision Related to their desire for an "equitable geographical distribution" of the Secretariat was the new nation's demand for adequate representation in such main organs of the United Nations as the Security Council and the Economic and Social Council. These nations pointed to the fact that, although the Organization's membership had doubled in 15 years, there had been no increase in the number of seats on the Security Council and the Economic and Social Council. Particularly galling to the new nations was the contention that the distribution of elective seats in the Security Council was governed by a "gentlemen's agreement" made before their own entry into the Organization.[106] They noted that

[105] One of the main obstacles to meeting the demands of the new nations more rapidly was the great shortage of trained personnel in these countries. In many instances those nations most vociferous in their demands were the same ones least willing to spare their most competent personnel for career service with the Secretariat.

[106] The "gentlemen's agreement" was an unwritten understanding among the Security Council's permanent members arrived at during the Assembly's first session in London in 1946. According to this informal understanding, the permanent members of the Security Council agreed for the purpose of electing the nonpermanent members of the Council to accept a tacit division of the world into 5 regions with these regions represented in the Council on the basis of the following formula: 2 seats for Latin America, 1 each for the British Commonwealth, the Middle East, Eastern Europe, and Western Europe. While the United States has claimed that this agreement was limited to the initial election, the Soviets claimed it was of indefinite length. See Bailey, Sydney D. *The General Assembly of the United Nations, A Study of Procedure and Practice.* Rev. ed. (New York: Frederick A. Praeger, 1964), pp. 158-67.

both the Security Council and the Economic and Social Council were mainly concerned with operations in Africa and Asia and that it was "therefore natural that those continents should claim proper representation in both Councils, in accordance with the principles of equality of all Member States, universality, justice, and the efficient working of the Organization."[107] During the Special Political Committee's consideration of the question at the fifteenth Assembly of increasing the membership of these organs no objection was raised to the result which the new nations sought; however, there was great dissension as to the method of obtaining this result. The Latin Americans vigorously objected to the proposals that greater African representation be immediately granted through the simple expedient of redistributing the existing number of seats. Colombia rejected such a distribution because "that would mean that some countries or areas would lose some of the representation which they had legitimately acquired. It was unthinkable that the greater consideration given to the needs of some countries should be prejudicial to the rights of others."[108] On the other hand, the Soviet bloc continued its implacable opposition to accepting any amendment of the Charter as long as the Peking Government was denied China's seat in the United Nations. The Soviet delegate told the Assembly, "If and when the Chinese people were rightfully represented in the United Nations, the problem would in his opinion be solved without any difficulties."[109] The considerable pressure that Mr. Morozov admitted had been brought to bear by the new nations on the Soviet Union had not altered this position. In fact, the Ukrainian delegate Mr. Udovichenko, mildly chided these nations for this pressure.

He sympathized with the eagerness of the new African States to exercise their rights; but he reminded them that the end of colonialism and their achievement of independence had been greatly assisted by the Chinese people's victory over imperialism. The African and Asian countries could use their influence to right the injustice done to China. He regretted that some countries, after voting to include the question of Chinese representation on the agenda of the General Assembly, had sponsored the two draft resolutions, which ignored the rights of China. . . . It had been said that

---

[107] Mr. Diallo Telli (Guinea), United Nations General Assembly *Official Records*, 15th Session, Special Political Committee, 192d meeting (Nov. 4, 1960), paras. 16 and 18.

[108] Mr. Noriega (Colombia), United Nations General Assembly *Official Records*, 15th Session, Special Political Committee, 187th meeting (Nov. 1, 1960), para. 2.

[109] Mr. Morozov (U.S.S.R.), United Nations General Assembly *Official Records*, 15th Session, Special Political Committee, 197th meeting (Nov. 10, 1960), para. 17.

one injustice should not be remedied by another; but in the present instance there was only one injustice—that committed against China by the
United States.[110]

These two separate sources of opposition to the new nations'
demands were forced into cooperation by the Afro-Asian tactic of
proposing in one draft resolution both a Charter amendment and an
immediate redistribution of the existing seats.[111] This combined
opposition was more than sufficient to defeat any such change at
the fifteenth session.

When 44 Afro-Asian states, 33 of them new nations, requested the
eighteenth session to re-examine the representation on the Economic
and Social Council and the Security Council, few circumstances
seemed to have changed.[112] The new nations still spoke in terms of
a redistribution of existing seats and/or an amendment increasing
the membership of the two organs. Those most favored by the existing "gentlemen's agreement" were opposed to any alteration of it
without increasing the number of seats. The Soviet bloc, while willing to redistribute the existing pie, remained opposed to any Charter
amendments increasing the number of elective seats until the Peking
Government had been seated. The Soviet spokesman, Mr. Fedorenko,
in attempting to divert the pressure of the new nations from the
Soviets to Peking, said,

The clarifying statements which the Soviet Union has received show that
the Government of the People's Republic of China does not approve of a
method of providing more equitable representation for the Afro-Asian
countries in the principal United Nations organs which would make it
necessary to increase the membership of those organs and make appropriate amendments in the United Nations Charter. . . . The Government
of the Soviet Union appreciates the position of the Government of the
People's Republic of China with regard to increasing the membership of
the principal United Nations organs. Now as before, the Soviet Government supports that Government's demand for the restoration of the lawful
rights of the People's Republic of China in the United Nations.[113]

---

[110] United Nations General Assembly *Official Records*, 15th Session, Special Political
Committee, 193d meeting (Nov. 7, 1960), para. 17.
[111] United Nations Document A/SPC/L.51 and Add. 1-5, Nov. 3, 4, 7, 8, 9, and 10,
1960; A/SPC/L.54 and Add. 1, Nov. 29 and 30, 1960; A/SPC/L.52 and Add. 1-3, Nov.
3, 4, 7, and 8, 1960; A/SPC/L.55 and Add. 1, Nov. 29 and 30, 1960.
[112] United Nations Document A/5520, Sept. 16, 1963, 6.
[113] United Nations Document A/SPC/96, Dec. 10, 1963, 6.

The Soviets' task was, however, suddenly made more onerous by Peking's duplicity or ambiguity in its communications with certain of the new nations regarding proposals for increasing the membership of the two Councils by Charter amendments. After the above statement by Mr. Fedorenko, the Guinean delegate, Mr. Diallo Telli, told the committee,

... all members of the Committee, and particularly those from Africa and Asia, had listened with all due attention to the Soviet representative's statement, which ruined all hope of achieving adequate representation of the States of Africa and Asia at the present session. . . . On 30 September 1963 the Minister for Foreign Affairs of the Republic of Guinea had said in the General Assembly that the restitution to the People's Republic of China of its legitimate rights and the just representation claimed by the countries of Africa and Asia were two different questions, which the Peking leaders had had the wisdom and foresight not to bind together. The Guinean Government had since been informed from an official source that that was in fact the position of the Peking leaders. It had also been informed publicly and solemnly that they were absolutely opposed to the injustice done to the countries of Africa and Asia by their present representation in the different organs of the United Nations.[114]

The Albanian delegate did not ease the extreme Soviet discomfort at being forced into a posture of being more Chinese than the Chinese when he told the committee,

The question of the equitable representation of the countries of Africa and Asia was intrinsically different from that of the restoration of the legitimate rights of the People's Republic of China. . . . The Albanian delegation did not think it fair that a Member should invoke the People's Republic of China to justify its own position in the present debate. Why should the People's Republic of China be saddled with a responsibility which was not its own . . .[115]

The Soviet Union was not the only permanent member of the Security Council which announced that it would not support the Afro-Asian amendments. France, the United Kingdom, and the United States joined in calling for a year's postponement of any vote, so that extensive consultations could take place as to what would be

[114] United Nations General Assembly *Official Records*, 18th Session, Special Political Committee, 423d meeting (Dec. 10, 1963), para. 47.
[115] Mr. Budo (Albania), United Nations General Assembly *Official Records*, 18th Session, 428th meeting (Dec. 14, 1963), paras. 21 and 22.

the exact distribution of seats under the new arrangements.[116] However, these requests were brushed aside and the Special Political Committee on December 16, 1963 approved two draft amendments to the Charter, one calling for an increase in the Security Council from 11 to 15 members and the other calling for an increase in the size of the Economic and Social Council from 18 to 27 members.[117] The draft concerning the Security Council was approved by a roll-call vote of 96 to 11, with 4 abstentions, and the draft on the Economic and Social Council by a vote of 95 to 11, with 4 abstentions. On both drafts 2 of the permanent members of the Security Council, France and the U.S.S.R. voted no and 2, the United Kingdom and the United States, abstained.[118] On the very next day, by virtually the same vote, the General Assembly adopted the 2 amendments and submitted them to the Members for ratification.[119]

After the Assembly had completed its action the Soviet Union attempted to shift to Peking the onus for its vote and the ultimate responsibility for whatever action it would eventually take with regard to ratifying the amendments. In a statement released on Dec. 23, 1963, the U.S.S.R. noted:

. . . if the Government of the People's Republic of China finds it possible to make a clear statement agreeing to the Charter amendments called for by the resolutions on increasing the membership of the Security Council and the Economic and Social Council . . . the Soviet Union will of course be able to give its approval to the amendments. . . .[120]

The Soviet statement went on to note an editorial in the Peking paper *Jenmin Jihpao* on December 18, 1963, which said that, if the Afro-Asian demands could not be met by redistributing the existing seats, "we [Peking] shall of course, in accordance with the position which

---

[116] United Nations General Assembly *Official Records*, 18th Session, 427th meeting (Dec. 14, 1963), paras. 49–51; paras. 43–48; paras. 12–21.

[117] United Nations Documents A/SPC/L.104/Rev. 1, Dec. 11, 1963; A/SPC/L.105, Dec. 10, 1963.

[118] The Republic of China voted in favor of the increase in the size of the Security Council, but did not participate in the vote on the increase in ECOSOC. This latter action was in retaliation for the Afro-Asian refusal to assure the Republic of China a seat in ECOSOC. Those voting against both drafts were Bulgaria, Byelorussian S.S.R., Cuba, Czechoslovakia, France, Hungary, Mongolia, Poland, Romania, Ukrainian S.S.R., and the U.S.S.R. Those abstaining on the two drafts were Portugal, South Africa, United Kingdom, and the United States.

[119] United Nations General Assembly Resolutions 1991A(XVIII), Dec. 17, 1963 and 1991B(XVIII), Dec. 17, 1963.

[120] United Nations Document A/5686, Dec. 31, 1963, 9.

we have always taken, support such amendments so that the demands of the Afro-Asian countries can really be met."[121]

The number of ratifications of these amendments gradually increased throughout 1964, along with the pressure on the permanent members of the Security Council to ratify the amendments. Although it was not until the late summer of 1965 that such action was completed, eventually the five permanent members altered their positions and permitted the long-sought increase in the membership of the two councils to take place in the fall of 1965. This long campaign, waged almost exclusively by those states that had joined the Organization since 1955, required the effective exercise of political influence on both the East and West. The extent and effectiveness of this influence was reflected in the extreme discomfort shown by the Soviet Union in being forced to oppose this campaign in order to demonstrate its fidelity to Peking. The speed with which the Soviet Union reversed its stand when Chinese duplicity was proven on the issue demonstrates the effectiveness of this political influence.

The active concern of the new nations with organizational questions grew out of the pragmatic view that existing structural inequities in the United Nations were hindering the successful pursuit of desired goals. A more favorable geographical distribution of the Secretariat, that is, more members of the Secretariat drawn from new nations, was sought in order to reduce what was viewed as an excessive Western orientation of this organ and to ensure their access to what they viewed as the "executive level" of the Organization.[122] Similarly, the desire for greater representation in the Security Council and the Economic and Social Council developed from the belief that only as voting members, rather than as nonvoting plead-

[121] *Ibid.*, p. 10. The Soviets added: "It should be noted that this was the first time China had taken that position, and that it did so after the vote on the draft resolutions calling for an increase in the membership of the Security Council and the Economic and Social Council and after the General Assembly had ended its session. . . . It can be stated unequivocally that if such a statement . . . had been made by the Government of the People's Republic of China while the matter was being discussed in the General Assembly, the Soviet Union would of course have voted for the resolutions submitted by the African and Asian countries." *Ibid.*

[122] Mr. Wachuku (Nigeria), United Nations General Assembly *Official Records*, 15th Session, 897th meeting (Oct. 10, 1960), para. 60. "As long as we have these problems—which are political—so long must we have in the Secretariat, on the thirty-eighth floor, an African who represents the legitimate views, protects the legitimate interests, and portrays to the Secretariat these yearnings of the people of Africa and the way in which they would like the problems of their continent to be solved—not viewing African problems with an alien eye."

ers, could the new nations obtain the action in regard to colonialism and economic development that they desired from these two organs. However, it should be noted that a strong emotional current of racial and cultural pride underlay the new nations' drive to obtain greater representation on the two councils. The new nations demonstrated no eagerness to join the Soviet bloc in attempting to demolish the fundamental framework of the Secretariat. The new nations accepted the legitimacy of the structure itself and used their influence to obtain alterations within the bounds of the system rather than replace the existing structure with a troika arrangement. Both by withholding their support from the troika, the majority reaction, and by actively supporting Hammarskjöld, publicly the minority reaction, the new nations were to a considerable extent the keystone in the Secretariat's ability to weather the storms of 1960–1962.

Extent of Influence—A Summary

In summarizing the scope and consistency with which the new nations have exercised their political influence over the panoply of issues faced by the Organization, the most significant factor to note is that these nations have brought their own distinctive set of priorities with them and have viewed the host of issues faced by the United Nations in terms of these priorities. Through the device of recasting a number of diverse issues into questions of colonialism or economic assistance, the new nations between 1960 and 1967 succeeded in narrowing the effective scope of the issues considered by the United Nations. Significantly for their effective exercise of influence, this recasting was done along precisely those lines where the new nations have exhibited the greatest strength. Basing their influence on the political bargaining power derived from the cold war, the new nations have used the formal voting power given them by the one-state-one-vote rule of the Assembly to secure United Nations action on their primary concerns.

Under the impetus of the new nations, colonialism became the chief concern of the United Nations. While unable to carry the Organization as far as they undoubtedly wished toward collective actions against the remaining colonial powers, the new nations were able to move it from general pronouncements of moral and legal rights to condemnations of specific nations, accompanied by requests for voluntary sanctions and, most recently, in the case of South Africa, to a host of preliminary steps designed to lead ultimately to enforcement action. The artful use of the Special Committee on Colonialism has enabled the new nations to maintain constant pressure on the remaining colonial areas. Perhaps the best example of the effectiveness of the new nations in exerting their influence on colonial issues has been their success in using the United Nations to strip Western-style colonialism of every element of legitimacy.

Economic aid and development is second only to colonialism in the interests of the new nations. Only limited success, however, has met their efforts in this area. Economic development is a subject that few are willing to oppose publicly, and the new nations have had great success in obtaining numerous Assembly and Economic and Social Council pronouncements on the desirability of more rapid economic development. Broad programs such as the "Development Decade" and more limited recommendations such as the levels of capital assistance required for development have been successfully extracted from the Assembly. Much more limited success met the attempts of the new nations to establish institutions commanding large financial resources to be applied to the development problem. By refusing to participate in the drafting of a statute for the United Nations Capital Development Fund and indicating that no contributions for it would be forthcoming, the developed nations effectively blocked the fund, although the Assembly had agreed in 1960 to its establishment "in principle." Between 1960 and 1967 the new nations were able to obtain a marked increase in the funds the United Nations system devoted to economic development, but even this increased level of assistance fell short of the level they felt was required by the magnitude of the problem. After arduous efforts the new nations formed a common alliance with the other developing nations on the importance of international trade to successful economic development. This common alliance overwhelmed the objections of the major trading nations and secured United Nations sponsorship for a conference on trade and development. The United Nations Conference on Trade and Development, in one of the few positive actions of the nineteenth Assembly, was made a permanent organ of the United Nations. If this alliance of the developing nations endures, it may well prove to have been the most significant political stroke of the new nations in the period between 1960 and 1967.

East-West issues have found the new nations, in general, fragmented. Moved by twin beliefs in the essential irrelevancy of the East-West conflict to their own goals and the dangers it poses to achieving these goals, many new nations have consistently abstained on East-West issues. Others, while voting with one or the other of the cold war protagonists, have attempted to maintain their independence from either by emphasizing the particular issue in question. For example, those new nations voting for the seating of the Peking Government emphasize the importance of obtaining universality of membership in order to ensure the maximum effectiveness of the Organization. Finally, a few of the new nations, Mongolia and the Philippines for example, are openly associated with either the East or the West. There is growing evidence that the disapproval with which the new nations view blatant attempts by the East and West to secure cold-war victories in the Assembly is reducing the number of such items coming before the Assembly. With respect to disarmament questions, the new nations, while showing a greater voting cohesion than on other East-West issues, have found their influence to be limited. While able to affect to some extent the tone of disarmament discussions, the new nations have found the substance of disarmament to be so intertwined with the most vital problems of great-power national security as to be beyond their influence.

The human rights activity of the United Nations has been viewed by the new nations as important and worthy of concern only insofar as it relates to colonialism and racialism. At the insistence of the new nations, self-determination has been repeatedly included in listings of human rights, thus giving the anticolonial forces another weapon to use in their struggle. Similarly, human rights activity directed at eliminating all forms of racial discrimination has been focused increasingly on the apartheid policies of South Africa. However, this monistic view of human rights activity has meant that the new nations have tended to avoid the aspects not directly related to colonialism and racialism. Thus they have not exercised as great an influence as they are capable of on such issues as the drafting of conventions on the rights of women and freedom of information.

Organizational questions have been viewed by the new nations primarily in an instrumental light. Increased representation was sought in the Secretariat and the councils for the purpose of obtaining satisfactory action on their decolonization and economic development demands. Both the wider geographical distribution of the Secretariat and the 1965 Charter amendments increasing the membership of the Security Council and the Economic and Social Council demonstrate the effectiveness with which the new nations have used their political influence to achieve their goals. On the other hand, the new nations offered little support to the Soviet bloc in its attempted emasculation of the Hammarskjöld-type Secretariat. Their lack of support for the Soviet troika was sufficient to deny the Soviets any hope of imposing such an arrangement on the Organization.

The record of the new nations with regard to that dimension of influence which has been directed at shaping the policy outputs of the United Nations is, in summary, largely one of successes. During this period the Organization's issue orientation, under the prodding of the new nations, became almost exclusively focused upon the problems of colonialism and economic aid and development. In both areas as a result of the activities of the new nations, a flood of resolutions has been passed, the verbal commitment of the Organization on these issues has been sharply escalated and new organs and institutions designed to foster action in these areas have been created. However, when it comes to assaying the impact of these actions on the international political environment, the influence of the new nations appears considerably less potent. Southern Africa remains a bastion of the retrograde colonial regimes and the international action that is currently underway in the area is probably more the result of the intemperate action of a white regime, Southern Rhodesia, than of the influence of the new nations. In spite of repeated resolutions of various United Nations organs calling upon the developed states to devote a larger share of their resources to the problems of the less developed states, such action has not been taken. The conclusion is inescapable that there is a considerable differentiation between the degree of influence that the new nations wield in shaping the policy outputs, such as resolutions, of the United Nations and their influence on the states that are the targets of these policy outputs.

Chapter VI

THE POLITICS OF DECOLONIZATION—
The Declaration on the Granting of Independence to Colonial
Countries and Peoples and the Special Committee on
Colonialism

From the time of the United Nations' founding, the problems associated with colonial territories have attracted its attention.[1] The potential extent of the problems facing the infant Organization in 1945
were enormous. Prior to the start of the Second World War there
were over 80 separate colonial territories including about one-third
of the population and covering one-third of the land area of the
world. Seven countries—Great Britain, the Netherlands, France,
Belgium, Portugal, Italy and Spain—with a combined population of
only 200 million people controlled in 1939 almost 700 million people
in their colonial possessions.[2]

Brief History of United Nations
Involvement before 1960

In common with all of the provisions of the Charter those dealing
with colonial territories were strongly influenced by the League's
provisions and experience.[3] However, of even greater influence than

---

[1] The debate at the San Francisco Conference that swirled around the extent to
which the Organization was to be concerned with colonial problems is cogently set
forth in Ruth B. Russell, *A History of the United Nations Charter, The Role of the
United States 1940–1945* (Washington, D.C.: The Brookings Institution, 1958), pp. 808–42.
[2] Emil J. Sady, *The United Nations and Dependent Peoples* (Washington, D.C.: The
Brookings Institution, 1956), p. 3.
[3] For an analysis of the League system, see H. Duncan Hall, *Mandates, Dependencies
and Trusteeships.* (Washington: Carnegie Endowment for International Peace, 1948),

the League on the shaping of the United Nations system for handling colonial issues was the drastically changed political environment of 1945. Actively engaged in drafting the Charter were a number of non-European countries overtly hostile to the prewar colonial system. In their opposition to this system, this group enjoyed the support of one of the great powers, the Soviet Union.[4] Another critical change in the political environment was that the Second World War had severed for the duration of the war the connections between the colonial powers and their possessions. And in this case absence had not made the heart grow fonder. At the time of San Francisco only the most tenuous of connections had been re-established in many cases, and in most colonial territories nascent revolutionary movements were struggling to prevent the reimposition of the prewar colonial order.

The United Nations Charter as drafted in this political context offers a two-pronged approach to colonial problems. First, in Chapters XII and XIII the trusteeship system, the direct successor of the League's mandate system, is set forth. This system, which was to cover "(a) territories now held under mandate; (b) territories which may be detached from enemy states as a result of the Second World War; and (c) territories voluntarily placed under the system by states responsible for their administration,"[5] offered the greatest amount of direct United Nations supervision. A Trusteeship Council, operating under the authority of the General Assembly and composed of governmental representatives, was set up to exercise the functions of the Organization with respect to trust territories. It was given the power to consider reports submitted by the administering power, to accept petitions without prior submission to the administering authority, and to make periodic visits to the trust territories.[6] The main

---

and Ernst B. Haas, "The Reconciliation of Conflicting Colonial Policy Aims: Acceptance of the League of Nations Mandate System," *International Organization*, 6 (Nov. 1952), 521–36.

[4] Of historical interest because of the anticolonial stance of the Soviet Union in the post-war period is Krishna Menon's assertion that it was the defeat of Russia by Japan in the Russo-Japanese War of 1905 that triggered the political drive of the colonial peoples of Asia. Mr. Menon contends that it was this defeat of a European Power by an Asian nation that gave the emotional self-confidence to Asian revolutionaries which was necessary to launch a political and social revolution against the dominant colonial powers. United Nations General Assembly *Official Records*, 15th Session, 944th meeting (Dec. 13, 1960), para. 96.

[5] United Nations Charter, Article 77 (1)

[6] *Ibid.*, Article 87.

emphasis of the trusteeship system as set forth in the Charter was on the "political, economic, social, and educational advancement of the inhabitants of the trust territories."[7]

As a counterpoint to the trusteeship system, the Charter in Chapter XI embodied a commitment by the Members controlling non-self-governing territories to "accept as a sacred trust the obligation to promote to the utmost . . . the well-being of the inhabitants of these territories."[8] Further, to achieve this goal these Members agreed to develop self-government, to assist in the progressive development of free political institutions, and to transmit regularly to the Secretary-General information on the economic, social, and educational conditions in these territories. The assumption by the Member States of international responsibilities for their colonial possessions was an important departure from the traditional order. It was in the Declaration of Chapter XI that one could most clearly glimpse the fundamental forces that were at work to change the colonial order. It embodied the first assertion, admittedly inchoate, of an international responsibility for the management of colonial territories outside the mandate or trusteeship system. It is from this acceptance of international responsibility that the assertion of institutionalized international accountability has developed.

In terms of the scope of application, the task of applying the elaborate provisions of the trusteeship system met with only limited success. In only 11 territories were the provisions of Chapters XII and XIII ever applied.[9] At its height there were more than eight times as many non-self-governing territories, containing over ten times as many people, outside the trusteeship system as in it.[10]

The Charter provisions for the Organization's supervision of the non-self-governing territories not placed under trusteeship are vague.

[7] United Nations Charter, Article 76. For a full exposition of the trusteeship system of the United Nations, see Chairmian Edwards Toussaint, *The Trusteeship System of the United Nations.* (New York: Frederick A. Praeger, 1956).

[8] United Nations Charter, Article 73. Also Article 1(2) declares that one of the purposes of the United Nations is "to develop friendly relations among nations based on respect for the principle of equal rights, and self-determination of peoples . . . ." Significantly, for later developments, this provision was sponsored at the San Francisco Conference by the Soviet Union.

[9] These territories were Cameroons (British); Cameroons (French); Nauru; New Guinea; North Pacific Islands; Rwanda Urundi; Somaliland; Tanganyika, Togoland (British); Togoland (French); Western Samoa. As of 1965 all but three—Nauru, New Guinea, and the North Pacific Islands—had become independent states.

[10] Harold Karan Jacobson, "The United Nations and Colonialism: A Tentative Appraisal," *International Organization,* 16, No. 1 (Winter 1962), 45.

It is only in Article 73e with its provisions for the transmission of certain information about these territories that a possible basis for an institutionalized supervision can be discerned. In the period 1946–1949 the General Assembly took actions to define the scope, nature, and procedures relating to the transmission of information under Article 73e. During the period 1949–1955 the General Assembly proceeded to establish its competence to examine the information transmitted by the administrative members and to make specific recommendations on conditions in the territories concerned. During this second period the Committee on Information from Non-Self-Governing Territories, composed equally of administering and nonadministering members, had the burden of initially examining the information received.[11] Between approximately 1955 and 1960 the General Assembly asserted its competence to decide when the obligation to transmit information had ceased and also to decide when there existed an obligation to transmit information under Article 73e. Unlike the case of the trust territories, the United Nations by 1960 had found no effective means for establishing direct contact with the vast majority of colonial territories falling only under Chapter XI. With the significant exception of the Portuguese territories, the administering powers had largely accepted the obligation to supply the United Nations with technical information, but this fell far short of the Organization's right to receive petitions from and send visiting missions to trust territories.

For reasons partly related to the small number of countries under the trusteeship system and more directly related to the strength of anticolonial forces in the Assembly, the period 1946–1960 was marked by a steady shift of active concern with colonial problems to the General Assembly. The Assembly during this period often took the Trusteeship Council to task for its timidity in dealing with the colonial powers. The Assembly also did not hesitate to consider colonial disputes that the Security Council dodged. Thus by the start

[11] An *ad hoc* committee was established by the General Assembly in 1946 to recommend procedures to be followed in the collection of this information. This *ad hoc* committee recommended and the Assembly agreed in 1948 to appoint a special committee to examine and to report on the information being transmitted. This special committee was renewed in 1949 and 1952. In 1955 the Assembly renamed the special committee the Committee on Information from Non-Self-Governing Territories. At the eighteenth session of the General Assembly in 1963 the Assembly dissolved the Committee on Information from Non-Self-Governing Territories and transferred its functions to the Special Committee on Colonialism.

of 1960 the Assembly through a decade and a half of active, probing concern with colonial problems had established for itself a dominant position in the Organization with respect to these problems.[12]

Precise assessment of the role of the United Nations in the profound changes that occurred in the colonial areas in the period from 1946 to 1960 is impossible. In some instances the ideological support derived from the principles of the Charter may have aided to a limited extent the growth of nascent nationalist movements in these territories. Quite possibly, the Trusteeship Council's activities and/or the possibility of United Nations concern with a particular colonial situation may have hastened the willingness of colonial powers to undertake reforms aimed at independence. However, these same activities by the Organization may have hardened the resolve of some colonial powers not to grant reforms under international pressure. The clearest contribution of the United Nations during this period was to provide an arena for the marshalling of a majority opinion hostile to a prolonged continuation of colonial rule in Africa and Asia.[13]

Mr. Khrushchev Makes a Declaration

Only a very little political acumen would have been required in the spring and summer of 1960 to foresee that the fifteenth session of the General Assembly convening in September 1960 would be decisively affected by the increased tempo of the disintegration of the colonial empires of Africa. Seventeen colonial territories were scheduled to gain their independence in time for admission to the Organization at that session; of this prospective batch of new nations only Cyprus was a non-African country, and it was in Africa that the colonial revolution was then at its acme. From past experience it was easy to guess that these countries newly emerging from the crucible of revolutionary action would be almost totally mesmerized by the compulsion to hasten the total end of colonialism in the underdeveloped world. In a body as politically oriented as the United

[12] For a succinct analysis of the reasons behind the increasing importance of the General Assembly in the handling of colonial problems, see Jacobson, "The United Nations and Colonialism: A Tentative Appraisal," International Organization, 16, No. 1 (Winter 1962), 38.
[13] Sady, The United Nations and Dependent Peoples, p. 44.

Nations the shifting voting balance in the Assembly resulting from this rush to independence of a whole continent could not go unnoticed. With over one-third of the Assembly by 1960 composed of nations who had achieved their independence after 1945, a dynamic potential existed for making the dominant concern of this group the dominant concern of the Organization. Additionally, by July 1960 the course of events in the Congo had assured the problems of Africa a central place in the upcoming Assembly's attention.

This, then, was the political context in which Nikita Khrushchev decided to seize the initiative on September 23, 1960, by requesting that an additional item, a "declaration on the granting of independence to colonial countries and peoples," be added to the agenda of the fifteenth session.[14] This draft declaration stridently proclaimed that in the colonial territories "the swish of the overseer's lash is heard; there heads fall under the executioner's axe."[15] With the intent of removing the multitude of injustices that the Soviets saw as flowing from the Western colonial system, the Soviet declaration went on to proclaim that all colonial countries "must be granted forthwith complete independence" and that all foreign bases in other states must be eliminated.

With the recommendation of the General Committee on September 28, 1960, that the Soviet item be placed on the agenda, the Assembly seemed assured of the first full-scale debate in its history on the broad question of colonialism, and the U.S.S.R. secured the credit for this accomplishment. In accordance with normal Assembly procedure, the General Committee recommended that this item be allocated to the First (Political and Security) Committee for its consideration. The Assembly accepted on October 10, 1960, the General Committee's recommendation to place the item on its agenda, but in a brilliant tactical maneuver the Soviet Union proposed that instead of allocating this item first to Committee it should be considered directly in plenary session.[16] The Soviets were well aware that plenary sessions of the Assembly are much more productive of world headlines and a wide audience. Additionally, with a crowded agenda such as that at the fifteenth session with almost 100 items to

---

[14] United Nations Document A/4501, Sept. 23, 1960.
[15] United Nations Document A/4502, Sept. 23, 1960, 3.
[16] United Nations Document A/L.312/Rev. 1, Oct. 12, 1960.

be considered, the Soviets had a genuine fear that the West would succeed in burying this item in Committee with the Assembly given time for only the most perfunctory debate after the headline-attracting Heads of Government had departed from New York. As Mr. Khrushchev himself said in the Assembly during the consideration of whether the Assembly should consider this item without prior Committee consideration,

The U.S.S.R. delegation has submitted this question for consideration by the most representative organ of the United Nations, the General Assembly in plenary meeting. It is quite clearly essential to hold the debate in this forum and no other, and at the highest level with the participation of the Heads of Government. Discussion of the problem of the elimination of the colonial system directly in plenary meeting with the participation of the Heads of Government and the Ministers for Foreign Affairs of Member States of the United Nations will invest the debate with the most authoritative character and secure the most favorable conditions for the successful solution of the problem within the framework of the United Nations.[17]

The Western position and the one supported by several Latin American countries was that no compelling reason existed for departing from normal parliamentary practice and that, in any case, a procedure such as that suggested by the Soviet Union would most likely degenerate into a propaganda battle.[18] Particularly adamant in their opposition to initial plenary consideration was the United Kingdom, the state with the largest number of remaining colonial possessions.

The Soviet proposal to shift the scene of debate to plenary session received strong support from the new nations, who were most directly concerned with the remnants of colonialism. Even relatively "pro-Western" new nations such as Nigeria gave unqualified support to the Soviet proposal.[19] However, foreshadowing things to come, several of the new nations from Asia noted 'that they were going along with this proposal more out of deference to their African comrades than from an acceptance of its logic. As Zulfikar Ali Bhutto of Pakistan noted,

[17] United Nations General Assembly *Official Records*, 15th Session, 902d meeting (Oct. 12, 1960), para. 25.
[18] For example, see United Nations General Assembly *Official Records*, 15th Session, 902d meeting (Oct. 12. 1960), para. 208 and 249.
[19] United Nations General Assembly *Official Records*, 15th Session, 902d meeting (Oct. 12, 1960). para. 181–84.

We feel that the First Committee is as important a forum as the Assembly in plenary session. However, the consensus of opinion, and especially those of our new comrades who have recently joined us from Africa, seems to be that this issue be discussed here in plenary, and in recognition of their wishes, we shall support the Soviet amendment that this issue, this very vital issue, be discussed in plenary.[20]

Thus the stage seemed to have been set for the first clash between the enlarged contingent of new nations, supported by the Soviet bloc and some Latin American states, and the West over what was in form, though probably not in essence, a procedural question. However, the United States in particular began to question the wisdom of risking the alienation of this group so early in the session over what was not a vital question. The clincher in what was essentially a Washington-London dialogue was the argument that colonialism was after all a two-edged sword with which the Soviet Union because of its domination of Eastern Europe could be slashed as often as the West.[21] On October 13, 1960, the Soviet proposal to allocate the item to the plenary was adopted by acclamation.[22] The Western support of this proposal can be attributed almost entirely to the influence of the new nations. On this particular issue there existed a dual basis for this influence. First, the West was very desirous of not estranging these nations. Secondly, through their alliance with the Soviet bloc and part of the Latin American group, the new nations had ensured that they would win on this issue regardless of the Western vote. These two forces working in tandem gave the new nations a victory on the question of which body was to consider a declaration on colonialism.

There was no reticence on the part of the Soviet Union in divulging to the General Assembly the strategy that underlay the formulation of their draft declaration. Mr. Khrushchev explained the strategy very concisely when he said:

[20] United Nations General Assembly *Official Records*, 15th Session, 902d meeting (Oct. 12, 1960), para. 245.

[21] It is ironical that, if the vote had been taken as scheduled on Oct. 12, 1960, the West would have probably voted against the Soviet proposal. However, the meeting had to be adjourned prematurely when the Rumanian delegate so angered the Assembly President, Frederick Boland of Ireland, by casting an aspersion on the independence of Ireland that the latter slammed his gavel down so hard that it broke, and without a gavel any meeting of the fifteenth session was impossible.

[22] United Nations General Assembly *Official Records*, 15th Session, 902d meeting (Oct. 12, 1960), para. 218.

I very much like the words of August Bebel, the social-democrat and leader of the German workers, who said, more or less, this: If the bourgeoise praise you, Bebel, think, in that case, what a stupid thing you must have done. If the bourgeoise reviles you, it means that you are truly serving the working class, the proletariat! If the colonialists now revile me, I am proud of it, because it means that I am truly serving the peoples which are struggling for their independence, for their freedom.[23]

And it was indeed a draft declaration formulated according to this precept that was to face the Assembly when it turned to the consideration of the item on November 28, 1960. These gratuitous insults were certainly not designed to gain the widest possible support for the draft. For example, the draft asked:

For what purposes do those who refuse to renounce colonial rule wage murderous war against peoples? Why are the freedom-loving aspirations of the enslaved peoples suppressed? Sometimes it is said that this is done in the interest of the "civilization" of the less developed countries to prepare them for self-government. But this is a lie given the guise of truth.[24]

As to the motivations of the colonial powers, the Soviet draft charged that

The main object of the colonial regime is in fact to secure enormous profits for big foreign monopolies, which have seized the key economic positions in the colonies and to extort their wealth by every possible means. Therefore, the entire economy of a colony is one of exploitation.[25]

While in somewhat more temperate language than the prologue, the operative paragraphs of the Soviet draft, phrased as "demands," were not in the bland diplomatic language of the Assembly, which is best suited to encompass the widest divergency in views and garner the most affirmative votes. The Soviet draft would have had the General Assembly proclaim the following demands:

1. All colonial countries and Trust and Non-Self-Governing Territories must be granted forthwith complete independence and freedom to build their own national States in accordance with the freely expressed will and desire of their peoples. The colonial system and colonial administration in all their forms must be completely abolished in order to offer the people of the territories concerned an opportunity to determine their own destiny and form of government.

[23] United Nations General Assembly *Official Records*, 15th Session, 902d meeting (Oct. 12, 1960), para. 218.
[24] United Nations Document A/4502, Sept. 23, 1960, 5.
[25] *Ibid.*, p. 6.

2. Similarly, all strongholds of colonialism in the form of possessions and leased areas in the territory of other States must be eliminated.

3. The Governments of all countries are urged to observe strictly and steadfastly the provisions of the United Nations Charter and of this Declaration concerning the equality and respect for the sovereign rights and territorial integrity of all States without exception, allowing no manifestation of colonialism or any special rights or advantage for some States to the detriment of other States.[26]

Once the decision had been taken to consider the Soviet item in plenary, informal talks began within the Afro-Asian group, which at that time included all the new nations in the United Nations except Israel. In spite of a wide range of opinion on the Soviet draft, a consensus was quickly reached that the Afro-Asian group should try to formulate, without prejudice to the Soviet draft, its own draft resolution on this item. At least three factors seem to have weighed heavily in this decision to draft an Afro-Asian proposal rather than to support the Soviet draft. Several of the North African and Arab states were of the opinion that the Soviet draft was too intemperate in its language and too extreme in its demands that all leased areas and bases be removed from foreign soil. Secondly, there was a belief based on political realism that the Soviet draft would have great difficulty in achieving the required vote in the General Assembly necessary for adoption. This belief stemmed from the view that Soviet sponsorship would result in a "cold war" vote in the Assembly, in which the Latin Americans would join the West in opposing the Soviet draft. Finally, there was an emotional belief that, as the nations with the most direct concern and experience with colonialism, the Latin Americans should be the ones to introduce and sponsor any Assembly resolution on colonialism.

Having decided to propose their own draft resolution on colonialism, the Afro-Asian group was next faced with the task of coming up with one that would reflect the diversity of opinion within their own membership.[27] At the fifteenth session the Afro-Asian group encompassed 45 countries, 33 of which were new nations in the sense of having achieved their independence in the post-1945 era. The task of preparing a preliminary draft for the consideration of the

---

[26] *Ibid.*, p. 13.

[27] This account of the negotiations leading to the adoption of the Declaration on Colonialism draws on contemporary press reports in the *New York Times* of Nov. 1960, the many revealing remarks made by the delegates during the debate on the question, and interviews conducted with delegates who participated in these negotiations.

larger group was delegated to a six-member drafting committee composed of Guinea, India, Iran, Indonesia, Nigeria, and Senegal. It is interesting to note that four of the members of this drafting committee—Guinea, Indonesia, Nigeria, and Senegal—were new nations; Nigeria was the newest Member having only been admitted to the United Nations on October 7, 1960. This drafting committee set to work in late October 1960 with 2 proposed drafts before it, 1 from Iran and 1 from Guinea. These 2 proposals represented the extremes within the larger Afro-Asian group. Iran proposed a moderate declaration of principles, which avoided direct mention of such controversial points as the Algerian war, deadlines for ending colonialism, and foreign bases. Guinea, on the other hand, proposed a draft much closer in tone and substance to the Soviet draft, one which in spirit was much closer to the expressed wishes of most of the new African states that had entered the Organization in 1960. India, in an attempt to find a middle ground between the Iranian and Guinean drafts, submitted a list of suggestions to the drafting group. Various countries pressed the drafting committee to incorporate views about which they felt special concern. Indonesia, for example, expended great efforts to obtain inclusion of a clause that would support it in its dispute with the Netherlands over West Irian. The drafting committee was unable to reach a conclusion on whether to fix a date for the final end of colonialism. However, they did agree to include specific mention of Algeria's right to independence. During its deliberations the drafting committee followed the general procedure of the Afro-Asian group itself and avoided voting, preferring to engage in extended discussions until a consensus was reached.

Finally, about November 2 the drafting committee had a provisional text ready for consideration by a larger working group before final presentation to the entire Afro-Asian group. During the period in which the struggle over a provisional text was taking place no attempt was made to consult groups outside the Afro-Asian group as to their views on the alternative texts, the feeling being that such consultations would only tend to splinter the Afro-Asian group itself.[28] Many modifications were made in the provisional text during

[28] The British were later to complain bitterly about this failure to consult until after a final text had been prepared. United Nations General Assembly *Official Records*, 15th Session, 947th meeting (Dec. 14, 1960), para. 48.

its consideration by the working group and the entire Afro-Asian group, and, on the whole, the newer nations of Africa who favored a draft close to the Soviet proposal lost more battles than they won at this stage. For example, the specific mention of Algeria's right to independence was deleted from the final version. As one of the more moderate members of the group explained it later,

There is no doubt, for example, that many of the co-sponsors of this draft declaration who have suffered greatly from the ravages of colonialism would have preferred a more expressive text, including clauses condemning colonialism in its most culpable aspects. However, in order to rally all currents of opinion in the Assembly in favor of a text acceptable to all the Members of the United Nations, they have, in a spirit of conciliation, accepted certain phrases of a much more moderate nature.[29]

The final draft in its preamble drew heavily upon the resolutions previously approved by Afro-Asian conferences at Bandung in 1955, Accra in 1958, and Addis Ababa in 1960, because they represented previously agreed-upon phraseology which would be accepted without extensive negotiation. The operative paragraphs of the final draft fluctuated between easily accepted platitudes and ambiguous phrases into which each sponsor could inject its own interpretation. First, an example of the former:

1. The subjection of peoples to alien subjugation, domination, and exploitation constitutes a denial of fundamental human rights . . .

Of the latter:

3. Inadequacy of political, economic, social, or educational preparedness should never serve as a *pretext* for delaying independence. [Emphasis added.]

Or:

7. All states shall observe faithfully and strictly the provisions of the Charter of the United Nations, the Universal Declaration of Human Rights and the present Declaration *on the basis of equality, noninterference in the internal affairs of all states and respect for the sovereign rights of all peoples and their territorial integrity.* [Emphasis added.][30]

This Afro-Asian draft differed from its Soviet counterpart in both tone and substance. Whereas the Soviet draft was both anticolonial

---

[29] Mr. Vakil (Iran), United Nations General Assembly *Official Records*, 15th Session, 926th meeting (Nov. 28, 1960), para. 75.
[30] United Nations Draft Resolution A/L323, No. 28, 1960.

and anti-Western, the Afro-Asian draft was only anticolonial and strenuously avoided attacks on specific Western countries. The tone was as measured, although slightly shrill, as the platitudes were general. Instead of proclaiming "the following demands" as in the Soviet draft, this draft only "declares." The substance of the operative paragraphs also differed. While the Soviet draft had demanded that all colonial territories "be granted forthwith complete independence and freedom," the Afro-Asian draft spoke of "immediate steps" to be taken to transfer power, implying that the transfer could proceed according to an orderly timetable. In contrast to the Soviet draft, no mention is to be found in this draft of any prohibition upon foreign bases.

With the approval in late November by the Afro-Asian caucus at the United Nations of a final draft resolution, the immediate problem became the placing of this resolution before the Assembly in time for the scheduled opening of debate on this item on November 28. With the exception of those few delegations who had such broad instructions that approval by their governments was not required before sponsoring such an important resolution, each delegation had to dispatch a copy of the final draft to its capital and wait for approval. This was a time-consuming process—so much so that only slightly more than half of the eventual sponsors of the resolution were listed on its initial submission to the Assembly.[31] The last state to become a sponsor, Somalia, was not added until December 6. Only Israel of the new nations then in the United Nations did not become a sponsor of this draft; this failure was due to lack of an invitation rather than any unsympathetic motives.

When the debate opened on November 28, the West immediately launched into an attack on Soviet domination of Eastern Europe designed to characterize this rule as the most despotic form of

[31] The sponsors with their date of inclusion were:
United Nations Document A/L.323, Nov. 28, 1960. Afghanistan, Burma, Cambodia, Ceylon, Chad, Cyprus, Ethiopia, Ghana, Guinea, India, Indonesia, Iran, Iraq, Jordan, Lebanon, Liberia, Libya, Morocco, Nepal, Nigeria, Pakistan, Saudi Arabia, Sudan, Togo, Tunisia, and Turkey.
United Nations Document A/L.323/Add.1, Nov. 28, 1960. Mali, United Arab Republic.
United Nations Document A/L.323/Add.2, Nov. 29, 1960. Laos, Senegal.
United Nations Document A/L.323/Add.3, Nov. 30, 1960. Congo (Brazzaville), Congo (Leopoldville), Dahomey, Ivory Coast, Niger, and Upper Volta.
United Nations Document A/L.323/Add.4, Nov. 30, 1960. Cameroon, Central African Republic, Federation of Malaya, and Madagascar.
United Nations Document A/L.323/Add. 5, Dec. 1, 1960. Gabon, the Philippines.
United Nations Document A/L.323/Add.6, Dec. 6, 1960. Somalia.

colonialism then in existence. Thus the British delegate, Mr. Ormsby-Gore, charged that:

The representative of the Soviet Union appears to wish to use this debate simply as another occasion for vilifying my country and other Administering Powers and for carrying the cold war into Africa. . . . I must warn him that if I chose to follow suit, I would have much better ammunition than he has. Since 1939, some 500 million people, formerly under British rule, have achieved freedom and independence, and their representatives sit here. In that same period, the whole or part of six countries, with a population of 22 million, have been forcibly incorporated into the Soviet Union; they include the world's three newest colonies: Lithuania, Estonia, and Latvia. . . . Countless efforts have been made by national movements in countries under Russian control to gain independence. All have been suppressed. In Central Asia, we have seen examples of a colonial policy, which as Mr. Khrushchev himself told us at great length earlier in the session [869th meeting], has in material terms been an outstanding success. He did not tell us of the mass deportations of populations and the ruthless suppression of nationalities which went with it. I shall not harrow the feeling of this Assembly by reciting the whole grisly catalogue; one or two examples must suffice. . . .[32]

The Western strategy which had been decided upon at the time of the decision to agree to direct plenary consideration of this item had been designed with the hope that the new nations would join the West in attacking the Soviet brand of colonialism. It was hoped that this would counter the more virulent Soviet attacks on Western colonialism. The results, however, of the British attack on Soviet colonialism were quite different from what had been expected.[33] This interjection of "cold-war propaganda" so early in the debate was particularly resented by the new nations of Africa. They made known their displeasure at what they viewed as a diversionary maneuver, not only publicly in the Assembly but also through diplomatic channels to Washington and London.[34] As a result of this

[32] United Nations General Assembly *Official Records*, 15th Session, 925th meeting (Nov. 28, 1960), para. 19.

[33] The results would not have been quite as unexpected if Sekou Toure's earlier eloquent plea for the Russians to avoid propaganda in this debate had not been misinterpreted as a one-sided warning applicable only to the Soviets. This plea by the President of Guinea was made during the earlier debate on the allocation of this agenda item. See United Nations General Assembly *Official Records*, 15th Session, 903d meeting (Oct. 13, 1960), para. 7-9.

[34] For examples of this displeasure in the General Assembly, see United Nations General Assembly *Official Records*, 15th Session, 929th meeting (Nov. 30, 1960), para. 140; and United Nations General Assembly *Official Records*, 15th Session, 926th meeting (Nov. 28, 1960), para. 115.

unexpected reaction from the new nations, the West quickly toned down and limited its references to Soviet colonialism and shifted the main line of its argument to a defense of the constructive aspects of Western colonialism. The tone set by New Zealand was much nearer the tone followed by the West during the remainder of the debate than Mr. Ormsby-Gore's opening statement. The New Zealand delegate reminded the Assembly that:

It is a fact worth recalling that the States which have borne the heaviest responsibilities for the administration of Trust and Non-Self-Governing Territories were among the founding Members of this Organization, and that they freely and voluntarily assumed the obligations which the Charter created. Their record of performance is symbolized by the presence among us of the representatives of many new States, which have been brought to independence by the United Kingdom, France, and other countries.[35]

In their effort to depict the more constructive aspects of colonialism, the Western nations received considerable support from Latin America. Appealing to the new nations to take a more balanced account of their colonial past, the Latin American representatives pointed to the constructive cultural and educational benefits of the system. They aptly noted that in many cases it was the language of the ex-colonial power that provided the principal bond uniting the new nations.[36]

Neither the West nor the Latin Americans found a willingness among the new nations to concede the possibility of some beneficial effects resulting from colonialism. The new nations almost as one depicted the colonial era as a time of treachery and deceit during which superior force and unquenchable greed suppressed highly developed native cultures. Their view of the history of colonialism was succinctly expressed by the Moroccan delegate when he said,

The history of colonial conquests, far from being a peak achievement, confronts us with quite different realities. It is nothing other than a stormy succession of wars and expeditions waged by Powers intoxicated by their economic and military potential, seeking to gain strategic positions and hankering for wealth and prestige. The struggles for power between these opposing powers . . . and their intrigues to partition whole conti-

[35] Mr. Shanahan (New Zealand), United Nations General Assembly *Official Records*, 15th Session, 932d meeting (Dec. 2, 1960), para. 4–5.
[36] United Nations General Assembly *Official Records*, 15th Session, 927th meeting (Nov. 29, 1960), para. 15–16; United Nations General Assembly *Official Records*, 15th Session, 929th meeting (Nov. 30, 1960), para. 74.

nents reflect little credit on the Powers involved and are certainly not a glorious page in the history of mankind.[37]

The Latin American assertions of the beneficial effects of colonialism came in for particularly vehement rejection by the new nations. Whereas the Latin Americans had presumed to speak on colonialism as fellow products of the system, the new nations would not accept this relationship and defended their exclusive right to speak as experts on colonialism. As the delegate of Mali said,

> The delegations which speak in this Assembly of their colonial experience or proclaim the benefits of colonialism can unfortunately only speak of the empire of their fathers' day; they speak of it as a heritage.
> If their countries were colonized at some time in history, they know it only from history books. Therein lies the fundamental differences between those delegations and ours, who have personal experience of colonial rule. Our knowledge is not based on hearsay or on what we learnt in school; we were for decades the living embodiment of that system. Ours was a generation which, on coming of age, did not have the right to vote in its own country.[38]

In the debate on the draft declaration the new nations by no means agreed on every aspect of the nature of colonialism. Most agreed that colonialism had contributed little that was positive to the development of their countries and that its main motivation had been economic and political greed. Similarly, there were divergent opinions among the new nations on the exact mechanics for the end of colonialism; these differences can be found in the Assembly debates on the draft. However, there was universal agreement among the new nations about the desirability of rapidly ending the colonial era and an acceptance of their broadly worded draft declaration as a legitimate instrument to achieve this goal. During the Assembly debate there was never any doubt that, in spite of internal division, the Afro-Asian nations would remain united behind their draft.

The Soviet bloc was far from silent during the debate on the agenda item that they had proposed. They maintained a withering fire against all forms of western colonialism. Foreign military bases and NATO assistance to countries engaged in colonial wars were

---

[37] United Nations General Assembly *Official Records*, 15th Session, 945th meeting (Dec. 13, 1960), para. 33.

[38] United Nations General Assembly *Official Records*, 15th Session, 931st meeting (Dec. 1, 1960), para. 27–28.

favorite subjects of this often vitriolic attack. However, despite the ferocity of this attack, the Soviet bloc was able to avoid incurring the odium of the new nations because it shared with these nations a common target, western colonialism. Often resorting to a liberal use of quotations from Afro-Asian delegates in the debate, the Soviets were always careful to direct the main thrust of their attacks against the common target. But while the Soviets and the new nations shared a common target, the Soviets were always more immoderate than the new nations in language, analysis, and proposals.[39] With regard to the Afro-Asian draft the Soviet Union during the debate publicly said very little beyond the fact that it applauded "the desire shown by the overwhelming majority of African and Asian delegations that measures should be taken . . . to advance the realization of that lofty goal—the complete liberation of the peoples of all colonies and dependent countries."[40] The Soviets continued publicly to press for the adoption of their own draft resolution. The new nations were quite happy to have the Soviet Union continue to urge its own more far-reaching resolution rather than publicly embrace their milder resolution. This happy configuration, which was to be repeated often on colonial issues during the next four years, enabled the new nations to appeal to their Western and Latin American colleagues as a voice of reason and restraint which if not supported would result in the victory of the more odious Soviet draft.[41]

During the debate, of course, negotiations—or as Marya Mannes termed it in a felicitous phrase, the fine art of corridor sitting[42]— continued. Although the Latin American states differed with the Afro-Asians in their assessment of the ultimate worth of colonialism and deplored the immoderate language of the newer nations, there was never any great concern by the new nations as to how the Latin American states would vote. The Latin American states repeatedly

[39] See Mr. Zorin's (U.S.S.R.) speech to the General Assembly, United Nations General Assembly *Official Records*, 15th Session, 939th meeting (Dec. 7, 1960), para. 19–74.
[40] *Ibid.*, para. 74.
[41] The Honduran delegation tried briefly to seize this role of moderation for itself by introducing a draft (United Nations Document A/L.324/Rev. 1 and 2, Dec. 1, 1960), which attempted to compromise the Western and Afro-Asian positions. However, both the Soviet bloc and the Afro-Asian group quickly indicated their determined opposition to this attempt, and Honduras did not press its draft to a vote. The importance of this otherwise unnoteworthy episode for an understanding of the Organization's political process is that, since the influx of new nations in 1960, the Afro-Asians have the voting power on the colonial issue on which they are united to deny a mediating role to any other group.
[42] Marya Mannes, "U.N.: The Fine Art of Corridor Sitting," *The Reporter*, Jan. 12, 1956, 30.

stated that as far as they were concerned it was "no longer a question of discussing whether or not colonialism must be brought to an end, but of determining the methods, time limits, and procedures by which the process of liquidation is to be effected."[43] Similarly, the belief at this time based on conversations with Eastern bloc delegates was that, when the time for the vote arrived, the Soviet Union would either withdraw its own draft in favor of the Afro-Asian version or after the vote on its own had been taken, and it had probably been defeated, it would vote in favor of the Afro-Asian version. The votes in greatest doubt, and hence the countries on which negotiations and pressure centered, were the Western European nations and the United States. The Scandinavian countries had supported the Afro-Asian draft during the debate, as had the Netherlands. In the case of the Netherlands this decision had been reached apparently in an effort to strengthen, or at least to avoid alienating, any potential support among the new nations in its dispute with Indonesia over West Irian. Ironically, the Netherlands in 1962 was to reproach the United States for attempting to curry favor with the new nations by tacitly supporting Indonesia in this same dispute. France was considered hopeless because of its involvement in the Algerian war. This left the United States and the United Kingdom as the principal targets of influence for the new nations. The British, during the debate on the draft, had left open the possibility of their eventually voting for it.[44] Similarly, Mr. Wadsworth had made United States support for the Afro-Asian draft seem a distinct possibility when he said,

It is equally fitting that . . . an effort should be made to state the sense of the General Assembly in a new declaration which accords with the circumstances of 1960. For that task no one among us is so well qualified as the nations of Africa and Asia, to most of whom this question is a matter of first-hand experience and who are the sponsors of the draft resolution before the Assembly. We of the United States wish to be in a position to support their declaration. We hope that whatever questions of language might remain can still be worked out. We applaud their initiative and the spirit which animates it.[45]

[43] Mr. Amadeo (Argentina), United Nations General Assembly *Official Records*, 15th Session, 927th meeting (Nov. 29, 1960), para. 18.
[44] United Nations General Assembly *Official Records*, 15th Session, 925th meeting (Nov. 28, 1960), para. 32.
[45] United Nations General Assembly *Official Records*. 15th Session, 937th meeting (Dec. 6, 1960), para. 17.

The British in particular wanted inserted into the Afro-Asian draft some mention of the positive contribution of the colonial powers and, more importantly, a recognition of the need for adequate preparations in the political, economic, and social realms before some form of self-determination was granted. In the fall of 1960 the British Government was in a period of extreme disquietude over the United Nations role in the Congo and was also feeling the burden of responsibility for the large number of colonial possessions it continued to administer. Both of these factors tended to restrict its willingness to approve an additional United Nations role in an area of intimate concern to itself. On the other hand, the sponsors of the draft resolution were both from a point of temperament and out of practical necessity unable to grant the compromises that the British desired. The new nations in 1960 could not afford the emotional disengagement necessary to praise publicly the salutary effects of colonialism. From a practical point of view, the 43 sponsors did not have the time to agree upon concessions among themselves, obtain approval from their governments, and then offer them to the British. In draft resolutions having long lists of sponsors the only feasible time to conduct negotiations is before the formal submission of such drafts.

In talks with the United States delegation, the new nations found a disquieting ambivalence. The United States delegation had only the strongest praise for the struggle of the colonial areas toward nationhood and was most solicitous toward their problems.[46] Also, the United States delegates in private conversation never failed to express their private support of the draft resolution. But when the conversation turned to how the United States would finally vote on the draft, a strange reticence prevailed. The United States, like Britain, expressed its preference for a draft in which greater recognition of the positive contribution of the colonial powers was given and which acknowledged the necessity of adequate preparation in the colonial territories before independence was granted. But no clear indication was ever given in the pre-vote debate as to how the United States would vote if such changes were not made.

[46] For one view of the attitude of the United States delegation, see Senator Wayne Morse (Oregon), "The United States in the United Nations: 1960—A Turning Point," *Supplementary Report to the Committee on Foreign Relations, United States Senate* (Washington, D.C., 1961), pp. 20–21.

On December 13, the day before the debate was to end on the various drafts, the Soviet Union introduced two amendments to the Afro-Asian draft. Mr. Zorin pointed out that the Soviet Union considered that both its own draft and the Afro-Asian draft expressed "a common platform and identical views on a number of vital questions" but that the latter had several defects which the Soviet amendments were designed to eliminate.[47] The first Soviet amendment called for setting the end of 1961 as a target date for the termination of colonialism, while the second amendment called for the Assembly to decide to put the question of the implementation of this resolution on the agenda of the sixteenth session.[48]

On December 14, 1960, after more than 70 states had spoken, the General Assembly voted on the drafts before it. The first draft to be voted upon was that of the Soviet Union. For purposes of voting, this draft was divided into two parts with the vote on the three operative paragraphs being taken first. These paragraphs of the Soviet draft, which called for the immediate granting of complete independence to all colonial possessions and the elimination of all foreign bases in the territory of other states, were defeated by a roll-call vote of 32 in favor, 35 against, and 30 abstentions.[49] On this vote 11 new nations, or 34.4 percent of the new nations voting, supported the Soviet draft, while only 3 new nations, or 9.4 percent of the new nations voting, voted against it. But the majority of the new nations voting, 18 representing 56.2 percent, abstained on this vote, and 1 new nation, Dahomey, was absent at the time of the vote. The

---

[47] United Nations General Assembly *Official Records*, 15th Session, 945th meeting (Dec. 13, 1960), para. 111.

[48] United Nations Document A/L.328, Dec. 13, 1960.

[49] United Nations General Assembly, *Official Records*, 15th Session, 947th meeting (Dec. 14, 1960), para. 29.

For: Morocco, Nepal, Poland, Romania, Saudi Arabia, Sudan, Togo, Ukrainian Soviet Socialist Republic, U.S.S.R., United Arab Republic, Yemen, Yugoslavia, Afghanistan, Albania, Bulgaria, Byelorussian S.S.R., Ceylon, Chad, Cuba, Czechoslovakia, Ethiopia, Ghana, Guinea, Hungary, India, Indonesia, Iraq, Jordan, Lebanon, Liberia, Libya, and Mali.

Against: Netherlands, New Zealand, Nicaragua, Niger, Norway, Panama, Philippines, Portugal, Spain, Sweden, Thailand, Turkey, United Kingdom, United States, Uruguay, Argentina, Australia, Belgium, Brazil, Canada, Chile, China, Colombia, Costa Rica, Denmark, El Salvador, France, Greece, Honduras, Iceland, Ireland, Israel, Italy, Japan, and Luxembourg.

Abstaining: Mexico, Nigeria, Pakistan, Paraguay, Peru, Senegal, Somalia, Tunisia, Upper Volta, Venezuela, Austria, Bolivia, Burma, Cambodia, Cameroon, Central African Republic, Congo (Brazzaville), Congo (Leopoldville), Cyprus, Dominican Republic, Ecuador, Federation of Malaya, Finland, Gabon, Guatemala, Haiti, Iran, Ivory Coast, Laos, and Madagascar.

second vote was on the remainder of the Soviet draft, which contained a vehement denunciation not only of colonialism but of the colonialist powers themselves. This section was overwhelmingly rejected by a roll-call vote of only 25 in favor to 43 against and with 29 abstentions.[50] Only 8 of the new nations voting, or 25 percent, supported this section of the Soviet declaration, while four, or 12.5 percent, opposed it. A clear majority of the new nations, 20 states representing 62.5 percent of the 32 new nations voting, abstained on the vote, and Dahomey was absent. Thus on the second vote, whereas only 30 percent of the Member States as a whole abstained, 62.5 percent of the new nations took this alternative. If the new nations' votes are disregarded entirely on this second vote, one finds that of the remaining 65 votes only 9, or 13.7 percent abstained. At least on this issue, it can be noted that, when the vote took on heavy overtones of a direct East-West clash, the new nations took shelter by abstaining.

Following the Rules of Procedure, the Assembly next turned to vote on the two Soviet amendments to the Afro-Asian draft. Quaison-Sackey of Ghana appealed to the Soviet Union on behalf of the Afro-Asian states to withdraw its amendments, particularly the one proposing a 1961 target date for the complete elimination of colonialism. Mr. Zorin in refusing this request clearly indicated what his country hoped to gain from such a vote when he stated his belief that "the voting should disclose the position of all countries and reveal who is interested in the speedy elimination of the colonial system."[51] Thus the Assembly proceeded to vote first on the Soviet

[50] United Nations General Assembly *Official Records,* 15th Session, 947th meeting (Dec. 14, 1960), para. 30.

For: Albania, Bulgaria, Byelorussian S. S. R., Ceylon, Cuba, Czechoslovakia, Ethiopia, Ghana, Guinea, Hungary, Iraq, Ivory Coast, Liberia, Madagascar, Mali, Morocco, Niger, Poland, Romania, Saudi Arabia, Ukrainian S.S.R., U.S.S.R., United Arab Republic, Yemen, and Afghanistan.

Against: Argentina, Australia, Belgium, Bolivia, Brazil, Canada, Chile, China, Colombia, Costa Rica, Denmark, Ecuador, El Salvador, Federation of Malaya, France, Greece, Guatemala, Honduras, Iceland, Iran, Ireland, Israel, Italy, Japan, Luxembourg, Netherlands, New Zealand, Nicaragua, Norway, Pakistan, Panama, Paraguay, Peru, Philippines, Portugal, Spain, Sweden, Thailand, Turkey, United Kingdom, United States, Uruguay, and Venezuela.

Abstaining: Austria, Burma, Cambodia, Cameroon, Central African Republic, Chad, Congo (Brazzaville), Congo (Leopoldville), Cyprus, Dominican Republic, Finland, Gabon, Haiti, India, Indonesia, Jordan, Laos, Lebanon, Libya, Mexico, Nepal, Nigeria, Senegal, Somalia, Sudan, Togo, Tunisia, Upper Volta, and Yugoslavia.

[51] United Nations General Assembly *Official Records,* 15th Session, 947th meeting (Dec. 14, 1960), para. 25.

amendment proposing a 1961 target date for the end of colonialism. It was rejected on a roll-call vote by 29 in favor, 47 against and with 22 abstentions.[52] Of the new nations nine, or 28.1 percent of the new nations voting, supported the Soviet amendment compared with ten, or 31.3 percent, who voted against it and 13, or 40.6 percent, who abstained on the vote. Unlike the previous votes on the Soviet draft, those abstaining could no longer muster an absolute majority, although they still represented a plurality. Voted on next was the second Soviet amendment, which would have placed the question of the implementation of the declaration on the agenda of the sixteenth session of the Assembly. This amendment, although it gained a simple majority, failed for lack of the required two-thirds majority with a vote of 41 in favor, 35 against, and with 22 abstentions.[53] An absolute majority of the new nations voting, 17 or 53.1 percent, favored the Soviet amendment, while only 5, or 15.6 percent, opposed it and 10, or 31.3 percent, abstained on the vote. While not abstaining as heavily on the Soviet amendments as on the Soviet draft, the new nations were splintered on these 2 votes. While the

[52] United Nations General Assembly *Official Records*, 15th Session, 947th meeting (Dec. 14, 1960), para. 32.

For: Iraq, Jordan, Lebanon, Liberia, Libya, Mali, Mexico, Morocco, Poland, Romania, Saudi Arabia, Somalia, Sudan, Togo, Tunisia, Ukrainian S.S.R., U.S.S.R., United Arab Republic, Yemen, Yugoslavia, Afghanistan, Albania, Bulgaria, Byelorussian S.S.R., Cuba, Czechoslovakia, Ethiopia, Guinea, and Hungary.

Against: Iran, Ireland, Israel, Italy, Ivory Coast, Japan, Laos, Luxembourg, Madagascar, Netherlands, New Zealand, Nicaragua, Niger, Norway, Pakistan, Panama, Peru, Philippines, Portugal, Spain, Sweden, Thailand, Turkey, Union of South Africa, United Kingdom, United States, Argentina, Australia, Belgium, Bolivia, Brazil, Canada, Chile, China, Colombia, Congo (Brazzaville), Costa Rica, Denmark, El Salvador, Federation of Malaya, France, Gabon, Greece, Guatemala, Honduras, and Iceland.

Abstaining: Indonesia, Nepal, Nigeria, Paraguay, Senegal, Upper Volta, Uruguay, Venezuela, Burma, Cambodia, Cameroon, Central African Republic, Ceylon, Chad, Congo (Leopoldville), Cyprus, Dominican Republic, Ecuador, Finland, Ghana, Haiti and India.

[53] United Nations General Assembly *Official Records*, 15th Session, 947th meeting (Dec. 14, 1960), para. 33.

For: Hungary, India, Iraq, Jordan, Lebanon, Liberia, Libya, Mali, Mexico, Morocco, Nepal, Nigeria, Poland, Romania, Saudi Arabia, Somalia, Sudan, Togo, Tunisia, Ukrainian S.S.R., U.S.S.R., United Arab Republic, Uruguay, Venezuela, Yemen, Yugoslavia, Afghanistan, Albania, Bulgaria, Burma, Byelorussian S.S.R., Cameroon, Ceylon, Chad, Congo (Leopoldville), Cuba, Cyprus, Czechoslovakia, Ethiopia, Ghana, and Guinea.

Against: Honduras, Iceland, Ireland, Italy, Ivory Coast, Japan, Luxembourg, Madagascar, Netherlands, New Zealand, Nicaragua, Niger, Norway, Pakistan, Portugal, Spain, Sweden, Thailand, Turkey, Union of South Africa, United Kingdom, United States, Australia, Belgium, Bolivia, Brazil, Canada, China, Colombia, Costa Rica, Denmark, Federation of Malaya, Finland, France, and Greece.

Abstaining: Haiti, Indonesia, Iran, Israel, Laos, Panama, Paraguay, Peru, Philippines, Senegal, Upper Volta, Argentina, Austria, Cambodia, Central African Republic, Chile, Congo (Brazzaville), Dominican Republic, Ecuador, El Salvador, Gabon, and Guatemala.

former French colonies showed a somewhat greater proclivity than their British counterparts for voting with the Soviets, there were numerous exceptions to this tendency.

With the voting on the Soviet amendments completed, the only thing that remained was the vote on the Afro-Asian draft itself. By this time there was certainly no doubt as to the vote's outcome, and the only element of suspense was provided by the uncertainty as to how the United States would vote. It was common knowledge in the Assembly that the United Kingdom and Portugal, two NATO allies of the United States, were exerting great pressure on the United States not to vote in favor of this draft. Similarly, few delegates who had discussed this draft with the members of the United States mission doubted its desire to support it. Thus on the final vote more than on any of the minor decisions preceding it, the United States was being asked to choose between its old ally, Great Britain, and the new nations of Africa and Asia.

By a roll-call vote of 89 in favor, none against, and with 9 abstentions, the Afro-Asian draft became General Assembly Resolution 1514(XV) a "Declaration on the Granting of Independence to Colonial Countries and Peoples."[54] Those abstaining were Australia, Belgium, the Dominican Republic, France, Portugal, Spain, the Union of South Africa, the United Kingdom, and the United States. The disquietude of the United States delegation at finding itself in the company of this retrograde group of colonial powers was not helped by the fact that the only Negro member of the delegation, Mrs. Zelma Watson George, stood up and applauded the adoption of the draft. After the vote Ambassador Wadsworth took the floor to explain the vote of the United States in the following terms:

[54] United Nations General Assembly *Official Records*, 15th Session, 947th meeting (Dec. 14, 1960), para. 34.

For: Haiti, Honduras, Hungary, Iceland, India, Indonesia, Iran, Iraq, Ireland, Israel, Italy, Ivory Coast, Japan, Jordan, Laos, Lebanon, Liberia, Libya, Luxembourg, Madagascar, Mali, Mexico, Morocco, Nepal, Netherlands, New Zealand, Nicaragua, Niger, Nigeria, Norway, Pakistan, Panama, Paraguay, Peru, Philippines, Poland, Romania, Saudi Arabia, Senegal, Somalia, Sudan, Sweden, Thailand, Togo, Tunisia, Turkey, Ukrainian S.S.R., U.S.S.R., United Arab Republic, Upper Volta, Uruguay, Venezuela, Yemen, Yugoslavia, Afghanistan, Albania, Argentina, Austria, Bolivia, Brazil, Bulgaria, Burma, Byelorussian S.S.R., Cambodia, Cameroon, Canada, Central African Republic, Ceylon, Chad, Chile, China, Colombia, Congo (Brazzaville), Congo (Leopoldville), Costa Rica, Cuba, Cyprus, Czechoslovakia, Denmark, Ecuador, El Salvador, Ethiopia, Federation of Malaya, Finland, Gabon, Ghana, Greece, Guatemala, and Guinea.

Against: None.

Abstaining: Portugal, Spain, Union of South Africa, United Kingdom, United States. Australia, Belgium, Dominican Republic, and France.

... The support of freedom is a concept springing from deeply held beliefs of the American people. We accordingly welcomed the underlying purpose of this resolution . . . which we understand to be the advancement of human freedom in the broadest sense. . . . Now there are difficulties in the language and thought of this resolution . . . which made it impossible for us to support it, because they seem to negate certain clear provisions of the United Nations Charter. . . . It is hard to understand why a resolution on this broad subject should be completely silent on the important contributions which the administering Powers, including my own Government, have made in the advancement of dependent peoples toward self-government or independence. The resolution is also heavily weighted towards complete independence as the only acceptable goal, thus ignoring the Charter provisions for self-government of dependent areas within larger political contexts. . . . I would call attention to a very wise statement which was made from this rostrum not long ago by the representative of India who, while discussing his delegation's position on another matter, said, "We do not feel that we could fully support it unless we could support every word of it." This is the major reason why the United States felt constrained to abstain on this particular vote. . . .[55]

While this was the formal explanation given for the United States abstention, the actual reason appears to have been a direct appeal from British Prime Minister Macmillan to Eisenhower to avoid placing the United Kingdom in an awkward position.[56] The final decision that the United States should abstain was made by Eisenhower against the advice of the entire United States delegation.[57]

What assessment can one make of the political influence exercised during this episode? Even without access to the Soviet archives, little extrapolation is needed to calculate that a considerable part was played in the initial Soviet decision to propose this agenda item and its accompanying draft declaration by the knowledge of the increasing numerical strength of the new nations in the Organization. Of

[55] United Nations General Assembly *Official Records*, 15th Session, 947th meeting (Dec. 14, 1960), para. 142–53.
[56] *New York Times*, Dec. 16, 1960, p. 4; Thomas J. Hamilton, "Colonialism at the U.N.," *New York Times*, Section IV, Dec. 18, 1960, 9.
[57] *Ibid.*; Senator Wayne Morse, "The United States in the United Nations: 1960— A Turning Point," *Supplementary Report to the Committee on Foreign Relations, United States Senate* (Washington, D.C., 1961), pp. 20–21. Arthur M. Schlesinger, Jr., *A Thousand Days: John F. Kennedy in the White House*, pp. 510–11: "Our delegation even had the concurrence of the State Department in Washington in its desire to vote for the resolution. But the British were opposed, and Harold Macmillan called Eisenhower by transatlantic telephone to request American abstention. When an instruction to abstain arrived from the White House, James J. Wadsworth, then our ambassador to the UN, tried to reach Eisenhower to argue the case. Eisenhower declined to accept his call."

course, a desire to harass the West at one of its most vulnerable points was probably not absent. But the reason that the Soviets believed this to be an effective means of harassment in 1960—they had never proposed a similar agenda item in the past—appears to be related to their empathy for the shifting balance of forces in the United Nations and for the concerns of the new nations. In this instance the Soviets seem to have taken the course that they did more out of a sensitivity to the latent influence than from any active use of this influence by the new nations.

The decision of the West not to oppose the acceptance of the Soviet agenda proposal and ultimately to vote in favor of its consideration in plenary without previous referral to a Main Committee involved a large element of active influence exercised by the new nations. For the West this decision meant a reversal of previous stands on the proper forum for the consideration of colonial issues and orderly Assembly procedure. Important considerations for the West were the facts that it had no desire to alienate such a large group over what the West viewed as a procedural issue and that the new nations with their allies had the voting strength to win in any case.

The new nations for their part made no real attempt to engage in negotiations concerning the contents of their draft until after it was fully formulated and was practically beyond change due to its large sponsorship. On this draft one can judge that the new nations expended very little influence in obtaining the support of the Soviet bloc; the Soviet bloc was willing to give its support in the hope of gaining for itself possible influence in the future. This presents the classic problem of attempting to measure the influence on someone who wants to be influenced. Similarly, with regard to the Latin American Members, little influence was required to obtain their support. Although the commitment of the Latin American states to the principle of decolonization perhaps lacked the emotional ardor of the new nations, the commitment was more than sufficient to ensure their support for the draft. It is, therefore, with the West that the new nations had the greatest need to exercise their political influence if they were to obtain their goal of a unanimously adopted resolution.

The result could not have been terribly disappointing. All of the Scandinavian countries, the Netherlands, Italy, Greece, and Canada voted in favor of the draft and there were no votes against it. In the case of the Scandinavian countries it is much more likely that their votes represented a genuine commitment to the principles enunciated in the draft than that they resulted from influence exercised by the new nations. However, in the case of the Netherlands, its decision to support the draft recognized the potential role of the new nations in its dispute with Indonesia over West Irian and apparently was designed to avoid alienating possible support for its position in this dispute.[58] The one common element in the decision of Italy, Greece and Canada to support the draft was an unwillingness to sacrifice developing relations with the new nations in defense of a system that most states admitted was doomed.[59] An important element in the new nations' influence was the strong feeling in the Assembly that the victory of the decolonization movement was inevitable. And while the principal colonial powers did abstain, that in itself was a form of victory in that the draft at question inter alia proclaimed "the necessity of bringing to a speedy and unconditional end colonialism in all its forms and manifestations." This unwillingness to be clearly stigmatized as being against the lofty principles enunciated in the draft is testimony, of sorts, to the possession of political influence by the new nations. Few had supposed in any case that the new nations had a great deal of influence on Portugal, Spain, and the Union of South Africa. Great Britain, probably the most progressive of all colonial powers, had again demonstrated its testiness on the issue of international responsibility for the administration of colonial possessions. It was really only with the United States that the new nations could have been disappointed with the results of their exercise of political influence. When the issue came down to one between fidelity to the principal ally of the United States and support of the new nations on a colonial declaration in the United Nations, the Eisenhower Administration supported Britain. But the loss was not without profit for the new nations. The abstention of the United States had focused attention on the nature of the choice and made clear that many even within the Administration would have

[58] United Nations General Assembly *Official Records*, 15th Session, 947th meeting (Dec. 14, 1960), para. 59–62.

[59] United Nations General Assembly *Official Records*, 15th Session, 947th meeting (Dec. 14, 1960), para. 36–44; United Nations General Assembly *Official Records*, 15th Session, 934th meeting (Dec. 3, 1960), para. 1–12; United Nations General Assembly *Official Records*, 15th Session, 937th meeting (Dec. 6, 1960), para. 69–89.

preferred to support the new nations. And perhaps most hopeful from the standpoint of the new nations, a new Administration that spoke of a new role for the United States in support of the national aspirations of the colonial and former colonial parts of the world was about to assume power in Washington.

A Special Committee Is Born

The progress toward the implementation of the Declaration on Colonialism in the period between its adoption at the fifteenth session and the opening of the sixteenth session was considerably less than remarkable. In fact, only one other country, Tanganyika, was scheduled to gain its independence in 1961, and this, too, was according to a previously announced timetable. As the sixteenth Assembly approached, there was not a case that could be pointed to as an example of the granting of independence to a colonial territory because of the Declaration. There still remained over 80 territories with a population of about 70 million who lacked complete independence.

No doubt being aware of the frustrations of the new nations at what seemed to be a dilatory response to the Assembly's call for immediate steps toward independence, the U.S.S.R. by a cable of August 28, 1961, requested the inclusion in the agenda of an item on "the situation with regard to the implementation of the Declaration on the granting of independence to colonial countries and peoples."[60] This initial submission was soon followed by a stinging memorandum that was both anticolonial and anti-imperialist, anticolonial in the sense that it attacked the colonial system of domination and anti-imperialist in the sense that it specifically attacked the colonial powers. A strident tone aimed more against the West than for independence of colonial territories permeated this document. It charged that the West was continuing to follow a "policy of terror and repression" in the remaining colonial areas and that the United States was using the North Atlantic Treaty Organization, the Central Treaty Organization, and the Southeast Asia Treaty Organization to maintain the colonial rule of its allies.[61]

A Soviet draft resolution designed to achieve the immediate end

[60] United Nations Document A/4859, Aug. 28, 1961.
[61] United Nations Document A/4889, Sept. 27, 1961.

of colonialism was submitted to the Assembly on October 9, 1961.[62] While its tone was less strident and the content less anti-Western than that of the memorandum, it certainly was not likely to comfort the administering powers. This draft called for "the immediate implementation" of the 1960 Declaration and declared "that the final and unconditional liquidation of colonialism in all its forms and manifestations must be implemented not later than the end of 1962." In addition, immediate elections on the basis of universal suffrage were to be held; all limitations on the fullest exercise of political rights were to be removed along with an immediate amnesty for all political prisoners; all troops of the administering powers were to be removed from the colonial territories; and all foreign military bases in Trust and Non-Self-Governing Territories were to be immediately dismantled. The Soviet draft also would have had the Assembly establish "a special commission to conduct a full and complete inquiry into the situation with respect to the implementation of the Declaration on the granting of independence to colonial countries and peoples and of the measure for carrying it into effect." In line with then current Soviet pressure for the reorganization of the United Nations, this special commission was to be composed according to the troika principle with the three main groups of states —Western, Socialist, and neutralist—having equal representation.

While the new nations continued to find Soviet talk of the immediate liquidation of colonialism congenial, they were even less willing in 1961 than in 1960 to abdicate what they saw as their personal responsibility for the management of this issue in the Assembly. The Nigerian delegate, Mr. Ngileruma, during the Assembly debate on this item stated very concisely what had often been said in private by the new nations as to the way they viewed the Soviet proposals.

My delegation must express its appreciation to the delegation of the Soviet Union for the interest and initiative which they have manifested in the problem of the speedy liquidation of the remnants of colonialism. However, my delegation feels compelled to add that we, and by "we" I mean the Africans and Asians who have worn the shoe of colonialism, know best how and when it pinches.[63]

---

[62] United Nations Document A/L.355, Oct. 9, 1961.
[63] United Nations General Assembly *Official Records*, 16th Session, 1066th meeting (Nov. 27, 1961), para. 107.

Behind the scene at the United Nations those who had "worn the shoe of colonialism" were actively engaged in preparing a draft resolution on the implementation of the 1960 Declaration. As in 1960 this feverish activity was centered on the Afro-Asian group, but unlike 1960 a sustained effort was made to involve a large number of delegations from outside their own group in the formative stage of drafting before formal submission by a long list of sponsors had ended hope of any real negotiations.[64] The new nations were showing increasing political sophistication in the delicate arts of drafting United Nations resolutions and organizing advanced support for such resolutions. The West, in particular the United States representative, Jonathan B. Bingham, played an active role in obtaining a draft that would embody the aspirations of the new states and be an effective means of peacefully ending the remnants of colonialism, while at the same time it would be acceptable to the administering powers. Mr. Subandrio of Indonesia aptly described the results:

We believe, first of all, that this draft—the result of extensive consultations and discussions—reflects a spirit of give and take and, in this respect, represents the widest possible area of agreement that can be obtained in this Assembly. For example, although my delegation believes it possible and desirable to end colonialism in two years . . . the authors of this draft resolution have taken into consideration the fact that a difference of opinion exists on this subject, not only within the African-Asian group itself but in this Assembly as a whole.[65]

The draft that emerged from this wide consultative process was

---

[64] For example, Mr. Gallin-Douathe (Central African Republic), United Nations General Assembly *Official Records*, 16th Session, 1066th meeting (Nov. 27, 1961), para. 124: ". . . first about draft resolution A/L.366 and Add.1–3. This was drafted by a large number of delegations, including delegations of countries which have colonial territories, particularly in Africa." Mr. Bingham (United States), United Nations General Assembly *Official Records*, 16th Session, 1066th meeting (Nov. 27, 1961), para. 24: "We are extremely grateful to the many sponsors of the draft resolution contained in document A/L.366 and Add.1–3 for their patient and painstaking efforts, over many weeks of arduous discussions, to arrive at a text which will both be acceptable, we believe, to the overwhelming majority of the Members of the United Nations and, more importantly, will work." Mr. Plimsoll (Australia), United Nations General Assembly *Official Records*, 16th Session, 1065th meeting (Nov. 27, 1961), para. 185: "First, regarding the draft resolution that is being submitted by Afghanistan and a group of other African-Asian States, the countries that are responsible for the submission of this proposal have gone to a great deal of trouble; they have consulted a large number of delegations from various groups, and as a result, we have before us a draft resolution which, I believe, commands a great deal of support throughout this Assembly."
[65] United Nations General Assembly *Official Records*, 16th session, 1065th meeting (Nov. 27, 1961), para. 151.

sponsored by 38 Afro-Asian states.[66] It is interesting to note, however, that 13 of the new nations were not listed as sponsors of this draft resolution. The failure of 2 of these states, Israel and Mongolia, to become co-sponsors is easily explained. Israel, because of its conflict with the Arab states, was simply not invited, and Mongolia had been admitted to the United Nations too late, October 27, 1961, to take part in the drafting of the resolution. The Sudan, on the other hand, declined to sponsor the draft because of a strongly held belief that the proposed size of the Special Committee was too large for any meaningful work to be accomplished.[67] Of the remaining 10 new nations who had declined to co-sponsor this draft, all were former French possessions and 9 were members of the moderate Brazzaville group,[68] and French pressure may have played some part in their decision not to co-sponsor the draft.

The draft itself was moderate in tone and its preamble hewed to the time-honored diplomatic tradition of using language that the Assembly had approved before, in this case the language of Resolution 1514(XV).[69] While reiterating and reaffirming the 1960 Declaration, the draft called upon the "States concerned to take action without further delay with a view to the faithful application and implementation of the Declaration." The draft also called for the establishment of a Special Committee, composed of 17 members to be nominated by the President of the General Assembly. The Special Committee was "to make suggestions and recommendations on the progress and extent of the implementation of the Declaration."

As in the case of most Assembly debates, the preceding negotiations had been so thorough that the debate contained few surprises and served largely to affirm publicly positions already stated privately. For the United States this provided the occasion for it to

[66] United Nations Document A/L.366 and Add.1–3, Nov. 21, 1961. Afghanistan, Burma, Cambodia, Cameroon, Ceylon, Congo (Leopoldville), Cyprus, Ethiopia, Federation of Malaya, Ghana, Guinea, India, Indonesia, Iran, Iraq, Japan, Jordan, Laos, Lebanon, Liberia, Libya, Mali, Morocco, Nepal, Niger, Nigeria, Pakistan, Philippines, Saudi Arabia, Senegal, Sierra Leone, Somalia, Syria, Thailand, Tunisia, Turkey, United Arab Republic, and Yemen.

[67] United Nations General Assembly *Official Records*, 16th Session, 1065th meeting (Nov. 27, 1961), para. 53.

[68] These 10 states were Central African Republic, Chad, Congo (Brazzaville), Dahomey, Gabon, Ivory Coast, Madagascar, Mauritania, Togo, and Upper Volta. Only Togo was not a member of the Brazzaville group. For a description of this group, see Hovet, *Africa in the United Nations*, pp. 91–8.

[69] United Nations Document A/L.366 and Add. 1–3, Nov. 21, 1961.

signal publicly a change from its 1960 decision not to support the Declaration on Colonialism. Mr. Jonathan Bingham, the United States representative responsible for colonial matters, clearly announced the position of the Kennedy administration when he told the Assembly:

. . . My country has associated itself with the principles of that historic Declaration. We shall be happy if, by our participation in this and future debates, as well as by our actions, both within and outside the United Nations, we can help to advance its great purposes.[70]

Thus the United States, which had abstained during the vote on the Declaration in 1960, was now not only associating with it but also announcing willingness to work for its implementation. Actually, the new Administration had publicly signaled its unwillingness to defend colonial powers at the cost of a loss of influence among the new nations during the Security Council debate in March 1961 on Angola. The decision of the United States to vote on March 15, 1961, in the Security Council with the Soviet Union, Liberia, Ceylon, and the United Arab Republic in favor of an inquiry into racial disorders in Angola marks the decisive shift in the United States position on colonial issues.[71] According to Schlesinger, Kennedy had decided to reverse the Eisenhower policy of "systematic deference to the old colonial power" before all possibilities of exercising influence on the new nations were lost, and the Angolan draft provided the first opportunity to indicate the new position.[72] In this new effort to associate itself with the aspirations of the new nations and in deference to their wishes, the United States reduced to a bare minimum references to "communist colonialism" in its interventions in the debate. In fact, when the United States finally felt sufficiently justified by repeated intemperate Soviet attacks on the United States to reply in kind, Adlai Stevenson submitted a memorandum for circulation and then revealed to the press that this form of submis-

[70] United Nations General Assembly *Official Records*, 16th Session, 1061st meeting (Nov. 22, 1961), para. 100.
[71] William J. Jordon, "State Department Divides over U.S. Vote on Angola," *New York Times*, Mar. 17, 1961, p. 1; Max Frankel, "U.S. Switched Its Tactics," *New York Times*, Mar. 17, 1961, p. 4.
[72] Arthur M. Schlesinger, Jr., *A Thousand Days: John F. Kennedy in the White House*, pp. 551–64. Schlesinger indicates that Kennedy also told deGaulle in June 1961 that the United States believed "that change in Africa was inexorable and the attempt to block it would only benefit the communists" and that therefore the United States had decided to take a progressive position in the United Nations. *Ibid.*, p. 352.

as to its effect on their own interest. However, the French said that they would be unable to vote in favor of the draft, even though they supported its purposes, because it was in violation of the Charter provisions concerning the obligations of administering powers to non-self-governing territories.[77] The French intervention in this debate was short and as inoffensive as possible and seemed designed to try to obtain the best of both possible worlds—that is, maintain the strict French interpretation of the Charter and maintain close relations with the new nations of Africa.

After more than three weeks of constant debate on colonialism, the Assembly on November 27, 1961, voted on the proposals before it. The first vote taken was on the controversial first Soviet amendment proposing a 1962 time limit for elimination of colonialism. The amendment was decisively defeated by a roll-call vote of 19 for, 46 against, and 35 states abstaining.[78] Of the new nations 6, or 16.7 percent of the new nations, supported the Soviet amendment, while only 4, or 11.1 percent, opposed it. However, as in 1960 on direct East-West clashes, the majority of the new nations, 26 or 72.2 percent, sought safety by abstaining on the vote. Those new nations supporting this Soviet amendment, with the exception of Mongolia, were all members of the Casablanca group of African states.[79] The 4 new nations, the Federation of Malaya, Israel, Pakistan, and Tunisia, voting against this amendment, all had close ties with the West, and notably only one was an African state. On the second Soviet amendment a roll-call vote was not requested, and it was

[77] United Nations General Assembly *Official Records*, 16th Session, 1065th meeting (Nov. 27, 1961), para. 24–36.

[78] United Nations General Assembly *Official Records*, 16th Session, 1066th meeting (Nov. 27, 1961), para. 147.

For: Ukrainian S.S.R., U.S.S.R., United Arab Republic, Yugoslavia, Albania, Bulgaria, Byelorussian S.S.R., Congo (Leopoldville), Cuba, Czechoslovakia, Ghana, Guinea, Hungary, Iraq, Mali, Mongolia, Morocco, Poland, and Romania.

Against: South Africa, Spain, Sweden, Thailand, Tunisia, Turkey, United Kingdom, United States, Uruguay, Venezuela, Argentina, Australia, Belgium, Dominican Republic, Ecuador, El Salvador, Federation of Malaya, France, Greece, Guatemala, Haiti, Iceland, Iran, Ireland, Israel, Italy, Japan, Luxembourg, Mexico, Netherlands, New Zealand, Nicaragua, Norway, Pakistan, Panama, Paraguay, Peru, and the Philippines.

Abstaining: Sudan, Togo, Upper Volta, Yemen, Afghanistan, Austria, Burma, Cambodia, Cameroon, Central African Republic, Ceylon, Chad, Congo (Brazzaville), Cyprus, Dahomey, Ethiopia, Finland, Gabon, India, Indonesia, Ivory Coast, Jordan, Laos, Lebanon, Liberia, Libya, Madagascar, Mauritania, Nepal, Niger, Nigeria, Saudi Arabia, Senegal, Sierra Leone, and Somalia.

[79] The Casablanca group consisted of Algeria, Ghana, Guinea, Mali, Morocco, and the United Arab Republic. This group was formed at Casablanca in January 1961 in response to events in the Congo. The group, in addition to supporting Lumumba in the struggle for power in the Congo, generally adopted the most radical position of any African group on colonial issues. See Hovet, *Africa in the United Nations*, pp. 54–56.

defeated on a show of hands by a vote of 22 in favor, 36 opposed, and 35 abstaining.[80] Thus even the second Soviet amendment, which was moderate in content, found its supposed beneficiaries, the new nations, unwilling to move decisively from passive abstention to active support at the cost of becoming associated with one side in the cold war. With the defeat of the Soviet amendments a roll-call vote easily passed the 38 power draft by a vote of 97 in favor, none opposed, 4 abstaining, and Portugal not participating.[81] Whereas 9 countries had abstained on the 1960 Declaration, 4 of these states, the United States, Australia, Belgium, and the Dominican Republic had voted in favor of the establishment of the Special Committee. The ranks of those willing to stand against overwhelming Assembly majorities on the question of a general commitment to end colonialism had substantially dwindled since the Charter was written in 1945.

In accordance with the Assembly's resolution, the President of the General Assembly named the following 17 states to the Special Committee: Australia, Cambodia, Ethiopia, India, Italy, Madagascar, Mali, Poland, Syria, Tanganyika, Tunisia, the U.S.S.R., the United Kingdom, the United States, Uruguay, Venezuela, and Yugoslavia.[82] Of the 17 members, 5 were new nations—the newest of these, Tanganyika, was so new that it had not even been a Member of the United Nations when this resolution was passed.[83] However, these 5

---

[80] United Nations General Assembly *Official Records*, 16th Session, 1066th meeting (Nov. 27, 1961), para. 148.

[81] United Nations General Assembly *Official Records*, 16th Session, 1066th meeting (Nov. 27, 1961), para. 149.

For: Saudi Arabia, Senegal, Sierra Leone, Somalia, Sudan, Sweden, Syria, Thailand, Togo, Tunisia, Turkey, Ukrainian S.S.R., U.S.S.R., United Arab Republic, United States, Upper Volta, Uruguay, Venezuela, Yemen, Yugoslavia, Afghanistan, Albania, Argentina, Australia, Austria, Belgium, Bolivia, Brazil, Bulgaria, Burma, Byelorussian S.S.R., Cambodia, Cameroon, Canada, Central African Republic, Ceylon, Chad, Chile, China, Colombia, Congo (Brazzaville), Congo (Leopoldville), Costa Rica, Cuba, Cyprus, Czechoslovakia, Dahomey, Denmark, Dominican Republic, Ecuador, El Salvador, Ethiopia, Federation of Malaya, Finland, Gabon, Ghana, Greece, Guatemala, Guinea, Haiti, Hungary, Iceland, India, Indonesia, Iran, Iraq, Ireland, Israel, Italy, Ivory Coast, Japan, Jordan, Laos, Lebanon, Liberia, Libya, Luxembourg, Madagascar, Mali, Mauritania, Mexico, Mongolia, Morocco, Nepal, Netherlands, New Zealand, Nicaragua, Niger, Nigeria, Norway, Pakistan, Panama, Paraguay, Peru, Philippines, Poland and Romania. Against: None.

Abstaining: South Africa, Spain, United Kingdom, and France.

Present and not voting: Portugal.

It thus became General Assembly Resolution 1654(XVI) of Nov. 27, 1961.

[82] United Nations General Assembly *Official Records*, 16th Session, 1094th meeting (Jan. 23, 1962), para. 3.

[83] Cambodia, Madagascar, Mali, Tanganyika, and Tunisia. The total years of experience as United Nations Members among the five as a whole were only 12 years.

in the United Nations' political process. These new nations are generally ex-colonial, nonwhite—in the 1960 influx, predominantly black—and possessed of a compelling desire to eradicate speedily the remaining bastions of European colonialism. In terms of social and economic criteria, many sectors of their societies are pre-modern, a fact that is only thinly disguised by the polite diplomatic euphemism of "developing countries," which is currently in vogue to describe this aspect of their condition. In terms of the lodestar of post-1945 international relations, the East-West conflict, the pre-ponderant majority of these new states, with varying degrees of consistency, attempt to follow the lesson of the African proverb, "When two elephants fight, it is the grass that suffers."[2] That the new nations arrived in significant numbers only after the provisions, procedures, and "gentlemen's agreements" that govern its operation had been adopted has been of great importance for the Organization.

These nations brought to the Organization their own distinctive set of goals with which to assess what should be the principal concerns of the United Nations. They view the Organization as the prime external instrument for obtaining the final demise of the crumbling European colonial empires and for preventing a vaguely perceived "neo-colonial" restoration. Closely associated with their demands for an end to colonialism is their personal commitment to eradicating that variant of racialism that maintains white superiority over black. As the end of colonialism has approached, the new nations have asserted more and more frequently, often in conjunction with other economically undeveloped nations, demands that the industrialized countries devote greater resources to raising the economic level of the "have-not South." The United Nations is viewed by the new nations both as the best available platform for advancing a claim to a greater share of the world's resources and as the most suitable operational instrument for carrying out this redistribution. Other problems and concerns traditionally dealt with by the United Na-tions, such as human rights, international law, and disarmament, have either been redefined by the new nations in such a way as to complement their primary goals or else have been largely ignored.

Much of the success of the new nations in effectively exercising

[2] Cecil V. Crabb, Jr., The Elephants and the Grass, A Study of Nonalignment (New York: Frederick A. Praeger, 1965), p. 2.

political influence in the United Nations analyzed in this study is owed to a propitious world political situation. One product of the cold war has been the creation of an environment in which either of the two major antagonists, the United States and the U.S.S.R., views a gain in support for the other as a defeat for itself. This attitude on the part of these two great powers has been reflected in active campaigns on their part to cultivate the support of the new nations. This great-power competition for support provided the new nations with numerous opportunities to advance their interests by playing off the East and the West against each other. Well aware of the bargaining advantages offered by the circumstances of the cold war, the new nations have not hesitated to employ this advantage to the fullest. The widest application of this tactic, and one that by and large was successful, was made on colonial questions. Repeated warnings were issued by the new nations that the obstinate attitude of the West on colonial questions was rapidly diminishing its influence with these new states and aiding the East in its courting of these states. There is particularly strong evidence that this tactic deserves much of the credit for the shift that occurred in the position of the United States in 1961 on colonial questions.

Another advantageous aspect of the political situation facing the new nations during this period was that their major goal, the independence of the remaining colonial areas, was largely under the control of the West. Most of the Western nations were more sensitive to public pressure than many other states because they found the role of colonial master a profoundly disturbing one to play. Reinforcing the disquietude of the West over its role as colonial master were the remarkably successful indigenous nationalist movements that were threatening, if not to evict the colonial powers, at least to make their continued rule extremely expensive in both blood and treasure. One cannot help but note the lesser success of the new nations with regard to economic aid, where these advantageous circumstances were not present.

In addition to a world political situation that was favorable to the new nations in their efforts to exercise influence, the United Nations itself provided a favorable environment for these efforts. First, the Organization's and its Members' commitments to the broad purposes and principles embodied in the Charter provided moral and legal

the interaction of conflicting national policies. This is not to deny that it may perform valuable tasks in areas of peace and security, decolonization or economic development, but rather to argue for a realization that the performance of such tasks rests on the approval or acquiescence of the Member States and does not have a significant life apart from their attitudes. Thus the shift after about 1955 in the primary emphasis of the Organization away from collective security and toward decolonization efforts is a natural result of its hyperdependency on the attitudes of the Member States.

In connection with this phenomenon, it seems also to be a characteristic of United Nations politics that secondary concerns either are recast in terms similar to the predominant emphasis or else gradually atrophy. Thus the traditional human rights activities of the Organization have lost their individual-oriented perspective and have become to a considerable extent only an adjunct to the decolonization struggle. On the other hand collective security has ceased for the present to be a meaningful concern of the Organization. As is strikingly indicated in the activities of the new nations, the politics of the United Nations is a politics of successive approximation toward goals involving a variable mix of private negotiations, public oratory, and voting. The circuitous tactics of these nations in regard to the remaining colonial areas of southern Africa have demonstrated the extent to which the patient application of such tactics can gradually lead to the desired goal. Of course, compromise is the very heart of this political process of successive approximation. The compromises are intra- as well as intergroup accommodations and often involve issues remote from the immediate concern of the negotiations. Thus the United States during the 1960's was forced to balance its support for its European allies in the military-political confrontation with the East against hoped-for influence with the new nations.

The experience of the new nations also provides an interesting insight into the limits of influence in the United Nations. Their greatest successes have been gained in obtaining endorsements of principles embodying broad transnational appeal, such as self-determination, freedom from hunger, and appeals for peace. Their greatest failures, on the other hand, have been in attempts to gain commitments of resources from the small group of states well-endowed with them to implement endorsements "in principle." Although the new nations have secured increased resources through the United Nations, their influence even when combined with the other underdeveloped countries did not secure the effective operationalizing of the United Nations Capital Development Fund. In the decolonization struggle, with the exception of southern Africa, this distinction has not been important, because the dynamism of the nationalist movement in the colonial areas was sufficient to accomplish their aims. But in southern Africa where ruthlessly applied internal suppression has emasculated the nationalist movements, the new nations have as yet been unable to move the other Members of the United Nations to back their moral commitments with effective collective action. While possessing sufficient influence to affect vitally the policy outputs of the United Nations, the new nations during the period under study did not possess sufficient influence to force the international political environment to conform to the standards of conduct established in United Nations resolutions. At its present stage of development the United Nations generally can have a significant international impact only to the extent that there is a congruence of influence patterns in the Organization and in the external international political environment. To the extent that this cogruence is absent, a group may have influence within the Organization sufficient to shape the policy outputs of the Organization but still be unable to obtain the fulfillment of the demands made in such outputs. This is largely the situation in which the new nations currently find themselves.

In summary, it can be said that the record of the new nations' exercise of political influence in the confines of the United Nations demonstrates a successful strategy of shifting the major focus of the Organization from one predominant concern to another. As a study in the political process of the United Nations this shift perhaps portends the methods of future shifts in focus. On the more immediate horizon, the alliance of the new nations with the other economically underdeveloped nations that began to emerge during this period may be the next shift in focus for the Organization.

—

Distribution According to Topic of Speeches Made by New Nations in Plenary and Main Committee Meetings of the General Assembly*

State	Topic										
	a	b	c	d	e	f	g	h	i	j	k
Fifteenth Session											
Cameroon	18	1	–	–	7	1	–	–	–	–	5
Central African Republic	1	2	–	–	2	–	2	–	1	–	3
Chad	10	2	3	–	3	–	–	–	–	–	4
Congo (Brazzaville)	8	1	1	–	5	–	–	–	–	–	4
Congo (Leopoldville)	2	2	–	–	10	–	–	–	–	–	1
Dahomey	2	–	–	–	1	–	–	–	–	–	7
Gabon	3	–	1	–	1	–	2	–	–	–	5
Ghana	35	12	22	9	13	10	5	2	2	5	30
Guinea	55	17	30	–	10	5	7	4	2	–	25
Ivory Coast	5	4	–	–	3	–	2	–	–	–	7
Libya	13	4	12	4	2	7	–	–	4	–	20
Madagascar	6	–	7	–	1	–	2	–	–	–	2
Mali	24	8	2	–	5	3	4	2	–	–	8
Morocco	32	4	16	7	5	4	2	3	4	2	31
Niger	1	–	–	–	2	–	–	–	–	–	5
Nigeria	23	10	19	8	7	2	9	–	1	–	18
Senegal	12	3	–	1	2	–	2	–	–	–	8
Somalia	7	3	12	–	–	–	3	–	–	–	6
Sudan	21	10	53	3	1	3	3	1	2	–	28
Togo	16	3	4	2	1	–	2	–	–	–	9
Tunisia	37	9	25	2	6	1	6	–	5	3	19
Upper Volta	7	–	1	–	1	–	–	–	1	–	4
Israel	12	1	13	8	1	3	3	–	11	7	28
Jordan	13	2	8	3	2	1	3	–	6	–	23
Burma	37	8	18	2	3	5	5	2	–	4	13

* This speech count is based on the *Official Records* of the General Assembly as indexed in *Index to Proceedings of the General Assembly,* 15th–21st Sessions (New York: United Nations, 1961, 1962, 1963, 1964, 1965, 1966, and 1967). For purposes of this count, when a speech dealt with more than one topic, each topic was counted as a separate speech.

a = Decolonization
b = South Africa
c = Economic Aid and Development
d = Human Rights
e = Congo
f = Disarmament

g = Representation in United Nations Organs
h = Chinese Representation
i = Refugees
j = International Law
k = Other

| | Topic | | | | | | | | | | |
State	*a*	*b*	*c*	*d*	*e*	*f*	*g*	*h*	*i*	*j*	*k*
Cyprus	21	2	10	3	1	17	–	2	2	–	25
Federation of Malaya	12	4	5	12	1	4	–	1	1	–	16
Indonesia	64	11	20	20	2	2	7	2	2	4	26
Laos	–	–	–	–	–	4	–	1	–	–	1
Mongolia	7	2	4	–	–	1	1	1	–	1	10
Pakistan	16	8	12	12	1	16	4	1	5	5	18
Philippines	31	14	14	9	–	6	4	3	–	1	21

Seventeenth Session

State	*a*	*b*	*c*	*d*	*e*	*f*	*g*	*h*	*i*	*j*	*k*
Algeria	11	8	24	7	1	6	–	2	3	1	17
Burundi	1	–	1	–	–	–	–	–	–	–	2
Cameroon	27	7	11	4	1	4	6	1	2	2	18
Central African Republic	11	5	15	1	1	4	4	2	3	–	10
Chad	3	2	15	–	–	4	–	–	–	–	–
Congo (Brazzaville)	15	2	5	4	1	4	–	1	–	–	4
Congo (Leopoldville)	9	2	3	8	–	3	–	–	–	3	4
Dahomey	13	–	3	1	–	–	–	–	1	1	2
Gabon	7	1	1	–	–	3	–	1	–	–	–
Ghana	65	19	34	20	2	11	5	2	3	7	36
Guinea	51	16	16	5	1	5	6	2	3	–	19
Ivory Coast	12	5	4	–	–	2	2	–	5	5	16
Libya	7	4	6	2	1	2	2	–	2	–	10
Madagascar	4	2	15	3	1	2	3	–	2	1	12
Mali	30	6	20	15	1	9	–	2	4	1	19
Mauritania	14	6	21	15	1	6	2	–	5	1	14
Morocco	13	3	27	4	–	2	1	–	4	–	7
Niger	13	3	6	3	1	2	–	–	1	–	4
Nigeria	42	10	29	12	2	10	6	–	1	2	25
Rwanda	–	–	1	–	–	–	–	1	3	–	4
Senegal	18	5	25	2	1	2	–	2	1	–	3
Sierra Leone	12	4	5	–	1	2	–	2	–	1	11
Somalia	16	13	3	–	1	4	–	2	–	1	7
Sudan	15	5	24	1	1	2	2	1	3	–	17
Tanganyika	22	4	15	5	–	2	–	–	2	1	4
Togo	16	6	12	5	1	2	4	–	3	–	14
Tunisia	24	3	39	7	1	3	4	1	7	7	21
Uganda	6	5	4	–	–	1	–	1	–	–	–
Upper Volta	6	2	2	3	1	2	–	1	–	–	–
Israel	6	2	16	6	1	5	4	1	15	7	24
Jordan	19	6	11	4	1	2	–	2	9	1	20

State	Topic										
	a	b	c	d	e	f	g	h	i	j	k
Burma	24	7	11	6	1	5	–	2	–	5	10
Cambodia	14	1	11	4	1	1	2	2	2	2	20
Ceylon	12	7	22	4	–	5	2	4	–	5	9
Cyprus	11	1	12	2	1	7	2	1	3	2	9
Federation of Malaya	9	5	15	7	1	4	–	1	1	–	14
Indonesia	40	5	25	17	–	7	4	2	1	4	15
Laos	1	–	1	–	1	2	–	1	–	–	3
Mongolia	7	4	11	4	1	10	1	2	1	2	15
Pakistan	5	5	45	6	–	5	2	–	6	5	23
Philippines	15	8	25	12	–	4	–	2	–	2	15
Jamaica	10	1	9	2	–	5	1	–	–	–	1
Trinidad and Tobago	5	3	–	–	–	–	–	–	–	–	2

Eighteenth Session

State	a	b	c	d	e	f	g	h	i	j	k
Algeria	13	9	18	5	1	2	2	2	5	5	4
Burundi	3	1	5	4	–	3	2	2	1	–	3
Cameroon	20	6	11	5	2	7	7	1	–	4	16
Central African Republic	4	1	5	2	2	3	4	2	3	–	9
Chad	5	2	9	2	1	4	–	–	–	–	1
Congo (Brazzaville)	9	4	4	–	2	1	2	–	1	1	1
Congo (Leopoldville)	11	6	1	–	2	1	3	–	3	1	11
Dahomey	15	3	3	–	–	2	2	–	1	1	2
Gabon	2	1	6	–	2	2	4	–	1	–	6
Ghana	40	12	25	21	3	12	18	3	2	20	15
Guinea	38	20	7	14	3	2	4	2	1	–	10
Ivory Coast	14	4	4	–	–	–	6	–	–	2	1
Kenya	–	–	–	–	–	–	–	–	–	–	1
Libya	9	3	16	2	–	3	3	–	3	1	7
Madagascar	8	4	17	8	2	6	3	1	1	3	7
Mali	18	8	10	2	1	8	10	2	2	1	13
Mauritania	20	8	13	4	–	3	2	–	3	–	7
Morocco	8	4	29	7	–	4	6	–	5	4	9
Niger	10	4	5	2	1	2	2	1	1	–	8
Nigeria	25	9	30	23	7	9	11	1	–	4	16
Rwanda	8	1	2	1	2	4	4	–	1	–	4
Senegal	17	6	16	16	1	3	2	1	1	–	5
Sierra Leone	8	2	4	1	1	2	4	2	–	–	6
Somali Republic	9	4	6	2	1	3	–	2	–	1	11
Sudan	19	9	14	6	3	5	8	1	2	–	5

State	Topic										
	a	b	c	d	e	f	g	h	i	j	k
Tanganyika	25	12	11	5	–	6	6	2	2	5	2
Togo	13	5	7	1	1	3	2	–	–	–	1
Tunisia	21	7	39	11	3	7	5	2	6	2	8
Uganda	11	4	8	9	2	6	2	1	1	1	5
Upper Volta	6	2	4	8	2	3	4	–	–	–	3
Zanzibar	–	–	–	–	–	–	–	–	–	–	1
Jamaica	3	2	16	6	1	7	3	–	–	5	6
Trinidad and Tobago	4	4	10	2	1	1	1	–	–	–	2
Burma	5	2	14	6	2	7	3	2	1	1	3
Cambodia	19	5	14	6	–	6	–	2	1	2	10
Ceylon	17	4	17	5	–	2	5	1	–	8	12
Indonesia	20	4	14	7	2	8	11	2	1	4	23
Laos	1	1	–	1	–	2	–	–	–	–	2
Malaysia	11	4	9	2	2	4	3	1	2	1	16
Mongolia	8	4	9	2	1	11	7	2	–	2	13
Pakistan	18	5	29	8	1	11	7	2	3	2	20
Philippines	9	5	25	7	1	6	3	1	–	2	22
Cyprus	8	1	10	5	2	10	5	1	1	8	15
Israel	6	3	22	28	3	4	5	1	8	1	17
Jordan	12	4	22	1	1	3	4	–	9	–	6
Kuwait	4	3	3	–	–	3	–	–	2	1	2
Nineteenth Session											
Algeria	4	1	4	1	1	2	–	1	–	–	17
Burundi	7	2	1	1	1	3	3	1	–	–	8
Cameroon	6	2	5	–	–	1	–	–	–	–	9
Central African Republic	3	1	4	–	1	4	3	1	1	–	9
Chad	5	2	3	–	1	1	3	–	–	–	9
Congo (Brazzaville)	2	1	3	–	1	–	–	1	–	–	2
Congo (Leopoldville)	–	–	–	–	1	–	–	–	–	–	1
Dahomey	8	3	8	1	–	8	1	1	–	–	3
Gabon	6	2	4	–	1	2	–	1	–	–	9
Ghana	10	2	6	–	1	2	3	1	1	1	8
Guinea	–	2	–	–	–	–	–	–	–	–	3
Ivory Coast	–	–	–	–	–	–	–	–	–	–	–
Kenya	6	1	4	–	1	–	3	1	–	–	6
Libya	6	3	3	–	–	6	3	–	1	–	5
Madagascar	3	1	5	1	–	1	–	–	1	1	8
Malawi	4	2	1	–	1	1	–	1	–	–	–
Mali	5	2	5	–	1	6	–	2	–	1	16

State	Topic										
	a	b	c	d	e	f	g	h	i	j	k
Mauritania	–	–	–	–	–	–	–	–	–	–	3
Morocco	2	1	2	–	1	–	–	1	1	–	17
Niger	2	2	3	–	1	4	–	1	–	–	8
Nigeria	3	3	3	–	2	8	–	1	1	–	7
Rwanda	–	–	–	–	–	–	–	–	–	–	1
Senegal	3	–	3	–	1	3	1	1	–	–	4
Sierra Leone	2	2	5	–	1	7	3	1	–	–	7
Somali Republic	6	2	3	–	1	5	–	1	–	–	8
Sudan	2	1	3	–	–	1	–	–	–	–	3
Tanzania	8	3	5	1	1	8	2	1	–	–	8
Togo	1	1	–	–	–	–	–	–	–	–	2
Tunisia	8	3	7	–	1	3	3	1	2	–	4
Uganda	3	3	3	–	1	4	1	1	3	–	2
Upper Volta	–	–	–	–	–	–	–	–	–	–	–
Zambia	3	1	1	–	–	3	–	1	–	–	4
Jamaica	1	2	11	1	–	1	1	–	–	1	4
Trinidad and Tobago	1	1	2	–	–	2	–	1	–	–	1
Burma	–	–	–	–	–	–	–	–	–	–	–
Cambodia	–	1	–	2	1	4	–	1	–	–	11
Ceylon	4	1	7	–	1	9	–	1	–	–	5
Indonesia	2	1	–	–	1	2	3	1	–	–	16
Laos	–	–	3	1	–	6	–	1	–	–	5
Malaysia	3	1	4	–	–	4	–	–	1	–	16
Mongolia	4	1	3	–	1	7	3	1	–	–	14
Pakistan	6	3	3	1	1	3	1	1	–	–	10
Philippines	1	1	3	1	–	4	–	1	–	–	10
Cyprus	6	1	7	2	1	5	–	–	1	1	19
Malta	1	–	5	1	–	–	–	–	–	–	2
Israel	1	1	5	–	3	3	–	1	2	–	14
Jordan	–	–	–	–	–	–	–	–	2	–	1
Kuwait	5	2	5	–	–	1	–	–	1	–	6
Twentieth Session											
Algeria	40	12	13	–	–	3	–	2	4	10	20
Burundi	–	–	–	1	–	–	–	–	–	1	2
Cameroon	15	5	19	11	–	8	3	1	1	6	17
Central African Republic	4	2	5	–	–	6	3	1	2	2	12
Chad	4	3	1	1	–	1	3	–	–	1	3
Congo (Brazzaville)	15	11	4	–	1	4	–	2	–	1	3
Congo (Democratic People's Republic)	8	–	2	16	–	3	–	1	1	4	3

State	Topic										
	a	*b*	*c*	*d*	*e*	*f*	*g*	*h*	*i*	*j*	*k*
Dahomey	8	3	10	1	1	8	3	–	2	5	12
Gabon	7	2	6	–	–	5	–	1	1	2	9
Gambia	–	–	–	–	–	–	–	–	–	–	3
Ghana	36	12	37	44	–	10	3	3	1	3	32
Guinea	27	17	19	9	–	3	1	3	3	4	27
Ivory Coast	8	3	11	8	–	2	3	2	4	1	5
Kenya	21	12	20	1	–	11	1	2	–	2	22
Libya	10	4	10	3	–	14	1	–	6	1	13
Madagascar	11	1	11	8	–	1	2	2	1	6	16
Malawi	1	–	3	3	–	–	1	1	–	–	6
Mali	33	8	21	4	–	8	–	1	3	10	22
Mauritania	11	–	12	33	–	1	–	3	3	–	11
Morocco	20	4	12	17	–	1	–	1	10	5	16
Niger	6	2	5	–	–	2	–	2	–	–	11
Nigeria	16	11	38	34	–	16	1	2	2	5	31
Rwanda	5	3	6	1	–	6	–	2	1	–	14
Senegal	22	1	34	19	–	1	3	1	2	2	29
Sierra Leone	14	–	7	7	–	–	–	2	–	–	13
Somali Republic	24	8	6	2	–	11	3	2	5	2	11
Sudan	17	5	22	8	–	8	–	2	5	–	10
Tanzania	24	8	8	24	–	12	1	2	1	8	27
Togo	14	4	6	2	–	7	–	2	2	1	18
Tunisia	21	7	25	9	–	7	3	2	2	3	22
Uganda	7	2	30	13	–	5	4	2	3	3	8
Upper Volta	1	–	6	10	–	–	–	–	–	2	7
Zambia	17	3	15	5	–	6	–	1	1	2	11
Jamaica	18	2	18	7	–	6	4	1	–	–	19
Trinidad and Tobago	9	4	6	11	–	2	–	–	–	–	6
Burma	4	–	4	4	–	5	–	2	2	1	8
Cambodia	–	–	–	1	–	–	–	7	–	–	14
Ceylon	14	3	19	5	–	1	–	4	–	6	20
Laos	3	–	–	1	–	2	–	–	–	–	8
Malaysia	8	4	13	10	–	3	1	2	5	3	34
Maldive Islands	–	–	–	–	–	–	–	–	–	–	1
Mongolia	8	6	13	6	–	9	5	2	–	3	11
Pakistan	27	9	20	10	–	7	–	2	5	3	29
Philippines	12	4	28	17	–	6	2	3	–	4	25
Singapore	6	–	8	–	–	1	–	2	–	–	7
Cyprus	17	7	7	6	–	15	–	–	5	4	23
Malta	–	–	24	–	–	10	1	1	–	–	7
Israel	9	4	32	21	–	3	1	–	23	14	28
Jordan	9	3	30	7	–	5	1	–	6	1	15
Kuwait	13	5	17	5	–	6	–	–	4	–	17

State						Topic					
	a	b	c	d	e	f	g	h	i	j	k
				Twenty-first Session								
Algeria	22	6	34	11	–	5	3	2	3	2	13
Botswana	1	1	–	–	–	–	–	1	–	–	1
Burundi	11	4	3	3	1	–	1	–	3	–	6
Cameroon	5	2	24	3	–	5	3	–	–	7	12
Central African Republic	3	3	7	4	–	5	3	2	1	1	5
Chad	2	2	8	2	–	2	–	1	–	–	5
Congo (Brazzaville)	16	3	1	20	–	4	1	3	–	–	8
Congo (Democratic People's Republic)	33	7	16	12	1	9	5	–	4	2	19
Dahomey	8	1	9	5	–	3	1	1	1	4	10
Gabon	7	2	13	–	–	3	–	1	–	–	3
Gambia	–	–	–	–	–	–	–	–	–	–	–
Ghana	43	10	44	20	–	2	2	2	1	10	15
Guinea	82	21	10	32	–·	3	2	3	4	2	40
Ivory Coast	12	3	21	5	–	2	1	–	1	2	11
Kenya	12	5	23	5	–	7	5	2	1	2	22
Lesotho	–	–	–	–	–	–	–	–	–	–	4
Libya	14	6	11	7	–	6	1	··	4	1	5
Madagascar	7	3	19	19	–	2	–	2	1	1	8
Malawi	11	3	1	1	–	2	1	1	–	2	4
Mali	28	10	5	14	–	3	–	2	2	5	11
Mauritania	16	3	3	13	–	3	1	1	1	–	4
Morocco	22	3	15	1	–	–	–	1	4	–	10
Niger	7	4	11	2	–	–	–	2	1	1	6
Nigeria	16	5	24	41	–	5	3	1	3	7	25
Rwanda	7	5	11	3	1	7	–	2	1	1	7
Senegal	20	4	27	17	–	1	4	1	1	–	18
Sierra Leone	21	5	12	5	–	6	–	1	1	3	6
Somali Republic	27	5	6	2	–	5	–	2	7	4	12
Sudan	25	6	28	6	–	3	2	–	3	3	11
Tanzania	53	9	22	19	–	7	3	2	2	10	32
Togo	21	2	3	6	–	1	–	2	–	1	8
Tunisia	12	6	19	28	·	7	1	2	5	3	13
Uganda	8	4	15	4	–	2	–	1	3	1	6
Upper Volta	3	2	11	15	–	4	–	1	1	1	7
Zambia	37	9	11	4	–	1	–	2	2	2	2
Barbados	–	–	–	–	–	–	–	–	–	–	1
Guyana	8	1	–	–	–	–	–	1	–	–	2
Jamaica	4	1	11	17	–	2	–	2	1	4	16

State	Topic										
	a	b	c	d	e	f	g	h	i	j	k
Trinidad and Tobago	5	3	26	–	–	–	–	2	1	1	9
Burma	1	1	12	–	–	6	–	2	–	2	12
Cambodia	–	–	–	1	–	–	–	2	–	–	11
Ceylon	33	2	23	9	–	9	3	2	1	5	16
Indonesia	7	2	8	2	–	4	–	1	1	1	7
Laos	1	1	–	–	–	2	–	–	–	–	4
Malaysia	27	2	13	6	–	4	–	2	2	1	9
Maldive Islands	1	2	1	–	–	–	–	–	–	–	4
Mongolia	2	4	8	5	–	6	–	2	–	3	25
Pakistan	23	6	44	40	–	13	4	3	3	3	21
Philippines	13	3	25	21	–	4	1	1	2	4	12
Singapore	2	2	8	–	–	2	–	2	–	–	3
Cyprus	7	3	5	11	–	11	2	–	–	4	21
Malta	–	–	17	–	–	7	2	1	–	–	15
Israel	17	5	26	14	–	7	1	2	5	15	23
Jordan	4	5	12	3	–	1	–	–	4	–	8
Kuwait	7	3	17	1	–	2	–	1	6	1	10

Selected Colonial Issues, Fifth–Eighteenth Sessions of the General Assembly*

Fifth Session

Res. 395(V). Treatment of people of Indian origin in the Union of South Africa. 2 December 1950 (33-6-21); Fr. - A; UK - A; US - Y.

Res. 395(V). Treatment of people of Indian origin in the Union of South Africa: Separate vote on paragraph 3, part 2 concerning the Group Areas Act. 2 December 1950 (35-13-12); Fr. - N; UK - N; US - N.

Res. 433(V). Annual report of the Trusteeship Council: Separate vote on draft paragraph 3 concerning the relation to the Assembly. 2 December 1950 (25-16-14); Fr. - N; UK - N; US - N.

Res. 436(V). Information on the implementation of Trusteeship Council and Assembly resolutions. 2 December 1950 (33-11-12); Fr. - N; UK - N; US - N.

Res. 446(V). Information on human rights in non-self-governing territories. 12 December 1950 (37-10-9); Fr. - A; UK - N; US - Y.

Res. 449(V). Question of South West Africa: part A. 13 December 1950 (45-6-5); Fr. - Y; UK - Y; US - Y.

Res. 449(V). Question of South Africa: part B. 13 December 1950 (30-10-16); Fr. - A; UK - N; US - Y.

Sixth Session

Res. 511(VE). Treatment of people of Indian origin in the Union of South Africa. 12 January 1952 (44-0-14); Fr. - A; UK - A; US - Y.

Document A/2061, 16 January 1952. Draft resolution on the participation of non-members in the Trusteeship Council. 361st plenary meeting, 18 January 1952 (28-18-10); Fr. - N; UK - N; US - N.

Res. 558(VI). Attainment by the Trust Territories of the objective of self-government. 18 January 1952 (38-8-11); Fr. - N; UK - N; US - A.

Res. 570A(VI). Question of South West Africa. 19 January 1952 (45-5-8); Fr. - Y; UK - Y; US - Y.

Seventh Session

Res. 615(VII). Treatment of people of Indian origin in the Union of South Africa. 5 December 1962 (41-1-15); Fr. - A; UK - A; US - Y.

Res. 616A(VII). The question of race conflict in South Africa resulting from the apartheid policies of the Government of the Union of South Africa. 5 December 1952 (35-1-23); Fr. - A; UK - A; US - A.

Res. 616A(VII). The question of race conflict in South Africa: separate vote on paragraph 1, establishing commission to study the conflict. 5 December 1952 (35-17-7); Fr. - N; UK - N; US - A.

Res. 646(VII). Renewal of the Committee on Information from Non-Self-Governing Territories: separate vote on part 2, paragraph 1 providing for auto-

*Fr. = France	N = No
UK = United Kingdom	A = Abstain
US = United States	O = Absent
Y = Yes	NP = Present but not participating

matic renewal of the committee. 10 December 1952 (11-18-30); Fr. - N; UK - N; US - N.

Res. 648(VII). Factors to be taken into consideration in deciding whether a Territory is or is not a Territory whose people have not yet attained a full measure of self-government. 10 December 1952 (36-15-7); Fr. - N; UK - N; US - N.

Res. 637A(VII). The rights of peoples and nations to self-determination. 16 December 1952 (40-14-6); Fr. - N; UK - N; US - N.

Res. 637A(VII). The rights of peoples and nations to self-determination: separate vote on preamble paragraph 1, concerning self-determination as a prerequisite to human rights. 16 December 1952 (38-13-9); Fr. - N; UK - N; US - N.

Res. 612(VII). The question of Morocco. 19 December 1952 (45-3-11); Fr. - O; UK - A; US - Y.

Eighth Session

Document A/2526, 22 October 1953. Draft resolution on question of Morocco: separate vote on paragraph 6 urging that Moroccan people have the right of free democratic political institutions. First Committee. 3 November 1953 (32-22-5); Fr. - O; UK - N; US - N.

Res. 719(VIII). Treatment of people of Indian origin in the Union of South Africa. 8 December 1953 (38-11-11); Fr. - A; UK - A; US - Y.

Document A/2530, 28 October 1953. Draft resolution on question of Tunisia. First Committee. 11 November 1953 (31-18-10); Fr. - O; UK - N; US - N.

Res. 748(VIII). Cessation of the transmission of information under Article 73e of the Charter in respect to Puerto Rico; separate vote on paragraph 6 concerning the competence of the General Assembly. 27 November 1953 (34-19-7); Fr. - N; UK - N; US - N.

Res. 749(VIII). Question of South West Africa: Part A. 28 November 1953. (46-1-12); Fr. - A; UK - A; US - A.

Res. 721(VIII). Question of race conflict in South Africa. 8 December 1953. (38-11-11); Fr. - N; UK - N; US - A.

Res. 721(VIII). Question of race conflict in South Africa: separate vote on paragraph 4(a) concerning the continuation of the commission. 8 December 1953. (38-15-7); Fr. - N; UK - N; US - A.

Ninth Session

Procedural proposal of General Committee to include question of apartheid policies of South Africa on agenda. 472d plenary meeting, 21 September 1954 (50-6-4); Fr. - N; UK - N; US - Y.

Procedural proposal of General Committee to include question of Cyprus on the agenda. 477th meeting. 24 September 1954 (30-19-11); Fr. - N; UK - N; US - A.

Procedural proposal of General Committee to include question of West Irian on the agenda. 477th meeting. 24 September 1954 (39-11-10); Fr. - N; UK - N; US - A.

Res. 844(IX). Procedure for the examination of reports and petition relating to the territory of South West Africa. 11 October 1954 (33-3-15); Fr. - N; UK - N; US - Y.

Res. 849(IX). Cessation of the transmission of information under Article 73e of the Charter in respect of Greenland: separate vote on last paragraph of the preamble concerning the competence of the Assembly. 22 November 1954 (38-15-4); Fr. - N; UK - N; US - N.

Res. 904(IX). Request for an advisory opinion of the ICJ on the voting procedure on questions relating to the reports concerning South West Africa. 23 November 1954 (25-11-21); Fr. - A; UK - N; US - A.

Document A/2831, 4 December 1954. Draft resolution on the question of West Irian: Separate vote on preamble. 10 December 1954 (34-21-5); Fr. - N; UK - N; US - A.

Res. 820(IX). Question of race conflict in South Africa. 14 December 1954 (40-10-10); Fr. - N; UK - N; US - A.

Res. 820(IX). Question of race conflict in South Africa: separate vote on paragraph 7 continuing the commission. 14 December 1954 (35-16-9); Fr. - N; UK - N; US - N.

Tenth Session

Procedural proposal of the General Committee to include the question of West Irian on the agenda, 532d plenary meeting. 3 October 1955 (31-18-10); Fr. - O; UK - N; US - A.

Res. 917(X). Question of race conflict in South Africa: separate vote on draft operative paragraph 7. 6 December 1955 (33-17-9); Fr. - N; UK - N; US - N.

Res. 946(X). Attainment by the Trust Territories of the objective of self-government or independence. 15 December 1955 (43-11-9); Fr. - N; UK - N; US - N.

Eleventh Session

Procedural proposal of General Committee to include question of apartheid policy of South Africa on agenda, 578th plenary meeting. 15 November 1956 (61-8-7); Fr. - N; UK - N; US - Y.

Procedural proposal of General Committee to include question of people of Indian origin in South Africa on the agenda, 578th plenary meeting. 15 November 1956 (63-2-13); Fr. - A; UK - A; US - Y.

Res. 1064(XI). Attainment of self-government or independence by Trust Territories. 26 February 1957 (45-14-16); Fr. - N; UK - N; US - N.

Document A/3565, 28 February 1957. Question of West Irian. 28 February 1957 (40-25-13); Fr. - N; UK - N; US - A.

Twelfth Session

Procedural proposal of the General Committee to include the question of the race conflict in South Africa on the agenda. 682d plenary meeting, 20 September 1957 (64-8-9); Fr. - N; UK - N; US - Y.

Procedural proposal of the General Committee to include the question of peoples of Indian origin in South Africa on the agenda. 682d plenary meeting, 20 September 1957 (63-2-16); Fr. - N; UK - A; US - Y.

Procedural proposal of the General Committee to include the question of West Irian on the agenda. 682d plenary meeting, 20 September 1957 (49-21-11); Fr. - N; UK - N; US - A.

Res. 1143(XII). Establishment of a Good Offices Committee on South West Africa. 25 October 1957 (50-10-20); Fr. - Y; UK - Y; US - Y.

Res. 1178(XII). Question of race conflict in South Africa. 26 November 1957 (59-6-14); Fr. - N; UK - N; US - A.

Res. 1129(XII). Treatment of people of Indian origin in South Africa. 26 November 1957 (61-0-15); Fr. - A; UK - A; US - Y.

Thirteenth Session

Res. 1245(XIII). Conditions in the Territory of South West Africa: separate vote on paragraph 3 expressing concern. 30 October 1958 (59-2-18); Fr. - A; UK - N; US - A.

Res. 1248(XIII). Race conflict in South Africa. 30 October 1958 (70-5-4); Fr. - N; UK - N; US - Y.

Res. 1248(XIII). Race conflict in South Africa: separate vote on paragraph 2 declaring discrimination to be inconsistent with the Charter. 30 October 1958 (70-3-5); Fr. - N; UK - A; US - Y.

Res. 1302(XIII). Treatment of people of Indian origin in the Union of South Africa. 10 December 1958 (69-0-10); Fr. - A; UK - A; US - Y.

Fourteenth Session

Res. 1375 (XIV). Question of the race conflict in South Africa. 17 November 1959 (62-3-7); Fr. - N; UK - N; US - Y.

Res. 1410(XIV). Dissemination of information on the United Nations in the Trust Territories. 5 December 1959 (67-0-13); Fr. - A; UK - A; US - A.

Res. 1460(XIV). Treatment of peoples of Indian origin in South Africa. 10 December 1959 (66-0-12); Fr. - A; UK - A; US - Y.

Fifteenth Session

Res. 1514(XV). Declaration on the granting of independence to colonial countries and peoples. 14 December 1960 (89-0-9); Fr. - A; UK - A; US - A.

Res. 1536(XV). Racial discrimination in non-self-governing territories. 15 December 1960 (88-0-2); Fr. - Y; UK - A; US - Y.

Res. 1541(XV). Principles which should guide Members in determining whether or not an obligation exists to transmit information called for under Article 73e of the Charter. 15 December 1960 (69-2-21); Fr. - A; UK - A; US - A.

Res. 1542(XV). Transmission of information under Article 73e of the Charter. 15 December 1960 (68-6-17); Fr. - N; UK - A; US - A.

Res. 1565(XV). Legal action to ensure the fulfillment of the obligation assumed by South Africa in respect to South West Africa. 18 December 1960 (86-0-6); Fr. - A; UK - A; US - Y.

Res. 1568(XV). Question of South West Africa: Separate vote on operative paragraph 3 depreciating policy of apartheid. 18 December 1960 (90-0-3); Fr. - Y; UK - A; US - Y.

Res. 1568(XV). Question of South West Africa. 18 December 1960 (78-0-15); Fr. - A; UK - A; US - A.

Res. 1579(XV). Question of the future of Rwanda-Urundi. 20 December 1960 (61-9-23); Fr. - N; UK - N; US - A.

Res. 1580(XV). Question of the Mwami. 20 December 1960 (50-24-19); Fr. - N; UK - N; US - N.

Res. 1593(XV). Appeal to member states which have particularly close and continuous relations with South Africa. 16 March 1961 (70-0-9); Fr. - A; UK - A; US - Y.

Procedural proposal to include the situation in Angola on the agenda. 23 March 1961 (79-2-8); Fr. - A; UK - A; US - Y.

Res. 1596(XV). Question of South West Africa. 7 April 1961 (83-0-9); Fr. - A; UK - A; US - Y.

Res. 1598(XV). Question of the race conflict in South Africa. 13 April 1961 (95-1-0); Fr. - Y; UK - Y; US - Y.

Res. 1605(XV). Question of the future of Rwanda-Urandi. 21 April 1961 (86-1-4); Fr. - A; UK - Y; US - Y.

Res. 1607(XV). Dissemination of information on the United Nations in the Trust Territories. 21 April 1961 (78-0-9); Fr. - A; UK - A; US - Y.

Sixteenth Session

Censure of South African Minister Eric Louw for General Debate Speech, 900th plenary meeting. 11 October 1961 (67-1-20); Fr. - NP; UK - NP; US - NP.

Res. 1650(XVI). The status of Algerians imprisoned in France. 15 November 1961 (62-0-31); Fr. - O; UK - A; US - A.

Res. 1654(XVI). Establishes Special Committee on Colonialism. 27 November 1961 (97 0-4); Fr. - A; UK - A; US - Y.

Res. 1663(XVI). Question of race conflict in South Africa. 28 November 1961 (97-2-1); Fr. - Y; UK - Y; US - Y.

Res. 1699(XVI). Non-compliance of Portugal with Chapter XI of Charter. 19 December 1961 (90-3-2); Fr. - A; UK - Y; US - Y.

Res. 1700(XVI). Renewal of the Committee on Information. 19 December 1961 (77-0-16); Fr. - A; UK - A; US - Y.

Res. 1724(XVI). Question of Algeria. 20 December 1961 (62-0-38); Fr. - O; UK - A; US - A.

Res. 1742(XVI). Situation in Angola. 30 January 1962 (99-2-1); Fr. - A; UK - Y; US - Y.

Res. 1745(XVI). Information from non-self-governing territories. 23 February 1962 (57-21-24); Fr. - N; UK - N; US - N.

Procedural proposal to include question of Southern Rhodesia on the agenda, 1109th plenary meeting. 12 June 1962 (62-26-15); Fr. - N; UK - N; US - N.

Res. 1746(XVI). Future of Rwanda-Urundi. 27 June 1962 (95-0-10); Fr. - Y; UK - Y; US - Y.

Res. 1747(XVI). Question of Southern Rhodesia. 28 June 1962 (71-1-27); Fr. - A; UK - NP; US - A.

Seventeenth Session

Res. 1761(XVII). Recommends sanctions and Security Council action against South Africa. 6 November 1962 (67-16-23); Fr. - N; UK - N; US - N.

Res. 1810(XVII). Approves procedures of Special Committee on Colonialism and its enlargement to 24 members. 17 December 1962 (101-0-4); Fr. - A; UK - A; US - Y.

Res. 1755(XVII). Calls for lifting of ban on ZAPU political party in Southern Rhodesia. 12 October 1962 (83-2-11); Fr. - A; UK - NP; US - A.

Res. 1760(XVII). Requests the United Kingdom to obtain a new constitution for Southern Rhodesia. 31 October 1962 (81-2-9); Fr. - A; UK - NP; US - A.

Document A/C.4/L.754, 15 November 1962. Requests Special Committee on Colonialism to consider the question of South West Africa and requests the Secretary-General to establish an effective UN presence in the Territory. Fourth Committee, 19 November 1962 (96-0-1); Fr. - Y; UK - Y; US - Y.

Res. 1807(XVII). Approves Special Committee's report on Portuguese Territories. 14 December 1962 (82-7-13); Fr. - N; UK - N; US - N.

Document A/C.4/L760, 10 December 1962. Establishes special training program for territories under Portuguese administration. Fourth Committee, 12 December 1962 (82-2-1); Fr. - Y; UK - Y; US - Y.

Res. 1819(XVII). Immediate independence for Angola and Security Council action. 18 December 1962 (57-14-18); Fr. - N; UK - N; US - N.

Eighteenth Session

Res. 1956(XVIII). Approves Special Committee on Colonialism's report and its continuance. 11 December 1963 (95-0-6); Fr. - A; UK - A; US - A.

Res. 1881(XVIII). Condemns South Africa for the policy of apartheid. 11 October 1963 (106-1-0); Fr. - Y; UK - Y; US - Y.

Res. 1899(XVIII). Right of South West Africa to self-determination and an oil and arms embargo against South Africa. 13 November 1963 (84-6-17); Fr. - N; UK - N; US - N.

Res. 1979(XVIII). Situation in South-West Africa is seriously disturbing international peace and requests Security Council consideration. 17 December 1963 (89-2-3); Fr. - A; UK - A; US - Y.

Res. 1913(XVIII). Notes Portugal's refusal to implement prior resolutions and requests Security Council consideration. 3 December 1963 (91-2-11); Fr. - A; UK - A; US - A.

Res. 1883(XVIII). Invites the United Kingdom not to transfer power to the current government of Southern Rhodesia. 14 October 1963 (90-2-13); Fr. - A; UK - NP; US - A.

Res. 1889(XVIII). Urges Members to use their influence with the United Kingdom to prevent the granting of independence to the current government of Southern Rhodesia. 6 November 1963; (73-2-19); Fr. - A; UK - NP; US - A.

Selected Colonial Issues, Twentieth and Twenty-first Sessions of the General Assembly*

Twentieth Session

Ghanian amendment deleting part of operative paragraph 3 of draft resolution A/C.4/L815 concerning the Cook Islands. Fourth Committee, 8 December 1965 (28-29-43); Fr. - N; UK - A; US - A.

Res. 2064(XX). Resolution considering transmission of information under Article 73e no longer necessary and reaffirming the continued responsibility of the United Nations. Plenary, 16 December 1965 (78-0-29); Fr. - A; UK - A; US - A.

Operative paragraph 2 of resolution requesting Spain to set the earliest possible date for the independence of Equatorial Guinea. Plenary, 16 December 1965 (77-4-26); Fr. - A; UK - A; US - A.

Operative paragraph 3 of draft resolution A/C.4/L.810/Add.2 considering the existence of military bases an obstacle to independence of twenty-six territories. Fourth Committee, 7 December 1965 (50-26-23); Fr. - N; UK - N; US - N.

Retention of words ". . . and, to this end, to enter into negotiations on the problems relating to sovereignty presented by these two Territories" in operative paragraph 2 of draft resolution A/6160 concerning Ifni and Spanish Sahara. Plenary 16 December 1965 (33-2-69); Fr. - A; UK - A; US - A.

Res. 2072(XX). Urgently requesting Spain to take immediately all necessary measures for liberation of Ifni and Spanish Sahara. Plenary, 16 December 1965 (100-2-4); Fr. - A; UK - A; US - A.

Res. 2105(XX). Continuing the Special Committee of 24 on the ending of colonialism and approving its report. Plenary, 20 December 1965 (74-6-27); Fr. - A; UK - N; US - N.

Res. 2111(XX). Calling for the Administering Authority to grant independence to Nauru not later than January 31, 1968 and to restore the island for habitation. Plenary, 21 December 1965 (84-0-25); Fr. - A; UK - A; US - A.

Res. 2112(XX). Calling upon Australia to fix an early date for the independence of New Guinea and Papua. Plenary, 21 December 1965 (86-0-22); Fr. - A; UK - A; US - A.

Operative paragraph 1 of draft resolution A/SPC/L.118/R appealing urgently to major trading partners of South Africa to cease their increasing economic collaboration with the Government of South Africa. Special Political Committee, 7 December 1965 (75-3-17); Fr. - A; UK - N; US - A.

Operative paragraph 6 of draft resolution A/SPC/L.118/R calling to the attention of the Security Council the fact that the situation in South Africa is a threat to international peace and security and that action under Chapter VII is essential. Special Political Committee, 7 December 1965 (70-12-13); Fr. - N; UK - N; US - N.

*Fr. = France   N = No
UK = United Kingdom   A = Abstain
US = United States   O = Absent
   Y = Yes   NP = Present but not participating

Operative paragraph 7 of draft resolution A/SPC/L.118/R deploring the actions of states which, through political, economic and military collaboration, are encouraging South Africa to persist in its racial policies. Special Political Committee, 7 December 1965 (72-4-19); Fr. - A; UK - N; US - A.

Res. 2054(XX). Calling for universal economic sanctions and cessation of political, economic and military collaboration with South Africa. Plenary, 15 December 1965 (80-2-16); Fr. - A; UK - A; US - A.

Ninth preambular paragraph of draft resolution A/C.4/L.812/R.1 noting with deep concern the serious threat to international peace and security in southern Africa which is further aggravated by the racist rebellion in Southern Rhodesia. Fourth Committee, 9 December 1965 (77-9-11); Fr. - N; UK - N; US - N.

Operative paragraph 2 of draft resolution A/C.4/L.812/R.1 endorsing the conclusions and recommendations of the Special Committee's report on South-West Africa. Fourth Committee, 9 December 1965 (63-10-24); Fr. - N; UK - N; US - N.

Operative paragraph 6 of draft resolution A/C.4/L.812/R.1 considering that any attempt to annex a part or the whole of South West Africa constitutes an act of aggression. Fourth Committee, 9 December 1965 (80-3-15); Fr. - A; UK - A; US - N.

Operative paragraph 8 of draft resolution A.C.4/L.812/R.1 condemning the policies of financial interests operating in South West Africa. Fourth Committee, 9 December 1965 (64-10-25); Fr. - N; UK - N; US - N.

Res. 2107(XX). Urging all states to sever diplomatic and consular relations, boycott all trades with Portugal and prevent sale and supply of arms to Portugal. Plenary, 21 December 1965 (66-26-15); Fr. - A; UK - N; US - N.

Operative paragraph 11 of draft resolution A/C.4/L.795/A.3 calling upon the United Kingdom to employ all necessary measures, "including military force," to implement the resolution. Fourth Committee, 1 November 1965 (68-27-9); Fr. - N; UK - O; US - N.

Res. 2022(XX). Calling on the United Kingdom to use all means, "including military force," to obtain certain objectives in Southern Rhodesia. Plenary, 5 November 1965 (82-9-18); Fr. - A; UK - O; US - N.

Res. 2024(XX). Condemning UDI by Southern Rhodesia. Plenary, 11 November 1965 (107-2-1); Fr. - A; UK - O; US - Y.

Operative paragraph 6 of draft resolution A/6089 considering immediate and complete removal of military bases in Aden essential to the people's liberation. Plenary, 5 November 1965 (64-22-25); Fr. - N; UK - N; US - N.

Res. 2023(XX). Urging the United Kingdom to abolish immediately the state of emergency in Aden; repeal restrictive laws; cease all repressive actions; and release political detainees. Plenary, 5 November 1965 (90-11-10); Fr. - N; UK - N; US - N.

Res. 2065(XX). Inviting the UK and Argentina to proceed without delay with negotiations recommended by the Special Committee with a view to finding a peaceful solution to the problem of the Falkland Islands. Plenary, 16 December 1965 (94-0-14); Fr. - A; UK - A; US - A.

Res. 2071(XX). Requesting the U.K. to end the State of emergency in British Guiana, release all political prisoners and take no action to delay the independence of the territory scheduled for May 26, 1966. Plenary, 16 December 1965 (87-0-19); Fr. - A; UK - A; US - A.

Twenty-first Session

Operative paragraph 11 of draft resolution A/L.506/A.2 which required colonial powers to dismantle their colonial military bases. Plenary, 13 December 1966 (58-23-21); Fr. - N; UK - N; US - N.

Res. 2189(XXI). Approving the work of the Special Committee of 24 and condemning policies of certain Administering Powers. Plenary, 13 December 1966 (76-7-20); Fr. - A; UK - N; US - N.

Res. 2226(XXI). Recommending that the Administering Authority fix the date of independence of Nauru not later than 31 January 1968, that the control of the phosphate industry be transferred to the control of the Nauruan people and that the island be restored for their habitation. Plenary, 20 December 1966 (85-2-27); Fr. - A; UK - N; US - A.

Operative paragraph 4 of draft resolution A/6624 calling upon the Administering Power of New Guinea and Papua to remove all discriminatory practices, to hold elections and to fix an early date for independence. Plenary, 20 December 1966 (70-16-28); Fr. - A; UK - N; US - N.

Res. 2227(XXI). Calling upon the Administering Power of New Guinea and Papua to hold elections, to fix an early date for independence and to refrain from utilizing the territory for military activities incompatible with the UN Charter. Plenary, 20 December 1966 (81-8-24); Fr. - A; UK - N; US - N.

Res. 2228(XXI). Calling upon the Administering Power of French Somaliland to ensure the right of self-determination on the basis of universal adult suffrage. Plenary, 20 December 1966 (95-1-18); Fr. - O; UK - A; US - A.

Res. 2229(XXI). Requesting the Administering Power of Ifni and Spanish Sahara to accelerate decolonization, to determine procedures for holding a referendum under UN auspices and to send a special mission to Spanish Sahara. Plenary, 20 December 1966 (105-2-8); Fr. - A; UK - Y; US - A.

Res. 2280(XXI). Requesting the Administering Power of Equatorial Guinea to hold a general election before independence. Plenary, 20 December 1966 (109-0-7); Fr. - A; UK - A; US - A.

Operative paragraph 4 of draft resolution A/6628 declaring that any attempt to disrupt the national unity and territorial integrity and to establish military bases in twenty-six non-self-governing territories is incompatible with the purposes of the UN Charter. Plenary, 20 December 1966 (72-18-27); Fr. - N; UK - N; US - N.

Draft resolution A/SPC/L.135/A. Requesting the main trading partners of South Africa to take urgent steps towards disengagement from South Africa and discouraging all states from close economic and financial relations with South Africa. Special Political Committee, 12 December 1966 (87-1-12); Fr. - A; UK - A; US - A.

Draft resolution A/SPC/L.136. Renewing the appeal to Governments, organizations and individuals for contributions to the UN Trust Fund for South Africa. Special Political Committee, 12 December 1966 (99-0-2); Fr. - Y; UK - Y; US - Y.

Res. 2145R(XXI). Deciding that South Africa's mandate over South West Africa is terminated; establishing a 14-member *Ad Hoc* Committee for South West Africa; calling upon the Government of South Africa to refrain from altering the present international status of South West Africa. Plenary, 27 October 1966 (114-2-3); Fr. - Y; UK - Y; US - Y.

Saudi Arabian draft resolution A/L.487/Rev. 1 declaring that "South Africa is a racist colonial Power and should only be considered as such by the United Nations." Plenary, 27 October 1966 (17-22-58); Fr. - A; UK - N; US - N.

Operative paragraph 3 of draft resolution A/C.4/L.842/Rev. 1. Condemning Portugal's policy of settling foreign immigrants in the Portuguese territories and of exporting African workers to South Africa. Fourth Committee, 5 December 1966 (71-13-20); Fr. - A; UK - N; US - N.

Operative paragraph 7 of draft resolution A/C.4/L.842/Rev. 1. Recommending that the Security Council make it obligatory for all states to implement the measures contained in GA Res. 2107(XX) concerning Portuguese territories. Fourth Committee, 5 December 1966 (66-19-18); Fr. - A; UK - N; US - N.

Res. 2184(XXI). Condemning Portuguese policies and recommending that the Security Council oblige all states to implement GE Res. 2107(XX) which urged severance of diplomatic relations, boycott of trade and prevention of supply of arms to Portugal. Plenary, 12 December 1966 (70-13-22); Fr. - A; UK - N; US - N.

Res. 2138(XXI). Condemning any agreement between the UK and Southern Rhodesia. Plenary, 22 October 1966 (86-2-18); Fr. - A; UK - A; US - A.

Operative paragraph 8 of draft resolution A/C.4/L.886/Add.3. Calling again upon the United Kingdom to take all necessary measures, including, in particular, the use of force to put an end to the Southern Rhodesian regime. Fourth Committee, 10 November 1966 (78-18-17); Fr. - A; UK - N; US - N.

Draft resolution A/C.4/L.836/Add.3. Calling upon the United Kingdom to take all necessary measures, including, in particular, the use of force to put an end to the Southern Rhodesian regime. Fourth Committee, 10 November 1966 (94-2-17); Fr. - A; UK - A; US - A.

Draft resolution A/C.4/L.833/Add.1. Reiterating grave concern over the threat to Basutoland, Bechuanaland and Swaziland posed by South Africa. Fourth Committee, 28 September 1966 (82-2-15); Fr. - A; UK - A; US - A.

Draft resolution A/C.4/L.841/Add.2. Approving the report of the Special Committee of 24 on Aden. Fourth Committee, 2 December 1966 (100-0-3); Fr. - A; UK - Y; US - Y.

Draft resolution A/C.4/L.844/Add.3. Endorsing the appointment of a sub-committee by the Special Committee of 24 to visit and study the situation in Fiji. Fourth Committee, 8 December 1966 (76-6-17); Fr. - A; UK - N; US - N.

Res. 2231(XXI). Asking the Administering Power to expedite, in consultation with Spain, the decolonization of Gibraltar. Plenary, 20 December 1966 (101-0-14); Fr. - A; UK - Y; US - Y.

United Nations Vote Tally on Selected Colonial Questions at the Sixteenth–Eighteenth Sessions of the General Assembly*

Country	1	2	3	4	5	6	7	8	9	10	11	12	13	14	15	16	17	18	19	20	21	22	23
Algeria	–	–	–	–	–	–	–	–	–	Y	Y	Y	Y	Y	Y	Y	Y	Y	Y	Y	Y	Y	Y
Burundi	–	–	–	–	–	–	–	–	–	Y	Y	Y	Y	Y	Y	Y	Y	Y	Y	O	Y	Y	O
Cameroon	Y	Y	Y	A	Y	Y	Y	Y	Y	Y	Y	Y	Y	Y	Y	Y	O	Y	Y	Y	O	Y	Y
Central African Republic	Y	O	Y	A	Y	Y	A	Y	Y	O	Y	Y	Y	Y	Y	Y	O	Y	Y	Y	Y	Y	Y
Chad	Y	Y	Y	A	Y	Y	A	Y	O	Y	Y	O	Y	Y	Y	Y	Y	Y	Y	Y	Y	Y	Y
Congo (Brazzaville)	Y	Y	Y	A	O	Y	A	Y	Y	Y	O	Y	Y	Y	O	Y	O	Y	Y	Y	Y	Y	Y
Congo (Leopoldville)	Y	Y	Y	Y	Y	Y	A	Y	Y	Y	Y	Y	Y	Y	Y	Y	Y	Y	Y	O	Y	Y	Y
Dahomey	Y	Y	Y	A	Y	Y	A	Y	Y	Y	Y	Y	O	Y	Y	Y	Y	Y	Y	Y	Y	Y	O
Gabon	Y	Y	Y	A	Y	O	A	Y	Y	O	Y	O	Y	Y	Y	O	O	Y	Y	O	Y	Y	O
Ghana	Y	Y	Y	Y	Y	Y	Y	Y	Y	Y	Y	Y	Y	Y	Y	Y	Y	Y	Y	Y	Y	Y	Y
Guinea	Y	Y	Y	Y	Y	Y	Y	Y	Y	Y	Y	O	Y	Y	Y	Y	Y	Y	Y	Y	Y	Y	Y
Ivory Coast	Y	O	Y	A	Y	Y	A	Y	Y	Y	Y	O	Y	Y	Y	Y	Y	Y	Y	Y	Y	Y	O
Kenya	–	–	–	–	–	–	–	–	–	–	–	–	–	–	–	–	–	–	Y	–	–	–	–
Libya	Y	Y	Y	A	Y	Y	A	Y	Y	Y	Y	O	Y	Y	Y	O	Y	Y	Y	Y	Y	Y	Y
Madagascar	Y	Y	Y	A	Y	Y	A	Y	Y	Y	Y	O	Y	O	Y	Y	Y	Y	Y	Y	Y	Y	Y
Mali	Y	Y	Y	Y	Y	Y	Y	Y	Y	Y	Y	Y	Y	Y	Y	Y	Y	Y	Y	Y	Y	Y	Y
Mauritania	–	O	Y	A	Y	O	A	Y	Y	Y	Y	Y	Y	Y	Y	Y	Y	Y	Y	Y	Y	Y	O
Morocco	Y	Y	Y	Y	Y	Y	Y	Y	Y	Y	Y	Y	Y	Y	Y	O	Y	Y	Y	Y	Y	Y	Y
Niger	Y	O	Y	A	Y	O	O	Y	Y	Y	Y	Y	Y	Y	Y	Y	Y	Y	Y	O	Y	Y	Y
Nigeria	Y	Y	Y	A	Y	Y	A	Y	Y	Y	Y	Y	Y	Y	Y	Y	Y	Y	Y	Y	Y	Y	Y
Rwanda	–	–	–	–	–	–	–	–	–	Y	O	O	Y	O	Y	O	Y	Y	Y	O	O	Y	Y
Senegal	Y	Y	Y	A	Y	Y	Y	Y	Y	Y	Y	Y	Y	Y	Y	O	Y	Y	Y	Y	Y	Y	O
Sierra Leone	Y	Y	Y	A	Y	Y	A	Y	Y	Y	Y	Y	Y	Y	Y	Y	Y	Y	Y	Y	Y	Y	O
Somali Republic	Y	Y	A	Y	Y	Y	Y	Y	Y	Y	Y	Y	Y	Y	Y	O	Y	Y	Y	O	Y	O	Y
Sudan	Y	Y	Y	A	Y	Y	Y	Y	Y	Y	Y	Y	Y	Y	O	Y	Y	Y	Y	O	Y	Y	Y
Tanganyika	–	–	–	–	–	–	Y	Y	Y	Y	Y	Y	Y	Y	Y	Y	Y	Y	Y	Y	Y	Y	Y
Togo	Y	Y	Y	A	A	Y	A	Y	Y	Y	Y	Y	Y	Y	Y	O	O	Y	Y	Y	Y	Y	O
Tunisia	Y	Y	Y	N	Y	Y	A	Y	Y	Y	Y	Y	Y	Y	Y	Y	Y	Y	Y	Y	Y	Y	Y

*Y = Yes, in favor
N = No, against
A = Abstained
O = Absent

NP = Present, but not participating
– = Vote taken prior to United Nations membership

Country	Issue Number																						
	1	2	3	4	5	6	7	8	9	10	11	12	13	14	15	16	17	18	19	20	21	22	23
Uganda	-	-	-	-	-	-	-	-	-	Y	Y	O	O	Y	Y	O	Y	Y	Y	Y	Y	Y	Y
Upper Volta	Y	Y	Y	A	Y	O	A	Y	Y	Y	Y	Y	Y	O	Y	Y	Y	Y	Y	O	Y	Y	O
Zanzibar	-	-	-	-	-	-	-	-	-	-	-	-	-	-	-	-	-	-	-	O	-	-	-
Jamaica	-	-	-	-	-	-	-	-	-	Y	Y	Y	Y	Y	Y	O	Y	Y	Y	Y	Y	Y	Y
Trinidad and Tobago	-	-	-	-	-	-	-	-	-	Y	Y	Y	Y	Y	Y	Y	Y	Y	Y	Y	Y	Y	Y
Burma	Y	Y	Y	A	A	Y	A	Y	Y	Y	Y	Y	Y	Y	Y	Y	Y	Y	Y	Y	Y	Y	Y
Cambodia	A	Y	Y	A	A	Y	A	Y	Y	Y	Y	Y	Y	Y	Y	Y	Y	Y	Y	Y	Y	Y	Y
Ceylon	Y	Y	Y	A	Y	Y	A	Y	Y	Y	Y	Y	Y	Y	Y	Y	Y	Y	Y	Y	Y	Y	Y
Indonesia	Y	Y	Y	A	Y	Y	Y	Y	Y	Y	Y	Y	Y	Y	Y	Y	Y	Y	Y	Y	Y	Y	Y
Laos	Y	Y	Y	A	A	Y	A	Y	A	Y	Y	Y	O	O	Y	Y	Y	Y	Y	Y	Y	Y	Y
Malaysia	Y	Y	Y	N	A	Y	A	Y	A	Y	Y	Y	Y	Y	Y	Y	Y	Y	Y	Y	Y	Y	Y
Mongolia	Y	Y	Y	Y	Y	Y	Y	Y	Y	Y	Y	Y	Y	Y	Y	Y	Y	Y	Y	Y	Y	Y	Y
Pakistan	A	Y	Y	N	Y	Y	A	Y	Y	Y	Y	Y	Y	Y	Y	Y	Y	Y	Y	Y	Y	Y	Y
Philippines	Y	Y	Y	N	A	Y	N	Y	Y	Y	Y	Y	Y	Y	Y	Y	Y	Y	Y	Y	Y	Y	Y
Cyprus	A	Y	Y	A	A	Y	A	Y	Y	Y	Y	O	Y	Y	Y	Y	Y	Y	Y	Y	Y	Y	Y
Israel	Y	A	Y	N	Y	Y	A	Y	Y	Y	Y	Y	Y	Y	Y	Y	Y	Y	Y	Y	Y	Y	Y
Jordan	Y	Y	Y	A	Y	Y	A	Y	Y	Y	Y	Y	Y	Y	Y	Y	Y	Y	Y	Y	Y	Y	Y
Kuwait	-	-	-	-	-	-	-	-	-	-	-	-	-	-	-	-	Y	Y	Y	Y	O	Y	Y
Afghanistan	Y	Y	Y	A	Y	Y	A	Y	Y	Y	Y	Y	Y	Y	Y	Y	Y	Y	Y	Y	Y	Y	Y
Ethiopia	Y	Y	Y	A	Y	Y	Y	Y	Y	Y	Y	Y	Y	Y	Y	Y	Y	Y	Y	O	Y	Y	Y
Liberia	Y	Y	Y	A	Y	Y	A	Y	Y	Y	Y	Y	Y	Y	O	Y	Y	Y	Y	O	Y	Y	Y
Greece	O	A	Y	N	N	Y	N	Y	N	N	Y	A	A	Y	A	A	Y	Y	A	Y	A	A	A
India	Y	Y	Y	A	A	Y	Y	Y	Y	Y	Y	Y	Y	Y	Y	Y	Y	Y	Y	Y	Y	Y	Y
Iran	Y	Y	Y	N	A	Y	N	Y	Y	Y	Y	Y	Y	Y	Y	Y	Y	Y	Y	Y	Y	Y	Y
Iraq	Y	Y	Y	Y	Y	Y	Y	Y	Y	Y	Y	Y	Y	Y	Y	Y	Y	Y	Y	O	Y	Y	Y
Lebanon	Y	Y	Y	A	A	Y	A	Y	Y	Y	Y	Y	Y	Y	Y	Y	Y	Y	Y	Y	Y	Y	Y
Nepal	Y	Y	Y	A	A	Y	A	Y	Y	Y	Y	Y	Y	Y	Y	Y	Y	Y	Y	O	Y	Y	Y
Saudi Arabia	Y	Y	Y	A	Y	O	A	Y	Y	Y	Y	Y	Y	O	O	O	O	Y	O	Y	Y	Y	Y
Syria	-	Y	Y	A	Y	Y	A	Y	Y	Y	Y	Y	Y	Y	Y	Y	Y	Y	Y	Y	Y	Y	Y
Turkey	Y	Y	Y	N	N	Y	N	Y	N	N	Y	A	A	Y	A	N	Y	Y	A	Y	A	A	A
U.A.R.	Y	Y	Y	Y	Y	Y	Y	Y	Y	Y	Y	Y	Y	Y	Y	Y	Y	Y	Y	Y	Y	Y	Y
Yemen	Y	Y	Y	A	Y	Y	A	Y	Y	Y	Y	Y	O	O	O	O	Y	Y	Y	O	Y	Y	Y
Republic of South Africa	N	A	A	N	N	N	N	N	N	N	A	N	N	N	P	N	N	A	N	N	N	O	N
Australia	A	A	Y	N	N	Y	N	Y	N	N	Y	A	A	Y	A	N	Y	Y	A	Y	Y	A	A
China	A	A	Y	N	N	Y	N	Y	A	Y	Y	Y	Y	Y	Y	Y	A	Y	Y	Y	Y	Y	Y
Japan	A	A	Y	N	N	Y	N	Y	A	N	Y	Y	A	Y	Y	A	Y	Y	A	Y	Y	A	A
New Zealand	A	A	Y	N	N	Y	N	Y	N	N	Y	Y	A	Y	A	N	Y	Y	A	Y	Y	A	A

Country	Issue Number																						
	1	2	3	4	5	6	7	8	9	10	11	12	13	14	15	16	17	18	19	20	21	22	23
Thailand	A	Y	Y	N	A	Y	N	Y	A	A	Y	Y	Y	Y	Y	Y	A	Y	Y	Y	Y	Y	Y
Argentina	Y	A	Y	N	N	Y	N	Y	A	A	Y	Y	Y	Y	Y	A	Y	Y	Y	Y	Y	Y	Y
Bolivia	Y	Y	Y	N	A	A	A	Y	A	A	Y	Y	Y	Y	Y	Y	Y	Y	Y	O	Y	Y	Y
Brazil	Y	A	Y	N	N	Y	N	Y	A	A	Y	Y	Y	Y	A	A	Y	Y	Y	Y	A	Y	Y
Chile	Y	A	Y	N	N	Y	N	Y	A	A	Y	Y	Y	Y	Y	A	Y	Y	Y	Y	Y	Y	Y
Colombia	A	A	Y	N	N	Y	N	Y	A	A	Y	Y	Y	Y	Y	O	Y	Y	Y	Y	Y	Y	Y
Costa Rica	A	A	Y	N	O	O	N	Y	A	A	Y	Y	Y	Y	Y	O	Y	Y	Y	Y	Y	Y	Y
Cuba	Y	Y	Y	Y	Y	Y	Y	Y	Y	Y	Y	Y	Y	Y	Y	O	Y	Y	Y	Y	Y	Y	Y
Dominican Republic	A	A	Y	N	N	Y	N	Y	A	A	Y	O	O	Y	A	A	Y	Y	Y	O	O	O	O
Ecuador	Y	O	Y	N	A	Y	N	Y	A	O	Y	Y	Y	Y	O	O	Y	Y	Y	Y	O	Y	Y
El Salvador	NP	A	Y	N	A	Y	N	Y	A	A	Y	Y	Y	Y	Y	O	O	Y	O	Y	O	O	O
Guatemala	A	A	Y	N	A	Y	N	Y	A	A	Y	Y	Y	Y	Y	O	O	Y	Y	Y	Y	Y	Y
Haiti	Y	O	Y	N	Y	Y	N	Y	Y	Y	Y	Y	Y	Y	Y	Y	O	Y	Y	O	Y	Y	O
Honduras	Y	O	O	O	A	O	N	Y	A	A	Y	Y	Y	Y	Y	A	O	O	O	O	Y	O	O
Mexico	Y	A	Y	N	A	Y	N	Y	A	Y	Y	Y	Y	Y	Y	A	Y	Y	Y	Y	Y	Y	Y
Nicaragua	A	O	Y	N	N	O	N	Y	O	Y	Y	O	O	O	O	O	Y	Y	O	Y	O	O	O
Panama	Y	A	Y	N	N	Y	N	Y	A	A	Y	Y	Y	Y	Y	Y	Y	Y	Y	Y	Y	Y	Y
Paraguay	O	O	Y	N	A	Y	N	Y	A	O	Y	Y	O	O	Y	O	Y	O	Y	Y	Y	Y	O
Peru	Y	A	Y	N	A	Y	N	Y	A	A	Y	O	O	O	Y	A	Y	Y	Y	Y	O	Y	Y
Uruguay	Y	A	Y	N	A	Y	N	Y	A	A	Y	Y	Y	Y	Y	O	Y	Y	Y	Y	Y	Y	Y
Venezuela	Y	A	Y	N	A	Y	N	Y	A	A	Y	Y	Y	Y	Y	Y	Y	Y	Y	Y	Y	Y	Y
Austria	A	Y	Y	A	N	Y	N	Y	N	A	Y	Y	A	Y	A	A	Y	Y	A	Y	Y	Y	A
Belgium	NP	A	Y	N	N	Y	N	Y	N	N	Y	A	A	Y	N	N	A	Y	A	Y	A	A	A
Canada	A	A	Y	N	N	Y	N	Y	N	N	Y	A	A	Y	A	N	Y	Y	A	Y	A	A	A
Denmark	NP	A	Y	N	N	Y	N	Y	N	A	Y	Y	A	Y	A	A	Y	Y	A	Y	Y	Y	A
Finland	A	Y	Y	A	N	Y	N	Y	N	A	Y	Y	A	Y	A	Y	A	Y	Y	A	Y	Y	A
France	NP	O	A	N	N	A	N	A	N	N	A	A	A	Y	N	N	A	Y	N	A	A	A	A
Iceland	NP	Y	Y	N	N	O	O	O	N	A	Y	Y	A	O	A	O	Y	Y	A	Y	Y	Y	A
Ireland	A	A	Y	N	N	Y	N	Y	A	N	Y	Y	Y	Y	Y	A	Y	Y	A	Y	Y	Y	O
Italy	A	A	Y	N	N	Y	N	Y	N	A	Y	Y	A	Y	A	N	Y	Y	A	Y	A	A	A
Luxembourg	O	A	Y	N	N	Y	N	Y	N	N	Y	A	A	O	O	N	Y	Y	A	Y	A	A	A
Netherlands	Y	A	Y	N	N	Y	N	Y	N	N	A	A	A	Y	N	N	A	Y	A	Y	A	A	A
Norway	NP	Y	Y	N	N	Y	N	Y	N	A	Y	Y	Y	Y	A	A	Y	Y	A	Y	Y	Y	A
Portugal	A	A	O	O	N	N	O	O	N	N	NP	N	N	A	N	N	O	O	N	N	N	N	N
Spain	A	A	A	N	N	N	N	N	N	N	A	A	A	Y	N	N	A	O	N	A	N	A	A
Sweden	NP	Y	Y	N	N	Y	N	Y	N	A	Y	Y	A	Y	Y	A	Y	Y	A	Y	Y	Y	A
United Kingdom	NP	A	A	N	N	Y	N	Y	N	N	A	NP	NP	Y	N	N	A	Y	N	A	A	NP	NP
United States	NP	A	Y	N	N	Y	N	Y	N	N	Y	A	A	Y	N	N	A	Y	N	Y	A	A	A
Albania	Y	Y	Y	Y	Y	Y	Y	Y	Y	Y	Y	Y	Y	Y	Y	Y	Y	Y	Y	Y	Y	Y	Y
Bulgaria	Y	Y	Y	Y	Y	Y	Y	Y	Y	Y	Y	Y	Y	Y	Y	Y	Y	Y	Y	Y	Y	Y	Y

Country	Issue Number																						
	1	2	3	4	5	6	7	8	9	10	11	12	13	14	15	16	17	18	19	20	21	22	23
Byelorussian S.S.R.	Y	Y	Y	Y	Y	Y	Y	Y	Y	Y	Y	Y	Y	Y	Y	Y	Y	Y	Y	Y	Y	Y	Y
Czechoslovakia	Y	Y	Y	Y	Y	Y	Y	Y	Y	Y	Y	Y	Y	Y	Y	Y	Y	Y	Y	Y	Y	Y	Y
Hungary	Y	Y	Y	Y	Y	Y	Y	Y	Y	Y	Y	Y	Y	Y	Y	Y	Y	Y	Y	Y	Y	Y	Y
Poland	Y	Y	Y	Y	Y	Y	Y	Y	Y	Y	Y	Y	Y	Y	Y	Y	Y	Y	Y	Y	Y	Y	Y
Romania	Y	Y	Y	Y	Y	Y	Y	Y	Y	Y	Y	Y	Y	Y	Y	Y	Y	Y	Y	Y	Y	Y	Y
Ukrainian S.S.R.	Y	Y	Y	Y	Y	Y	Y	Y	Y	Y	Y	Y	Y	Y	Y	Y	Y	Y	Y	Y	Y	Y	Y
U.S.S.R.	Y	Y	Y	Y	Y	Y	Y	Y	Y	Y	Y	Y	Y	Y	Y	Y	Y	Y	Y	Y	Y	Y	Y
Yugoslavia	Y	Y	Y	Y	Y	Y	Y	Y	Y	Y	Y	Y	Y	Y	Y	Y	Y	Y	Y	Y	Y	Y	Y

Issue Number	Issue
1	Censure of South African Foreign Minister Eric Louw for General Debate Speech. 900th plenary meeting, 11 October 1961 (67-1-20).
2	Resolution 1650(XVI). Requesting France to recognize imprisoned Algerians as political prisoners. 15 November 1961 (62-0-31).
3	Resolution 1654(XVI). Thirty-eight Power draft establishing Special Committee on Colonialism. 27 November 1961 (97-0-4).
4	Soviet amendment to Thirty-eight Power draft on colonialism, setting a 1962 time for the elimination of all colonialism. 1066th plenary meeting, 27 November 1961 (19-46-36).
5	Sanctions and expulsion paragraphs of African resolution on apartheid. Document A/4968, 1067th plenary meeting, 28 November 1961 (48-31-22). Failed for lack of two-thirds majority.
6	Resolution 1699 (XVI). Concerning failure of Portugal to report to United Nations on its Non-Self-Governing Territories. 19 December 1961 (90-3-2).
7	Bulgarian-Polish draft resolution calling for sanctions against Portugal. Document A/L.383, 1102nd plenary meeting, 30 January 1962 (26-43-32).
8	Resolution 1742(XVI). Afro-Asian resolution calling for self-determination in Angola. 30 January 1962 (99-2-1).
9	Resolution 1745(XVI). Request for the Special Committee on Colonialism to consider whether Southern Rhodesia is fully self-governing. 23 February 1962 (57-21-24).
10	Resolution 1761(XVII). Recommends sanctions and Security Council action against South Africa because of apartheid. 6 November 1962 (67-16-23).
11	Resolution 1810(XVII). Approves procedures of Special Committee on Colonialism and its enlargement to twenty-four members. 17 December 1962 (101-0-4).
12	Resolution 1755(XVII). Calls for lifting of ban on ZAPU Political Party in Southern Rhodesia and the release of ZAPU President. 12 October 1962 (83-2-11).

Issue Number	Issue

13 Resolution 1760(XVII). Requests the United Kingdom to obtain a new constitution for Southern Rhodesia. 31 October 1962 (81-2-9).

14 Document A/C.4/L.754, 15 November 1962. Requests Special Committee on Colonialism to consider the question of South West Africa and requests the Secretary-General to establish an effective United Nations presence in the Territory. Fourth Committee. 19 November 1962 (96-0-1).

15 Resolution 1807(XVII). Approves Special Committee's report on Portuguese Territories and requests a halt in the sale and supply of arms to Portugal. 14 December 1962 (82-7-13).

16 Resolution 1819 (XVII). Supports immediate independence for Angola and requests Security Council action. 18 December 1962 (57-14-18).

17 Resolution 1956(XVIII). Approves Special Committee on Colonialism's report and its continuance. 11 December 1963 (95-0-6).

18 Resolution 1881(XVIII). Condemns South Africa for the policy of apartheid and requests the release of all political prisoners. 11 October 1963 (106-1-0).

19 Resolution 1899(XVIII). Affirms right of South West Africa to self-determination and calls for an oil and arms embargo against South Africa. 13 November 1963 (84-6-17).

20 Resolution 1979(XVIII). Finds that the situation in South-West Africa is seriously disturbing international peace and requests Security Council consideration. 17 December 1963 (89-2-3).

21 Resolution 1913(XVIII). Notes refusal of Portugal to implement prior resolutions and requests Security Council consideration. 3 December 1963 (91-2-11).

22 Resolution 1883(XVIII). Invites the United Kingdom not to transfer power to the present government of Southern Rhodesia. 14 October 1963 (90-2-13).

23 Resolution 1889. Urges Members to use their influence with the United Kingdom to prevent the granting of independence to the present government of Southern Rhodesia and calls on the United Kingdom not to grant independence to this government. 6 November 1963 (73-2-19).

United Nations Vote Tally on Selected Colonial Questions at the Twentieth Session of the General Assembly*

Country	1	2	3	4	5	6	7	8	9	10	11	12	13	14	15	16	17	18	19	20	21	22	23	24	25
Algeria	Y	A	Y	Y	Y	Y	Y	Y	Y	Y	Y	Y	Y	Y	Y	Y	Y	Y	Y	Y	Y	Y	Y	Y	Y
Botswana	–	–	–	–	–	–	–	–	–	–	–	–	–	–	–	–	–	–	–	–	–	–	–	–	–
Burundi	O	Y	Y	O	O	Y	Y	Y	Y	O	O	O	Y	O	O	O	O	Y	Y	Y	Y	Y	Y	Y	O
Cameroon	Y	Y	Y	Y	Y	Y	Y	Y	Y	Y	Y	Y	Y	Y	Y	Y	Y	Y	Y	Y	Y	Y	Y	Y	Y
Central African Republic	A	Y	Y	A	Y	Y	Y	Y	Y	Y	Y	Y	Y	Y	Y	Y	Y	Y	Y	Y	Y	Y	Y	Y	Y
Chad	A	O	O	Y	O	O	Y	Y	Y	Y	Y	Y	Y	Y	Y	Y	Y	Y	Y	Y	Y	Y	Y	O	O
Congo (Brazzaville)	Y	A	Y	O	A	Y	Y	Y	Y	Y	Y	Y	O	Y	Y	Y	Y	Y	Y	Y	Y	Y	Y	Y	Y
Congo (Leopoldville)	Y	A	Y	Y	A	Y	Y	Y	Y	Y	Y	Y	Y	Y	Y	Y	Y	Y	Y	Y	Y	Y	Y	Y	Y
Dahomey	Y	Y	Y	Y	A	Y	O	Y	Y	Y	Y	Y	Y	Y	Y	Y	Y	Y	Y	Y	Y	Y	Y	Y	Y
Gabon	O	Y	A	O	A	Y	Y	Y	Y	Y	Y	Y	Y	O	O	O	O	Y	Y	Y	Y	Y	Y	Y	Y
Gambia	O	O	O	O	O	O	O	O	O	O	O	O	O	O	O	O	O	Y	O	O	O	O	O	O	O
Ghana	Y	A	Y	Y	Y	Y	Y	Y	Y	Y	Y	Y	Y	Y	Y	Y	O	Y	Y	Y	Y	Y	Y	Y	Y
Guinea	A	Y	Y	Y	Y	Y	Y	Y	Y	Y	Y	Y	Y	Y	Y	Y	Y	Y	Y	Y	Y	Y	Y	Y	Y
Ivory Coast	A	Y	Y	A	Y	Y	Y	Y	Y	O	O	O	Y	Y	Y	Y	Y	Y	Y	Y	Y	A	Y	Y	Y
Kenya	Y	A	Y	Y	Y	Y	Y	Y	Y	Y	Y	Y	Y	Y	Y	Y	Y	Y	Y	Y	Y	Y	Y	Y	Y
Lesotho	–	–	–	–	–	–	–	–	–	–	–	–	–	–	–	–	–	–	–	–	–	–	–	–	–
Libya	A	Y	Y	Y	Y	Y	Y	Y	Y	Y	Y	Y	Y	Y	Y	Y	Y	Y	Y	Y	Y	Y	Y	Y	Y
Madagascar	A	Y	Y	A	A	Y	Y	Y	Y	Y	Y	Y	O	Y	Y	Y	Y	Y	Y	Y	A	Y	Y	Y	Y
Malawi	A	Y	Y	O	A	Y	Y	O	O	O	O	O	O	O	O	O	O	O	O	O	Y	Y	Y	Y	Y
Mali	A	Y	Y	Y	Y	Y	Y	Y	Y	Y	Y	Y	Y	Y	Y	Y	Y	Y	Y	Y	Y	Y	Y	Y	Y
Mauritania	A	Y	Y	Y	Y	Y	Y	Y	Y	Y	Y	Y	Y	Y	Y	Y	Y	Y	Y	Y	Y	Y	Y	Y	Y
Morocco	A	Y	Y	Y	Y	Y	Y	Y	Y	Y	Y	Y	Y	Y	Y	Y	Y	Y	Y	Y	Y	Y	Y	Y	Y
Niger	A	Y	Y	A	Y	Y	Y	Y	Y	Y	Y	Y	Y	Y	Y	Y	Y	Y	Y	Y	Y	Y	Y	Y	Y
Nigeria	N	Y	Y	Y	Y	Y	Y	Y	Y	Y	Y	Y	Y	Y	Y	Y	Y	Y	Y	Y	Y	Y	Y	Y	Y
Rwanda	N	Y	Y	Y	A	Y	Y	Y	Y	Y	Y	Y	Y	Y	Y	Y	Y	Y	Y	Y	Y	Y	Y	Y	Y
Senegal	A	A	Y	A	Y	Y	Y	Y	Y	Y	Y	Y	Y	Y	Y	Y	Y	Y	Y	Y	Y	Y	Y	Y	Y
Sierra Leone	A	Y	Y	Y	Y	Y	Y	Y	Y	Y	Y	Y	Y	Y	Y	Y	Y	Y	Y	Y	Y	Y	Y	Y	Y
Somali Republic	Y	A	Y	Y	O	O	Y	Y	Y	Y	Y	Y	Y	Y	Y	Y	Y	Y	Y	Y	Y	Y	Y	Y	Y

*Y = Yes, in favor
N = No, against
A = Abstained
O = Absent
NP = Present, but not participating
– = Vote taken prior to United Nations membership

215

Country	1	2	3	4	5	6	7	8	9	10	11	12	13	14	15	16	17	18	19	20	21	22	23	24	25
Sudan	Y	A	Y	Y	Y	Y	Y	Y	Y	Y	Y	Y	Y	Y	Y	Y	Y	Y	Y	Y	Y	Y	Y	Y	Y
Tanzania	Y	O	Y	Y	O	O	Y	Y	Y	Y	Y	Y	O	Y	Y	Y	Y	Y	Y	Y	Y	Y	Y	Y	O
Togo	A	Y	Y	A	Y	Y	O	Y	Y	Y	Y	Y	Y	Y	Y	Y	Y	Y	Y	Y	Y	Y	Y	Y	Y
Tunisia	Y	A	Y	Y	Y	Y	Y	Y	Y	Y	Y	Y	Y	Y	O	O	Y	Y	Y	Y	Y	Y	Y	Y	Y
Uganda	Y	A	Y	Y	Y	Y	O	Y	Y	Y	Y	Y	O	Y	Y	Y	Y	Y	Y	Y	Y	Y	Y	Y	Y
Upper Volta	A	Y	Y	A	Y	Y	Y	Y	Y	O	O	O	Y	Y	Y	Y	Y	Y	Y	Y	Y	Y	Y	Y	Y
Zambia	Y	Y	Y	Y	Y	Y	Y	Y	Y	Y	Y	Y	Y	O	O	O	O	O	Y	Y	Y	Y	Y	Y	Y
Barbados	-	-	-	-	-	-	-	-	-	-	-	-	-	-	-	-	-	-	-	-	-	-	-	-	-
Guyana	-	-	-	-	-	-	-	-	-	-	-	-	-	-	-	-	-	-	-	-	-	-	-	-	-
Jamaica	N	Y	Y	Y	A	Y	Y	Y	Y	Y	Y	Y	Y	Y	Y	Y	Y	Y	A	Y	Y	Y	Y	Y	Y
Trinidad and Tobago	O	A	Y	O	O	Y	A	Y	Y	Y	Y	Y	Y	Y	Y	Y	Y	Y	Y	Y	Y	Y	Y	Y	Y
Burma	A	Y	Y	Y	A	Y	Y	Y	Y	Y	Y	Y	Y	Y	Y	Y	Y	Y	Y	Y	Y	Y	Y	Y	Y
Cambodia	O	O	O	O	O	O	O	O	O	O	O	O	O	O	O	O	O	O	O	O	O	O	O	O	O
Ceylon	N	Y	Y	Y	A	Y	O	Y	Y	Y	Y	Y	O	Y	Y	Y	Y	Y	Y	Y	Y	A	Y	Y	Y
Indonesia	-	-	-	-	-	-	-	-	-	-	-	-	-	-	-	-	-	-	-	-	-	-	-	-	-
Laos	O	O	O	O	O	O	Y	Y	Y	O	O	O	O	O	O	O	O	A	O	Y	Y	A	Y	O	O
Malaysia	N	Y	Y	A	A	Y	Y	Y	Y	Y	Y	Y	Y	Y	Y	Y	Y	Y	Y	Y	Y	A	Y	Y	Y
Maldive Islands	O	Y	Y	O	A	Y	O	Y	Y	O	O	O	O	O	O	O	O	O	O	Y	Y	A	Y	Y	Y
Mongolia	Y	A	Y	Y	A	Y	Y	Y	Y	Y	Y	Y	Y	Y	Y	Y	Y	Y	Y	Y	Y	Y	Y	Y	Y
Pakistan	N	Y	Y	Y	Y	Y	Y	Y	Y	Y	Y	Y	Y	Y	Y	Y	Y	Y	Y	Y	Y	Y	Y	Y	Y
Philippines	N	Y	A	N	A	Y	A	Y	Y	Y	Y	Y	Y	Y	Y	Y	Y	A	Y	Y	Y	A	Y	Y	Y
Singapore	O	O	O	O	O	O	Y	Y	O	O	O	O	O	O	O	O	O	Y	O	Y	Y	Y	Y	O	O
Cyprus	Y	O	O	Y	O	O	Y	Y	Y	Y	Y	Y	O	Y	Y	Y	Y	Y	Y	Y	Y	Y	Y	O	O
Malta	O	O	O	O	O	O	O	O	O	O	O	O	O	O	O	O	O	O	O	O	O	O	O	O	O
Israel	A	Y	Y	A	A	Y	Y	A	Y	Y	Y	Y	Y	Y	Y	Y	Y	Y	Y	Y	Y	N	A	Y	Y
Jordan	A	Y	A	Y	A	Y	Y	Y	Y	Y	Y	Y	Y	Y	Y	Y	Y	Y	Y	Y	Y	Y	Y	Y	Y
Kuwait	A	Y	A	Y	Y	Y	O	Y	Y	Y	Y	Y	Y	Y	Y	Y	Y	Y	Y	Y	Y	Y	Y	Y	Y
South Yemen	-	-	-	-	-	-	-	-	-	-	-	-	-	-	-	-	-	-	-	-	-	-	-	-	-
Afghanistan	A	Y	Y	Y	Y	Y	Y	Y	Y	Y	Y	Y	Y	Y	Y	Y	Y	Y	Y	Y	Y	Y	Y	Y	Y
Ethiopia	A	Y	Y	Y	Y	Y	Y	Y	Y	Y	Y	Y	Y	Y	Y	Y	Y	Y	Y	Y	Y	Y	Y	Y	Y
Liberia	N	Y	Y	Y	Y	Y	Y	Y	Y	Y	Y	Y	Y	Y	Y	Y	Y	Y	Y	Y	Y	Y	Y	Y	Y
Greece	N	Y	Y	N	A	Y	Y	Y	Y	A	A	Y	Y	Y	A	Y	A	A	A	Y	Y	A	Y	Y	Y
India	A	Y	Y	Y	A	Y	Y	Y	Y	Y	Y	Y	Y	Y	Y	Y	Y	Y	Y	Y	Y	Y	Y	Y	Y
Iran	A	Y	Y	A	Y	Y	Y	Y	Y	Y	Y	Y	Y	Y	Y	Y	Y	Y	Y	Y	Y	Y	Y	Y	Y
Iraq	A	Y	Y	Y	A	Y	Y	Y	Y	Y	Y	Y	Y	Y	Y	Y	Y	Y	Y	Y	Y	Y	Y	Y	Y
Lebanon	O	Y	A	O	Y	Y	Y	Y	Y	Y	Y	Y	Y	O	O	O	O	O	Y	Y	Y	Y	Y	Y	Y
Nepal	N	Y	Y	Y	Y	Y	Y	Y	Y	Y	Y	Y	Y	Y	Y	Y	Y	Y	Y	O	Y	A	Y	Y	Y

Issue Number

Country	1	2	3	4	5	6	7	8	9	10	11	12	13	14	15	16	17	18	19	20	21	22	23	24	25
Saudi Arabia	A	Y	Y	Y	A	Y	Y	Y	Y	Y	Y	Y	Y	Y	Y	Y	Y	Y	Y	Y	Y	Y	Y	Y	Y
Syria	Y	A	Y	Y	Y	Y	Y	Y	Y	Y	Y	Y	Y	Y	Y	Y	Y	Y	Y	Y	Y	Y	Y	Y	Y
Turkey	N	Y	Y	N	A	Y	Y	Y	Y	Y	Y	Y	Y	Y	A	Y	A	A	Y	Y	Y	A	Y	Y	Y
U.A.R.	Y	Y	Y	Y	Y	Y	Y	Y	Y	Y	Y	Y	Y	Y	Y	Y	Y	Y	Y	Y	Y	Y	Y	Y	Y
Yemen	Y	A	Y	Y	Y	Y	Y	Y	Y	Y	Y	Y	Y	Y	Y	Y	Y	Y	Y	Y	Y	Y	Y	Y	Y
South Africa	N	A	A	N	A	A	N	A	A	O	O	O	N	N	N	N	N	N	N	N	N	N	N	A	A
Australia	N	A	Y	N	A	Y	N	A	A	N	N	N	A	N	N	A	N	N	N	N	Y	N	N	A	A
China	N	Y	Y	N	A	Y	A	Y	A	Y	A	A	Y	A	A	Y	A	A	A	Y	Y	A	Y	Y	Y
Japan	N	Y	Y	N	A	Y	A	Y	A	A	A	Y	A	A	A	Y	A	A	A	Y	Y	A	A	Y	Y
New Zealand	N	Y	Y	N	A	Y	N	A	A	A	N	A	A	N	N	A	N	N	N	N	Y	N	N	A	Y
Thailand	N	Y	Y	N	A	Y	Y	Y	Y	Y	Y	Y	Y	Y	Y	Y	Y	A	Y	Y	Y	A	Y	Y	Y
Argentina	A	Y	Y	A	A	Y	Y	Y	Y	Y	A	A	Y	Y	A	Y	A	N	A	Y	Y	A	Y	Y	A
Bolivia	A	Y	N	N	A	Y	Y	A	Y	O	O	O	O	Y	A	Y	A	N	N	O	O	O	O	Y	Y
Brazil	A	Y	A	N	A	Y	A	Y	Y	Y	A	A	Y	A	Y	Y	A	N	N	A	Y	N	Y	Y	Y
Chile	A	Y	Y	A	A	Y	Y	Y	Y	Y	Y	Y	Y	Y	A	Y	A	A	A	Y	Y	A	Y	Y	Y
Colombia	A	Y	N	A	A	Y	Y	Y	Y	Y	A	Y	Y	Y	A	A	A	N	N	Y	Y	A	Y	Y	A
Costa Rica	A	Y	A	A	A	Y	A	Y	Y	Y	Y	Y	Y	A	A	Y	A	N	N	A	Y	A	Y	Y	A
Cuba	Y	A	Y	Y	A	Y	Y	Y	Y	Y	Y	Y	Y	Y	Y	Y	Y	Y	Y	Y	Y	Y	Y	Y	Y
Dominican Republic	O	Y	A	O	A	Y	A	Y	Y	O	O	O	Y	Y	A	Y	A	A	O	Y	Y	A	Y	Y	A
Ecuador	A	O	O	O	A	Y	O	O	O	O	O	O	O	Y	Y	Y	O	N	A	Y	Y	Y	O	O	Y
El Salvador	A	Y	A	Y	A	Y	A	Y	Y	O	O	O	O	Y	A	A	A	N	N	A	Y	A	Y	Y	A
Guatemala	A	Y	A	N	A	Y	A	Y	Y	O	O	O	Y	Y	A	A	A	N	N	A	Y	N	Y	Y	A
Haiti	O	Y	O	N	O	O	Y	Y	Y	Y	Y	Y	Y	O	O	O	O	O	Y	Y	Y	A	Y	Y	O
Honduras	A	Y	A	A	A	Y	A	O	O	O	O	O	O	O	O	O	O	N	N	Y	Y	A	Y	Y	A
Mexico	A	Y	Y	A	A	Y	Y	Y	Y	A	A	A	Y	Y	A	Y	A	N	N	A	Y	A	Y	Y	Y
Nicaragua	O	Y	A	A	A	Y	A	O	O	O	O	O	Y	O	O	O	O	O	O	O	O	O	O	Y	A
Panama	A	Y	A	A	A	Y	A	O	O	Y	Y	Y	Y	Y	A	Y	A	O	N	A	Y	Y	Y	Y	A
Paraguay	O	Y	A	O	A	Y	A	A	Y	O	O	O	O	O	O	O	O	N	O	O	Y	O	O	Y	A
Peru	A	Y	A	A	A	Y	Y	A	Y	O	O	O	Y	O	O	O	A	N	N	Y	Y	A	Y	Y	A
Uruguay	A	Y	A	A	A	Y	Y	Y	Y	O	O	O	Y	Y	A	Y	Y	N	A	Y	O	A	Y	Y	Y
Venezuela	A	Y	A	A	A	Y	Y	Y	Y	A	A	A	Y	Y	A	Y	A	N	A	Y	Y	A	Y	Y	A
Austria	N	Y	A	A	A	Y	A	A	A	A	N	A	A	A	A	A	A	N	N	A	Y	N	A	Y	Y
Belgium	N	Y	A	N	A	Y	A	A	A	A	N	N	A	A	N	A	N	N	N	N	Y	N	N	Y	Y
Canada	N	Y	Y	N	A	Y	A	A	A	A	N	A	A	N	N	A	N	N	N	N	Y	N	N	A	Y
Denmark	N	Y	Y	N	A	Y	A	A	A	A	Y	A	Y	Y	A	A	A	A	N	A	Y	N	A	A	Y
Finland	N	Y	Y	A	A	Y	A	A	A	A	A	A	A	A	A	Y	A	A	N	A	Y	N	A	A	Y
France	N	A	A	N	A	A	A	A	A	A	N	A	A	N	N	A	N	A	N	A	A	A	N	N	A

		Issue Number																							
Country	1	2	3	4	5	6	7	8	9	10	11	12	13	14	15	16	17	18	19	20	21	22	23	24	25
Iceland	O	Y	Y	O	A	Y	A	A	A	A	A	A	A	O	O	O	O	O	O	A	Y	N	N	A	Y
Ireland	N	Y	Y	N	A	Y	A	A	A	A	N	A	A	A	N	Y	N	A	N	A	Y	N	N	Y	Y
Italy	N	Y	A	N	A	Y	A	A	A	Y	N	A	A	N	A	A	A	N	N	A	Y	N	N	Y	Y
Luxembourg	O	Y	A	O	A	Y	A	A	A	O	O	O	A	O	O	O	O	N	O	N	Y	N	N	Y	Y
Netherlands	N	Y	A	N	A	Y	A	A	A	A	N	A	A	A	A	A	A	A	N	N	Y	N	N	A	Y
Norway	N	Y	Y	N	A	Y	A	A	A	A	A	A	A	A	A	Y	A	A	N	A	Y	N	N	A	Y
Portugal	A	A	N	N	N	N	N	A	A	N	N	N	N	N	N	N	N	N	N	N	N	N	N	A	A
Spain	N	Y	N	N	N	N	A	A	A	Y	A	A	Y	A	A	A	A	N	N	A	Y	Y	Y	Y	A
Sweden	N	Y	Y	N	A	Y	A	A	A	A	A	A	Y	Y	A	A	A	A	N	A	Y	N	N	A	Y
United Kingdom	A	A	A	N	A	A	N	A	A	N	N	N	A	N	N	A	N	N	O	O	O	N	N	A	A
United States	A	A	A	N	A	A	N	A	A	A	N	A	A	N	N	N	N	N	N	N	Y	N	N	A	A
Albania	O	O	O	O	O	O	Y	O	O	Y	Y	Y	Y	O	O	O	O	Y	Y	Y	Y	Y	Y	O	O
Bulgaria	Y	A	Y	Y	A	Y	Y	Y	Y	Y	Y	Y	Y	Y	Y	Y	Y	Y	Y	Y	Y	Y	Y	Y	Y
Byelorussian S.S.R.	Y	A	Y	Y	A	Y	Y	Y	Y	Y	Y	Y	Y	Y	Y	Y	Y	Y	Y	Y	Y	Y	Y	Y	Y
Czechoslovakia	Y	A	Y	Y	A	Y	Y	Y	Y	Y	Y	Y	Y	Y	Y	Y	Y	Y	Y	Y	Y	Y	Y	Y	Y
Hungary	Y	A	Y	Y	A	Y	Y	Y	Y	Y	Y	Y	Y	Y	Y	Y	Y	Y	Y	Y	Y	Y	Y	Y	Y
Poland	Y	A	Y	Y	A	Y	Y	Y	Y	Y	Y	Y	Y	Y	Y	Y	Y	Y	Y	Y	Y	Y	Y	Y	Y
Romania	Y	A	Y	Y	A	Y	Y	Y	Y	Y	Y	Y	Y	Y	Y	Y	Y	Y	Y	Y	Y	Y	Y	Y	Y
Ukrainian S.S.R.	Y	A	Y	Y	A	Y	Y	Y	Y	Y	Y	Y	Y	Y	Y	Y	Y	Y	Y	Y	Y	Y	Y	Y	Y
U.S.S.R.	Y	A	Y	Y	A	Y	Y	Y	Y	Y	Y	Y	Y	Y	Y	Y	Y	Y	Y	Y	Y	Y	Y	Y	Y
Yugoslavia	Y	Y	Y	Y	Y	Y	Y	Y	Y	Y	Y	Y	Y	Y	Y	Y	Y	Y	Y	Y	Y	Y	Y	Y	Y

Issue Number	Issue

1　Ghanian amendment deleting part of operative paragraph 3 of draft resolution A/C.4/L.815 concerning the Cook Islands. Fourth Committee, 8 December 1965 (28-29-43).

2　Resolution 2064(XX), considering transmission of information under Article 73e no longer necessary and reaffirming the continued responsibility of the U.N. Plenary, 16 December 1965 (78-0-29).

3　Operative paragraph 2 of resolution requesting Spain to set the earliest possible date for the independence of Equatorial Guinea. Plenary, 16 December 1965 (77-4-26).

4　Operative paragraph 3 of draft resolution A/C.4/L.810/Add.2 considering the existence of military bases an obstacle to independence of twenty-six territories. Fourth Committee, 7 December 1965 (50-26-23).

Issue Number	Issue
5	Retention of words, ". . . and, to this end, to enter into negotiations on the problems relating to sovereignty presented by these two Territories" in operative paragraph 2 of draft resolution A/6160 concerning Ifni and Spanish Sahara. Plenary, 16 December 1965 (33-2-69).
6	Resolution 2072(XX) urgently requesting Spain to take immediately all necessary measures for liberation of Ifni and Spanish Sahara. Plenary, 16 December 1965 (100-2-4).
7	Resolution 2105(XX) continuing the Special Committee of 24 on the ending of colonialism and approving its report. Plenary, 20 December 1965 (74-6-27).
8	Resolution 2111(XX) calling for the Administering Authority to grant independence to Nauru not later than January 31, 1968 and to restore the island for habitation. Plenary, 21 December 1965 (84-0-25).
9	Resolution 2112(XX) calling upon Australia to fix an early date for the independence of New Guinea and Papua. Plenary, 21 December 1965 (86-0-22).
10	Operative paragraph 1 of draft resolution A/SPC/L.118/R appealing urgently to major trading partners of South Africa to cease their increasing economic collaboration with the Government of South Africa. Special Political Committee, 7 December 1965 (75-3-17).
11	Operative paragraph 6 of draft resolution A/SPC/L.118/R calling to the attention of the Security Council the fact that the situation in South Africa is a threat to international peace and security and that action under Chapter VII is essential. Special Political Committee, 7 December 1965 (70-12-13).
12	Operative paragraph 7 of draft resolution A/SPC/L.118/R deploring the actions of states which, through political, economic and military collaboration, are encouraging South Africa to persist in its racial policies. Special Political Committee, 7 December 1965 (72-4-19).
13	Resolution 2054(XX) calling for universal economic sanctions and cessation of political, economic and military collaboration with South Africa. Plenary, 15 December 1965 (80-2-16).
14	Ninth preambular paragraph of draft resolution A/C.4/L.812/R.1 noting with deep concern the serious threat to international peace and security in southern Africa which is further aggravated by the racist rebellion in Southern Rhodesia. Fourth Committee, 9 December 1965 (77-9-11).
15	Operative paragraph 2 of draft resolution A/C.4/L.812/R.1 endorsing the conclusions and recommendations of the Special Committee's report on South West Africa. Fourth Committee, 9 December 1965 (63-10-24).
16	Operative paragraph 6 of draft resolution A/C.4/L.812/R.1 considering that any attempt to annex a part or the whole of South West Africa constitutes an act of aggression. Fourth Committee, 9 December 1965 (80-3-15).
17	Operative paragraph 8 of draft resolution A/C.4/L.812/R.1 condemning the policies of financial interests operating in South West Africa. Fourth Committee, 9 December 1965 (64-10-25).
18	Resolution 2107(XX) urging all states to sever diplomatic and consular

Issue Number	*Issue*

relations, boycott all trade with Portugal and prevent sale and supply of arms to Portugal. Plenary, 21 December 1965 (66-26-15).

19 Operative paragraph 11 of draft resolution A/C.4/L.795/A.3 calling upon the United Kingdom to employ all necessary measures, "including military force," to implement the resolution. Fourth Committee, 1 November 1965 (68-27-9).

20 Resolution 2022(XX) calling on the United Kingdom to use all means, "including military force," to obtain certain objectives in Southern Rhodesia. Plenary, 5 November 1965 (82-9-18).

21 Resolution 2024(XX) condemning U.D.I. by Southern Rhodesia. Plenary, 11 November 1965 (107-2-1).

22 Operative paragraph 6 of draft resolution A/6089 considering immediate and complete removal of military bases in Aden essential to the people's liberation. Plenary, 5 November 1965 (64-22-25).

23 Resolution 2023(XX) urging the United Kingdom to abolish immediately the State of Emergency in Aden; repeal restrictive laws; cease all repressive actions; and release political detainees. Plenary, 5 November 1965 (90-11-10).

24 Resolution 2065(XX) inviting the United Kingdom and Argentina to proceed without delay with negotiations recommended by the Special Committee with a view to finding a peaceful solution to the problem of the Falkland Islands. Plenary, 16 December 1965 (94-0-14).

25 Resolution 2071(XX) requesting the United Kingdom to end the State of Emergency in British Guiana, release all political prisoners, and take no action to delay the independence of the territory scheduled for May 26, 1966. Plenary, 16 December 1965 (87-0-19).

United Nations Vote Tally on Selected Colonial Questions at the Twenty-first Session of the General Assembly*

Country	1	2	3	4	5	6	7	8	9	10	11	12	13	14	15	16	17	18	19	20	21	22
Algeria	Y	Y	Y	Y	Y	Y	Y	Y	Y	Y	Y	Y	Y	Y	Y	Y	Y	Y	Y	Y	Y	Y
Botswana	O	O	O	O	O	O	O	O	O	O	O	O	O	O	O	O	N	Y	–	O	O	O
Burundi	O	O	Y	Y	Y	Y	Y	Y	Y	Y	Y	Y	Y	Y	Y	Y	Y	Y	Y	Y	Y	Y
Cameroon	Y	Y	Y	Y	Y	Y	Y	Y	Y	Y	Y	Y	Y	Y	Y	Y	Y	Y	Y	Y	Y	Y
Central African Republic	A	Y	Y	Y	Y	Y	A	Y	Y	Y	Y	Y	Y	Y	O	Y	Y	Y	O	Y	Y	Y
Chad	O	O	Y	Y	Y	A	Y	Y	Y	Y	Y	Y	Y	Y	Y	Y	Y	Y	Y	Y	O	Y
Congo (Brazzaville)	O	O	Y	Y	Y	Y	Y	Y	Y	Y	Y	Y	O	O	O	Y	Y	Y	Y	O	O	Y
Congo (Leopoldville)	Y	Y	Y	Y	Y	Y	Y	Y	Y	Y	Y	Y	Y	Y	Y	Y	Y	Y	Y	Y	A	Y
Dahomey	Y	Y	Y	Y	Y	A	Y	Y	Y	Y	Y	Y	O	O	Y	Y	Y	Y	Y	Y	Y	Y
Gabon	A	Y	Y	Y	Y	A	Y	Y	Y	O	O	Y	O	O	Y	Y	Y	O	O	O	Y	Y
Gambia	O	O	O	O	O	O	O	O	O	O	O	O	Y	Y	O	Y	Y	Y	O	Y	Y	O
Ghana	Y	Y	Y	Y	Y	Y	Y	Y	Y	Y	Y	Y	Y	Y	Y	Y	Y	Y	Y	Y	A	Y
Guinea	Y	Y	Y	Y	Y	Y	Y	Y	Y	Y	Y	Y	Y	Y	Y	Y	Y	Y	Y	Y	Y	Y
Ivory Coast	Y	Y	Y	Y	Y	Y	Y	Y	A	Y	Y	Y	Y	Y	Y	Y	Y	Y	Y	Y	A	Y
Kenya	Y	Y	Y	Y	Y	Y	Y	Y	Y	Y	Y	Y	Y	Y	Y	Y	Y	Y	Y	Y	Y	Y
Lesotho	O	O	O	O	O	Y	Y	Y	Y	O	O	O	O	O	O	O	O	O	–	O	O	Y
Libya	Y	Y	Y	Y	Y	Y	Y	Y	Y	Y	Y	Y	Y	Y	Y	Y	Y	Y	Y	Y	Y	Y
Madagascar	A	Y	A	A	A	A	Y	Y	A	Y	Y	Y	Y	Y	Y	Y	Y	Y	Y	Y	Y	Y
Malawi	A	A	Y	Y	Y	Y	Y	Y	Y	A	A	A	A	A	A	O	O	O	A	Y	A	Y
Mali	Y	Y	Y	Y	Y	Y	Y	Y	Y	Y	Y	Y	Y	Y	Y	Y	Y	Y	Y	Y	Y	Y
Mauritania	Y	Y	Y	Y	Y	Y	Y	Y	Y	Y	Y	Y	Y	Y	Y	Y	Y	Y	Y	Y	Y	Y
Morocco	Y	Y	Y	Y	Y	Y	Y	Y	Y	Y	Y	Y	Y	Y	Y	Y	Y	Y	Y	Y	Y	Y
Niger	Y	Y	Y	Y	Y	A	Y	Y	Y	Y	Y	Y	Y	Y	Y	Y	Y	Y	Y	Y	Y	Y
Nigeria	Y	Y	Y	Y	Y	Y	Y	Y	Y	Y	Y	Y	Y	Y	Y	Y	Y	Y	Y	Y	Y	Y
Rwanda	Y	Y	Y	Y	Y	Y	Y	Y	Y	Y	Y	Y	Y	Y	O	Y	Y	Y	Y	Y	Y	Y
Senegal	Y	Y	Y	Y	Y	A	Y	Y	Y	Y	Y	Y	Y	Y	Y	Y	Y	Y	Y	Y	Y	Y
Sierra Leone	Y	Y	Y	Y	Y	Y	Y	Y	Y	Y	Y	Y	Y	Y	Y	Y	Y	Y	Y	Y	Y	Y
Somali Republic	Y	Y	Y	Y	Y	Y	Y	Y	Y	Y	Y	Y	Y	'Y	Y	Y	Y	Y	Y	Y	Y	O
Sudan	Y	Y	Y	Y	Y	Y	Y	Y	Y	Y	Y	Y	Y	Y	Y	Y	Y	Y	Y	Y	Y	Y
Tanzania	Y	Y	Y	Y	Y	Y	Y	Y	Y	Y	Y	Y	Y	Y	Y	Y	Y	Y	Y	Y	Y	Y
Togo	Y	Y	Y	Y	Y	Y	Y	Y	Y	Y	Y	Y	Y	Y	Y	Y	Y	Y	Y	O	N	Y

*Y = Yes, in favor
N = No, against
A = Abstained
O = Absent
NP = Present, but not participating
– = Vote taken prior to United Nations membership

| Country | \multicolumn{22}{c}{Issue Number} |
| --- | 1 | 2 | 3 | 4 | 5 | 6 | 7 | 8 | 9 | 10 | 11 | 12 | 13 | 14 | 15 | 16 | 17 | 18 | 19 | 20 | 21 | 22 |

Country	1	2	3	4	5	6	7	8	9	10	11	12	13	14	15	16	17	18	19	20	21	22
Tunisia	Y	Y	Y	Y	Y	Y	Y	Y	Y	Y	Y	Y	Y	Y	Y	Y	Y	Y	Y	Y	O	Y
Uganda	O	O	Y	Y	Y	Y	Y	Y	Y	Y	O	O	Y	Y	Y	O	Y	Y	Y	Y	Y	Y
Upper Volta	Y	Y	Y	Y	Y	A	Y	Y	Y	O	Y	Y	Y	Y	O	O	Y	Y	O	O	O	Y
Zambia	Y	Y	Y	Y	Y	Y	Y	Y	Y	Y	Y	Y	Y	Y	Y	Y	Y	Y	Y	Y	Y	Y
Burma	Y	Y	Y	Y	Y	Y	Y	Y	Y	Y	Y	Y	Y	Y	Y	Y	Y	Y	Y	Y	Y	Y
Cambodia	O	O	Y	Y	Y	O	Y	Y	Y	O	O	Y	O	O	O	O	O	O	Y	Y	O	Y
Ceylon	Y	Y	Y	Y	Y	Y	Y	Y	Y	Y	Y	Y	Y	Y	Y	Y	Y	Y	Y	Y	Y	Y
Indonesia	Y	Y	Y	Y	Y	Y	Y	Y	Y	Y	Y	Y	Y	Y	Y	O	Y	Y	Y	O	Y	Y
Laos	O	O	A	A	A	Y	Y	Y	A	Y	Y	Y	O	O	O	O	Y	Y	O	O	O	Y
Malaysia	A	Y	Y	A	A	Y	Y	Y	Y	Y	Y	Y	Y	Y	Y	Y	Y	Y	Y	Y	O	Y
Maldive Islands	O	O	Y	A	A	Y	Y	Y	A	O	O	Y	Y	Y	Y	Y	Y	Y	O	Y	Y	Y
Mongolia	Y	Y	Y	Y	Y	Y	Y	Y	Y	Y	Y	Y	Y	Y	Y	Y	Y	Y	Y	Y	Y	A
Pakistan	Y	Y	Y	Y	Y	Y	Y	Y	Y	Y	Y	Y	Y	Y	Y	Y	Y	Y	Y	Y	Y	Y
Philippines	N	Y	Y	Y	Y	Y	Y	Y	N	Y	Y	Y	Y	Y	Y	Y	Y	Y	Y	Y	Y	Y
Singapore	Y	Y	Y	Y	Y	Y	Y	Y	Y	Y	Y	Y	O	O	Y	Y	Y	Y	Y	O	O	Y
Cyprus	O	O	Y	Y	Y	Y	Y	Y	Y	Y	Y	Y	Y	Y	Y	Y	Y	Y	Y	Y	Y	Y
Malta	N	N	O	O	O	O	O	O	O	O	O	O	Y	O	O	O	O	O	O	O	O	O
Israel	A	A	A	A	A	A	Y	Y	A	Y	Y	Y	Y	Y	Y	Y	Y	Y	Y	Y	Y	Y
Jordan	Y	Y	Y	Y	Y	Y	Y	Y	Y	Y	Y	Y	Y	Y	Y	O	Y	Y	Y	Y	Y	Y
Kuwait	Y	Y	Y	Y	Y	Y	Y	Y	Y	O	O	Y	Y	Y	Y	Y	Y	Y	Y	O	Y	Y
South Yemen	–	–	–	–	–	–	–	–	–	–	–	–	–	–	–	–	–	–	–	–	–	–
Afghanistan	Y	Y	Y	Y	Y	Y	O	Y	Y	Y	Y	Y	Y	Y	Y	Y	O	Y	Y	Y	Y	Y
Ethiopia	Y	Y	Y	Y	Y	Y	Y	Y	Y	Y	Y	Y	Y	Y	Y	Y	Y	Y	Y	Y	Y	Y
Liberia	Y	Y	Y	Y	Y	Y	Y	Y	Y	Y	Y	Y	Y	Y	Y	Y	Y	Y	Y	Y	A	Y
Greece	N	Y	A	A	A	Y	Y	Y	N	Y	Y	Y	A	A	A	Y	A	Y	Y	Y	Y	Y
India	Y	Y	Y	Y	Y	Y	Y	Y	Y	Y	Y	Y	Y	Y	Y	Y	Y	Y	Y	Y	Y	Y
Iran	A	Y	Y	Y	Y	Y	Y	Y	A	Y	Y	Y	Y	Y	A	Y	Y	Y	Y	Y	Y	Y
Iraq	Y	Y	O	Y	Y	Y	Y	Y	Y	Y	Y	Y	Y	Y	Y	Y	Y	Y	Y	Y	Y	Y
Lebanon	O	O	Y	Y	Y	Y	Y	Y	Y	Y	Y	Y	Y	Y	Y	Y	Y	Y	O	Y	Y	Y
Nepal	O	O	Y	Y	Y	Y	Y	Y	Y	Y	Y	Y	Y	Y	Y	Y	Y	Y	Y	Y	Y	Y
Saudi Arabia	Y	Y	Y	Y	Y	Y	Y	Y	Y	Y	Y	Y	Y	Y	Y	Y	Y	Y	Y	Y	Y	Y
Syria	Y	Y	Y	Y	Y	Y	Y	Y	Y	Y	Y	Y	Y	Y	Y	Y	Y	Y	Y	Y	Y	Y
Turkey	A	Y	Y	A	Y	Y	Y	Y	A	Y	Y	Y	A	N	A	Y	Y	Y	Y	Y	Y	Y
U.A.R.	Y	Y	Y	Y	Y	Y	Y	Y	Y	Y	Y	Y	Y	Y	Y	Y	Y	Y	Y	Y	Y	Y
Yemen	Y	Y	Y	Y	O	Y	Y	Y	Y	O	O	Y	Y	Y	Y	O	Y	Y	O	O	Y	Y
Austria	A	A	A	N	A	A	Y	Y	A	A	Y	Y	N	N	N	A	N	A	A	Y	A	Y
Belgium	N	A	A	N	A	A	A	Y	N	A	Y	Y	N	N	N	A	N	A	A	O	O	A
Canada	N	A	A	N	N	Y	Y	Y	N	A	Y	Y	N	N	N	A	N	A	A	Y	A	Y
Denmark	N	A	A	N	A	Y	Y	Y	N	Y	Y	Y	A	N	A	A	N	A	A	Y	A	Y
Finland	A	A	A	A	A	Y	Y	Y	A	Y	Y	Y	A	N	A	A	N	A	A	Y	A	Y

Country	Issue Number																					
	1	2	3	4	5	6	7	8	9	10	11	12	13	14	15	16	17	18	19	20	21	22
France	N	A	A	A	A	O	A	A	N	A	Y	A	A	A	A	A	A	A	A	A	A	A
Iceland	N	A	A	A	A	Y	Y	Y	N	Y	Y	Y	O	O	A	A	N	A	A	O	O	Y
Ireland	A	A	A	N	A	Y	Y	Y	A	Y	Y	Y	A	A	Y	A	N	A	Y	Y	A	Y
Italy	N	A	A	A	A	A	Y	Y	A	A	Y	Y	N	N	A	A	N	A	Y	Y	A	Y
Luxembourg	N	A	A	N	A	A	Y	Y	N	O	O	Y	O	O	N	A	O	O	O	O	O	Y
Netherlands	N	A	A	N	A	A	Y	Y	N	A	Y	Y	N	N	N	A	N	A	A	Y	A	Y
Norway	N	A	A	N	A	Y	Y	Y	N	Y	Y	Y	A	N	A	A	N	A	A	Y	A	Y
Portugal	N	N	A	N	N	N	N	A	N	N	A	N	N	N	N	N	N	N	N	Y	N	A
Spain	Y	Y	Y	Y	Y	Y	N	A	Y	Y	Y	Y	N	N	N	Y	A	A	Y	Y	Y	Y
Sweden	N	A	A	N	A	Y	Y	Y	N	Y	Y	Y	A	N	A	A	N	A	A	Y	A	Y
United Kingdom	N	N	N	N	N	A	Y	A	N	A	Y	A	N	N	N	A	N	A	A	Y	N	Y
United States	N	N	A	N	N	A	A	A	N	A	Y	Y	N	N	N	A	N	A	A	Y	N	Y
Albania	Y	Y	Y	Y	Y	Y	Y	Y	Y	Y	Y	Y	Y	Y	Y	Y	O	O	Y	Y	Y	O
Bulgaria	Y	Y	Y	Y	Y	Y	Y	Y	Y	Y	Y	Y	Y	Y	Y	Y	Y	Y	Y	Y	Y	A
Byelorussian S.S.R.	Y	Y	Y	Y	Y	Y	Y	Y	Y	Y	Y	Y	Y	Y	Y	Y	Y	Y	Y	Y	Y	A
Czechoslovakia	Y	Y	Y	Y	Y	Y	Y	Y	Y	Y	Y	Y	Y	Y	Y	Y	Y	Y	Y	Y	Y	A
Hungary	Y	Y	Y	Y	Y	Y	Y	Y	Y	Y	Y	Y	Y	Y	Y	Y	Y	Y	Y	Y	Y	A
Poland	Y	Y	Y	Y	Y	Y	Y	Y	Y	Y	Y	Y	Y	Y	Y	Y	Y	Y	Y	Y	Y	A
Romania	Y	Y	Y	Y	Y	Y	Y	Y	Y	Y	Y	Y	Y	Y	Y	Y	Y	Y	Y	Y	Y	A
Ukrainian S.S.R.	Y	Y	Y	Y	Y	Y	Y	Y	Y	Y	Y	Y	Y	Y	Y	Y	Y	Y	Y	Y	Y	A
U.S.S.R.	Y	Y	Y	Y	Y	Y	Y	Y	Y	Y	Y	Y	Y	Y	Y	Y	Y	Y	Y	Y	Y	A
Yugoslavia	Y	Y	Y	Y	Y	Y	Y	Y	Y	Y	Y	Y	Y	Y	Y	Y	Y	Y	Y	Y	Y	Y

Issue Number	Issue

1 Operative paragraph 11 of draft resolution A/L.506/A.2 which required colonial powers to dismantle their colonial military bases. Plenary, 13 December 1966 (58-23-21).

2 Resolution 2189(XXI) approving the work of the Special Committee of 24 and condemning policies of certain Administering Powers. Plenary, 13 December 1966 (76-7-20).

3 Resolution 2226(XXI) recommending that the Administering Authority fix the date of independence of Nauru not later than 31 January 1968, that the control of the phosphate industry be transferred to the control of the Nauruan people, and that the island be restored for their habitation. Plenary, 20 December 1966 (85-2-27).

4 Operative paragraph 4 of draft resolution A/6624 calling upon the Administering Power of New Guinea and Papua to remove all discriminatory practices, to hold elections, and to fix an early date for independence. Plenary, 20 December 1966 (70-16-28).

5 Resolution 2227(XXI) calling upon the Administering Power of New

Issue Number	Issue

Guinea and Papua to hold elections, to fix an early date for independence, and to refrain from utilizing the territory for military activities incompatible with the U.N. Charter. Plenary, 20 December 1966 (81-8-24).

6 Resolution 2228(XXI) calling upon the Administering Power of French Somaliland to ensure right of self-determination on the basis of universal adult suffrage. Plenary, 20 December 1966 (95-1-18).

7 Resolution 2229(XXI) requesting the Administering Power of Ifni and Spanish Sahara to accelerate decolonization, to determine procedures for holding a referendum under U.N. auspices, and to send a special mission to Spanish Sahara. Plenary, 20 December 1966 (105-2-8).

8 Resolution(XXI) requesting the Administering Power of Equatorial Guinea to hold a general election before independence. Plenary, 20 December 1966 (109-0-7).

9 Operative paragraph 4 of draft resolution A/6628 declaring that any attempt to disrupt the national unity and territorial integrity and to establish military bases in twenty-six non-self-governing territories is incompatible with the purposes of the U.N. Charter. Plenary, 20 December 1966 (72-18-27).

10 Draft resolution A/SPC/L.135/A requesting the main trading partners of South Africa to take urgent steps towards disengagement from South Africa and discouraging all states from close economic and financial relations with South Africa. Special Political Committee, 12 December 1966 (87-1-12).

11 Draft resolution A/SPC/L.136 renewing the appeal to Governments, organizations and individuals for contributions to the U.N. Trust Fund for South Africa. Special Political Committee, 12 December 1966 (99-0-2).

12 Resolution 2145(XXI) deciding that South Africa's mandate over South West Africa is terminated; establishing a fourteen-member Ad Hoc Committee for South West Africa; calling upon the Government of South Africa to refrain from altering the present international status of South West Africa. Plenary, 27 October 1966 (114-2-3).

13 Operative paragraph 3 of draft resolution A/C.4/L.842/Rev. 1 condemning Portugal's policy of settling foreign immigrants in the Portuguese territories and of exporting African workers to South Africa. Fourth Committee, 5 December 1966 (71-13-20).

14 Operative paragraph 7 of draft resolution A/C.4/L.842/Rev. 1 recommending that the Security Council make it obligatory for all states to implement the measures contained in G.A. Res. 2107(XX) concerning Portuguese territories. Fourth Committee, 5 December 1966 (66-19-18).

15 Resolution 2184(XXI) condemning Portuguese policies and recommending that the Security Council oblige all states to implement G.A. Res. 2107(XX) which urged severance of diplomatic relations, boycott of trade, and prevention of supply of arms to Portugal. Plenary, 12 December 1966 (70-13-22).

16 Resolution 2138(XXI) condemning any agreement between the United Kingdom and Southern Rhodesia. Plenary, 22 October 1966 (86-2-18).

Issue Number	Issue

17 Operative paragraph 8 of draft resolution A/C.4/L.836/Add.3 calling again upon the United Kingdom to take all necessary measures, including, in particular, the use of force to put an end to the Southern Rhodesian regime. Fourth Committee, 10 November 1966 (78-18-17).

18 Draft resolution A/C.4/L.836/Add.3 calling upon the United Kingdom to take all necessary measures, including, in particular, the use of force to put an end to the Southern Rhodesian regime. Fourth Committee, 10 November 1966 (94-2-17).

19 Draft resolution A/C.4/L.833/Add.1 reiterating grave concern over the threat to Basutoland, Bechuanaland, and Swaziland posed by South Africa. Fourth Committee, 28 September 1966 (82-2-15).

20 Draft resolution A/C.4/L.841/Add.2 approving the report of the Special Committee of 24 on Aden. Fourth Committee, 2 December 1966 (100-0-3).

21 Draft resolution A/C.4/L.844/Add.3 endorsing the appointment of a sub-committee by the Special Committee of 24 to visit and study the situation in Fiji. Fourth Committee, 8 December 1966 (76-6-17).

22 Resolution 2231(XXI) asking the Administering Power to expedite, in consultation with Spain, the decolonization of Gibraltar. Plenary, 20 December 1966 (101-0-14).

Vote Tally on Selected East-West Issues before the Fifteenth Session of the General Assembly*

Country	Issue Number 1	2	3	4	5	6	7	8	9
Cameroon	O	O	Y	Y	A	A	O	A	A
Central African Republic	Y	Y	A	N	A	O	A	A	A
Chad	Y	Y	Y	Y	A	A	A	A	Y
Congo (Brazzaville)	O	O	Y	N	N	Y	O	A	A
Congo (Leopoldville)	O	O	O	A	N	Y	Y	O	A
Dahomey	Y	Y	Y	N	N	Y	A	A	A
Gabon	Y	Y	Y	N	N	O	Y	A	A
Ghana	Y	Y	N	A	Y	Y	A	N	Y
Guinea	Y	Y	N	A	Y	A	N	N	Y
Ivory Coast	Y	Y	Y	N	N	O	A	A	N
Libya	Y	Y	A	Y	Y	O	A	A	Y
Madagascar	Y	Y	Y	N	N	A	A	A	A
Mali	O	O	N	A	Y	O	O	N	Y
Morocco	Y	Y	N	A	Y	A	N	N	Y
Niger	Y	Y	Y	N	N	Y	A	A	A
Nigeria	Y	O	O	Y	A	Y	A	N	Y
Senegal	Y	Y	Y	Y	A	Y	Y	N	A
Somali Republic	Y	Y	A	Y	A	Y	A	A	Y
Sudan	Y	Y	A	Y	Y	Y	Y	N	Y
Togo	Y	Y	N	Y	A	A	A	A	Y
Tunisia	Y	Y	A	Y	A	Y	Y	A	Y
Upper Volta	O	O	O	Y	N	O	O	A	Y
Burma	Y	Y	A	Y	Y	Y	A	N	Y
Cambodia	Y	Y	A	A	A	A	A	N	Y
Ceylon	Y	Y	N	A	Y	A	A	N	Y
Indonesia	Y	Y	N	A	Y	A	A	N	Y
Laos	Y	Y	Y	A	A	O	A	A	A
Malaysia	Y	Y	A	Y	A	Y	Y	A	A
Pakistan	Y	Y	A	Y	A	Y	Y	Y	N
Philippines	A	Y	Y	Y	N	A	A	Y	N
Cyprus	Y	Y	Y	Y	N	Y	A	A	A
Israel	Y	Y	A	Y	N	Y	Y	A	N
Jordan	Y	Y	Y	Y	Y	O	A	Y	A

*Y = Yes, in favor
N = No, against
A = Abstained
O = Absent
NP = Present, but not participating
– = Vote taken prior to United Nations membership

Country	Issue Number								
	1	*2*	*3*	*4*	*5*	*6*	*7*	*8*	*9*
Afghanistan	Y	Y	N	A	Y	A	A	N	Y
Ethiopia	Y	Y	A	Y	Y	O	A	N	Y
Liberia	Y	Y	A	Y	A	Y	Y	Y	A
Greece	A	Y	Y	Y	N	Y	Y	Y	N
India	Y	Y	N	A	Y	A	A	N	Y
Iran	Y	Y	A	Y	A	Y	Y	Y	A
Iraq	Y	Y	N	A	Y	N	A	N	Y
Lebanon	Y	Y	A	Y	Y	N	A	Y	Y
Nepal	Y	Y	Y	Y	A	O	A	N	Y
Saudi Arabia	Y	Y	N	Y	Y	N	A	A	Y
Turkey	A	A	Y	Y	N	Y	Y	Y	N
United Arab Republic	Y	Y	N	A	Y	N	A	N	Y
Yemen	Y	Y	N	A	Y	N	A	N	Y
South Africa	A	Y	Y	A	N	A	A	Y	A
Australia	A	Y	Y	Y	N	Y	Y	Y	N
China	A	Y	Y	Y	N	A	Y	Y	N
Japan	Y	Y	Y	Y	N	Y	Y	Y	N
New Zealand	Y	Y	Y	Y	N	Y	Y	Y	N
Thailand	Y	Y	Y	Y	N	Y	Y	Y	N
Argentina	Y	Y	Y	Y	N	Y	Y	Y	N
Bolivia	A	Y	Y	Y	N	Y	A	Y	Y
Brazil	A	Y	Y	Y	N	Y	Y	Y	Y
Chile	Y	Y	Y	Y	N	A	Y	Y	Y
Colombia	A	Y	Y	A	N	A	Y	Y	N
Costa Rica	Y	Y	Y	Y	N	A	O	Y	N
Cuba	Y	Y	N	A	Y	A	A	N	Y
Dominican Republic	A	Y	Y	Y	A	O	A	Y	A
Ecuador	Y	Y	Y	Y	N	Y	A	Y	Y
El Salvador	A	Y	Y	Y	N'	Y	A	Y	N
Guatemala	A	Y	Y	Y	N	A	A	Y	N
Haiti	A	Y	Y	Y	N	Y	A	Y	O
Honduras	Y	Y	Y	Y	N	Y	A	Y	N
Mexico	Y	Y	Y	A	N	A	A	Y	Y
Nicaragua	A	Y	Y	Y	N	O	Y	Y	N
Panama	Y	Y	Y	Y	N	Y	Y	Y	N
Paraguay	A	Y	Y	Y	N	O	Y	Y	N
Peru	A	Y	Y	Y.	N	Y	A	Y	N
Uruguay	A	Y	Y	Y	N	Y	Y	Y	N
Venezuela	Y	Y	A	Y	N	A	A	Y	N

Country	Issue Number								
	1	2	3	4	5	6	7	8	9
Austria	Y	Y	Y	Y	N	Y	Y	A	A
Belgium	A	A	Y	A	N	A	A	Y	N
Canada	Y	Y	A	Y	N	Y	Y	Y	N
Denmark	Y	Y	Y	Y	N	Y	Y	N	A
Finland	Y	Y	A	Y	A	Y	Y	N	A
France	A	A	Y	A	N	A	A	Y	N
Iceland	Y	Y	Y	Y	N	O	Y	A	A
Ireland	Y	Y	A	Y	N	Y	Y	N	Y
Italy	A	Y	Y	Y	N	Y	Y	Y	N
Luxembourg	A	Y	Y	Y	N	Y	Y	Y	N
Netherlands	A	Y	Y	Y	N	Y	Y	Y	N
Norway	Y	Y	Y	Y	N	Y	Y	N	A
Portugal	A	Y	Y	A	N	N	Y	A	A
Spain	A	A	Y	A	N	A	A	Y	A
Sweden	Y	Y	A	Y	N	Y	Y	N	A
United Kingdom	A	Y	Y	Y	N	Y	Y	Y	N
United States	A	A	Y	Y	N	Y	Y	Y	N
Albania	Y	Y	N	N	Y	N	N	N	Y
Bulgaria	Y	Y	N	N	Y	N	N	N	Y
Byelorussian S.S.R.	Y	Y	N	N	Y	N	N	N	Y
Czechoslovakia	Y	Y	N	N	Y	N	N	N	Y
Hungary	Y	Y	N	N	Y	N	N	N	Y
Poland	Y	Y	N	N	Y	N	N	N	Y
Romania	Y	Y	N	N	Y	N	N	N	Y
Ukrainian S.S.R.	Y	Y	N	N	Y	N	N	N	Y
U.S.S.R.	Y	Y	N	N	Y	N	N	N	Y
Yugoslavia	Y	Y	N	A	Y	A	A	N	Y

Issue Number	Issue
1	Resolution 1576(XV). Requests all Governments to make every effort to prevent the wider dissemination of nuclear weapons. 20 December 1960 (68-0-26).
2	Resolution 1577(XV). Urges continuation of the voluntary suspension of the testing of nuclear weapons. 20 December 1960 (88-0-5).
3	Resolution 1498(XV). Accepts the credentials of the Congo delegation issued by President Kasavubu, the Head of State. 22 November 1960 (53-24-19).
4	Resolution 1600(XV). Sponsored by seventeen Afro-Asian States, it urges the immediate release of all members of the Congolese Parliament and its convening without delay and appoints a Commission of Conciliation. 15 April 1961 (60-16-23).
5	Document A/L.341 and Corr. 1. U.S.S.R. draft resolution which would have

Issue Number	Issue

(1) declared that no action violating the unity, political independence, or territorial integrity of the Congo would be allowed; (2) required the Congolese Parliament to resume work within twenty-one days; (3) requested the UN Command to ensure the safety of the members of Parliament. 15 April 1961 (29-53-17).

6   Document A/C.5/L.638/Rev. 1. Draft resolution recognizing that the Congo expenses "constitute 'expenses of the Organization' within the meaning of Article 17, paragraph 2, of the Charter" and apportioning the 1960 expenses. Fifth Committee, 15 December 1960 (45-15-25).

7   Resolution 1590(XV). Authorizes the Secretary-General to incur $24 million in commitments in 1961 for the Congo operation. 20 December 1960 39-11-44).

8   Resolution 1493(XV). Rejects U.S.S.R. request for the inclusion of an agenda item on Chinese representation and decides not to consider at the fifteenth session any proposals to change the seating of China. 8 October 1960 (42-34-22).

9   Document A/C.1/L.275. Mexican draft resolution calling upon all States to ensure that their territories were not used to promote a civil war in Cuba and asking them to cooperate, in the spirit of the Charter, in a search for a peaceful solution to the problem. First Committee, 21 April 1961 (42-31-25).

Vote Tally on Selected East-West Issues before the Sixteenth Session of the General Assembly*

Country	Issue Number												
	10	11	12	13	14	15	16	17	18	19	20	21	22
Cameroon	Y	Y	Y	Y	Y	A	Y	Y	Y	A	Y	N	A
Central African Republic	Y	Y	Y	Y	A	A	Y	Y	Y	A	Y	A	A
Chad	Y	Y	Y	Y	A	A	Y	Y	O	O	Y	A	O
Congo (Brazzaville)	O	Y	Y	Y	Y	A	O	O	O	O	Y	A	A
Congo (Leopoldville)	Y	Y	Y	Y	A	A	O	O	O	A	Y	A	A
Dahomey	O	O	O	Y	O	O	Y	Y	Y	Y	Y	A	O
Gabon	O	Y	O	Y	A	A	O	O	Y	O	O	N	A
Ghana	Y	Y	Y	Y	A	A	N	A	A	A	N	Y	A
Guinea	Y	Y	Y	Y	N	N	O	A	A	N	N	Y	A
Ivory Coast	Y	Y	O	Y	A	A	Y	Y	Y	A	Y	A	A
Libya	Y	Y	Y	Y	A	A	A	A	A	A	Y	N	A
Madagascar	O	Y	Y	Y	A	A	Y	Y	Y	A	Y	N	N
Mali	Y	A	Y	Y	N	N	N	A	A	N	N	Y	A
Mauritania	–	Y	Y	Y	–	–	Y	Y	Y	A	Y	N	A
Morocco	Y	O	Y	Y	A	A	A	A	A	A	N	Y	A
Niger	Y	Y	O	Y	Y	A	Y	Y	Y	A	Y	A	O
Nigeria	Y	Y	Y	Y	A	A	A	A	A	A	A	A	A
Senegal	Y	Y	Y	Y	A	A	O	A	Y	A	Y	N	A
Sierra Leone	O	Y	Y	Y	–	–	A	A	A	A	A	Y	A
Somali Republic	Y	O	Y	Y	A	A	A	A	A	A	A	Y	A
Sudan	Y	Y	Y	Y	A	A	A	A	A	A	N	Y	A
Tanganyika	–	–	–	–	–	–	O	O	O	O	A	N	A
Togo	Y	Y	Y	Y	A	A	A	A	A	A	O	A	A
Tunisia	Y	Y	Y	Y	A	A	A	A	A	O	N	A	A
Upper Volta	Y	Y	Y	Y	Y	A	Y	Y	Y	A	Y	A	A
Burma	Y	Y	Y	Y	A	Y	A	A	A	A	N	Y	A
Cambodia	A	Y	Y	Y	A	A	A	A	A	A	N	Y	A
Ceylon	A	Y	Y	Y	A	N	A	A	A	N	N	Y	A
Indonesia	A	Y	Y	Y	N	N	N	A	A	N	N	Y	A
Laos	Y	Y	Y	O	Y	Y	Y	Y	Y	Y	Y	N	O
Malaysia	Y	Y	Y	A	Y	Y	Y	Y	Y	Y	Y	N	N
Mongolia	–	N	N	Y	–	–	N	N	N	N	N	Y	Y
Pakistan	Y	Y	Y	A	A	Y	Y	Y	A	Y	A	Y	N

*Y = Yes, in favor
N = No, against
A = Abstained
O = Absent
NP = Present, but not participating
– = Vote taken prior to United Nations membership

Country	\multicolumn{13}{c}{Issue Number}
	10	11	12	13	14	15	16	17	18	19	20	21	22
Philippines	Y	Y	Y	A	Y	Y	Y	Y	Y	Y	Y	N	N
Cyprus	Y	Y	Y	Y	Y	Y	Y	Y	Y	Y	A	A	N
Israel	Y	Y	Y	A	Y	A	Y	Y	Y	A	Y	A	N
Jordan	O	Y	Y	Y	A	O	A	Y	Y	A	Y	N	A
Afghanistan	Y	Y	Y	Y	A	A	N	A	A	A	N	Y	A
Ethiopia	Y	Y	Y	Y	A	A	O	A	A	A	N	Y	A
Liberia	Y	Y	Y	Y	Y	Y	Y	Y	Y	A	Y	N	A
Greece	Y	Y	N	N	Y	Y	Y	Y	Y	Y	Y	N	N
India	A	Y	Y	Y	A	A	A	A	A	A	N	Y	A
Iran	Y	Y	Y	A	Y	Y	Y	Y	Y	Y	Y	N	N
Iraq	A	Y	Y	Y	A	A	N	A	A	N	N	Y	A
Lebanon	Y	Y	Y	Y	A	A	A	A	A	A	Y	A	A
Nepal	Y	Y	Y	Y	A	Y	A	A	A	A	N	Y	A
Saudi Arabia	A	Y	Y	Y	A	A	O	O	A	O	Y	A	A
Syria	Y	Y	Y	Y	–	–	A	A	A	A	N	Y	A
Turkey	Y	Y	A	N	Y	Y	Y	Y	Y	Y	Y	N	N
United Arab Republic	Y	Y	Y	Y	A	A	A	A	A	A	N	Y	A
Yemen	Y	Y	Y	Y	A	A	A	A	A	A	N	Y	A
South Africa	Y	Y	N	N	A	Y	Y	Y	Y	Y	Y	N	N
Australia	Y	Y	N	N	Y	Y	Y	Y	Y	Y	Y	N	N
China	Y	Y	N	N	Y	Y	Y	Y	Y	Y	Y	N	N
Japan	Y	Y	Y	Y	Y	Y	Y	Y	Y	Y	Y	N	N
New Zealand	Y	Y	A	N	Y	Y	Y	Y	Y	Y	Y	N	N
Thailand	Y	Y	Y	A	Y	Y	Y	Y	Y	Y	Y	N	N
Argentina	Y	Y	Y	A	Y	Y	Y	Y	Y	Y	Y	N	N
Bolivia	Y	Y	Y	A	Y	Y	Y	Y	Y	Y	Y	N	N
Brazil	Y	Y	Y	A	Y	Y	Y	Y	Y	Y	Y	N	N
Chile	Y	Y	Y	A	Y	Y	Y	Y	Y	Y	Y	N	N
Colombia	Y	Y	Y	A	Y	Y	Y	Y	Y	Y	Y	N	N
Costa Rica	Y	Y	Y	N	Y	Y	Y	Y	Y	Y	Y	N	N
Dominican Republic	Y	Y	Y	O	Y	Y	O	Y	Y	Y	Y	N	N
Ecuador	Y	Y	Y	A	Y	Y	Y	Y	O	Y	Y	N	N
El Salvador	Y	Y	Y	A	O	O	Y	Y	Y	Y	Y	N	N
Guatemala	Y	Y	Y	N	A	Y	Y	Y	Y	Y	Y	N	N
Haiti	O	Y	A	A	Y	Y	Y	Y	Y	Y	Y	N	N
Honduras	Y	Y	Y	A	Y	Y	O	Y	O	Y	Y	N	N
Mexico	Y	Y	Y	Y	Y	Y	Y	Y	O	Y	Y	N	N
Nicaragua	O	O	Y	N	Y	Y	O	Y	Y	Y	Y	N	N
Panama	Y	Y	Y	A	Y	Y	Y	Y	Y	Y	Y	N	N
Paraguay	Y	Y	Y	A	Y	Y	Y	Y	Y	Y	Y	N	N
Peru	Y	Y	Y	A	Y	Y	Y	Y	Y	Y	Y	N	N

Country	\multicolumn{13}{c}{Issue Number}
	10	11	12	13	14	15	16	17	18	19	20	21	22
Uruguay	Y	Y	Y	A	Y	Y	Y	Y	Y	Y	Y	N	N
Venezuela	Y	Y	Y	A	Y	Y	Y	Y	Y	Y	Y	N	N
Austria	Y	Y	Y	A	Y	Y	A	Y	Y	Y	A	A	N
Belgium	Y	Y	A	N	Y	Y	Y	Y	Y	Y	Y	N	N
Canada	Y	Y	Y	N	Y	Y	Y	Y	Y	Y	Y	N	N
Denmark	Y	Y	Y	A	Y	Y	Y	Y	Y	Y	N	Y	N
Finland	Y	Y	Y	A	A	A	A	A	A	A	N	Y	A
France	Y	Y	N	N	A	Y	Y	Y	A	Y	Y	N	N
Iceland	Y	Y	Y	A	Y	Y	Y	Y	Y	Y	Y	A	N
Ireland	Y	Y	Y	N	Y	Y	Y	Y	Y	Y	Y	N	N
Italy	Y	Y	N	N	Y	Y	Y	Y	Y	Y	Y	N	N
Luxembourg	O	Y	N	N	Y	Y	Y	Y	Y	Y	Y	N	N
Netherlands	Y	Y	A	N	Y	Y	Y	Y	Y	Y	Y	A	N
Norway	Y	Y	Y	A	Y	Y	Y	Y	O	Y	N	Y	N
Portugal	Y	Y	N	N	A	Y	O	O	O	O	Y	A	N
Spain	Y	Y	A	N	A	Y	Y	Y	A	Y	N	Y	N
Sweden	Y	Y	Y	A	Y	Y	Y	Y	Y	Y	Y	Y	N
United Kingdom	Y	Y	A	N	Y	Y	Y	Y	Y	Y	Y	N	N
United States	Y	Y	N	N	Y	Y	Y	Y	Y	Y	Y	N	N
Albania	A	N	N	Y	N	N	N	N	N	N	N	Y	Y
Bulgaria	A	N	N	Y	N	N	N	N	N	N	N	Y	Y
Byelorussian S.S.R.	A	N	N	Y	N	N	N	N	N	N	N	Y	Y
Czechoslovakia	A	N	N	Y	N	N	N	N	N	N	N	Y	Y
Hungary	A	N	N	Y	N	N	N	N	N	N	N	Y	Y
Poland	A	N	N	Y	N	N	N	N	N	N	N	Y	Y
Romania	A	N	N	Y	N	N	N	N	N	N	N	Y	Y
Ukrainian S.S.R.	A	N	N	Y	N	N	N	N	N	N	N	Y	Y
U.S.S.R.	A	N	N	Y	N	N	N	N	N	N	N	Y	Y
Yugoslavia	A	Y	Y	Y	N	N	N	A	A	N	Y	Y	Y

Issue Number	Issue
10	Resolution 1629(XVI). Approved Atomic Radiation Committee's Report which contained criticism of Soviet nuclear testing. 20 October 1961 (75-0-17).
11	Resolution 1632(XVI). Appeal to U.S.S.R. not to explode 50-megaton bomb. 27 October 1961 (87-11-1).
12	Resolution 1648(XVI). Calls for uncontrolled moratorium on nuclear testing. Sponsored by India. 6 November 1961 (71-20-8).
13	Resolution 1653(XVI). Afro-Asian sponsored ban on the use of nuclear weapons. 24 November 1961 (55-20-26).

Issue	
Number	*Issue*

14 Document A/4882, 22 September 1961. General Committee recommendation that the Assembly put "the Question of Tibet" on its agenda. 25 September 1961 (48-14-35-).

15 Document A/4882, 22 September 1961. General Committee recommendation that the Assembly put "The Question of Hungary" on its agenda. 25 September 1961 (51-15-30).

16 Motion in the First Committee by the United States not to seat North Korea. First Committee. 19 December 1961 (54-17-22).

17 Resolution 1740(XVI). Reaffirms earlier United Nations resolutions on the unification of Korea and extends the mandate of the Commission for the Unification and Rehabilitation of Korea. 20 December 1961 (60-11-27).

18 Resolution 1723(XVI). Recognizes the right of self-determination for Tibet. 20 December 1961 (56-11-29).

19 Resolution 1741(XVI). Deplores the continued disregard by the U.S.S.R. and Hungary of "the General Assembly resolutions concerning the situation in Hungary." 20 December 1961 (49-17-32).

20 Resolution 1668(XVI). Declares the question of Chinese representation to be an important question within the meaning of Article 18. 15 December 1961 (61-34-7).

21 Document A/L.360, 27 October 1961. Soviet draft calling for removing the Republic of China and the seating of the People's Republic of China. 15 December 1961 (37-48-19).

22 Document A/C.1/L.309, 2 February 1962. Czechoslovakian-Romanian draft calling upon the United States to end its interference in the internal affairs of Cuba and all actions directed against Cuba's territorial integrity and political independence. First Committee, 15 February 1962 (11-50-39).

Vote Tally on Selected East-West Issues before the Seventeenth
and Eighteenth Sessions of the General Assembly*

Country	Issue Number									
	23	24	25	26	27	28	29	30	31	32
Algeria	A	–	Y	A	A	A	Y	Y	Y	A
Burundi	A	O	N	Y	A	A	Y	Y	Y	A
Cameroon	A	N	N	Y	Y	A	N	N	N	Y
Central African Republic	O	N	N	Y	Y	A	N	N	N	Y
Chad	A	O	N	O	Y	A	N	N	N	Y
Congo (Brazzaville)	O	A	O	Y	Y	A	N	N	A	Y
Congo (Leopoldville)	O	NP	A	Y	O	A	N	N	N	Y
Dahomey	A	N	N	Y	Y	A	N	N	A	Y
Gabon	A	O	N	Y	Y	O	N	N	N	O
Ghana	A	N	Y	A	A	A	Y	Y	Y	A
Guinea	A	NP	Y	A	A	N	Y	Y	O	A
Ivory Coast	A	N	N	Y	Y	A	N	N	N	Y
Libya	A	A	O	O	O	A	N	N	O	A
Madagascar	A	N	N	Y	Y	A	N	N	N	Y
Mali	NP	N	Y	A	A	NP	Y	Y	Y	A
Mauritania	A	N	A	Y	Y	A	N	A	N	Y
Morocco	A	A	Y	A	O	A	Y	Y	Y	A
Niger	A	N	N	Y	Y	A	N	N	A	Y
Nigeria	A	A	A	A	A	A	A	A	A	A
Rwanda	O	O	N	Y	Y	A	N	N	N	Y
Senegal	A	N	A	A	A	A	N	N	A	A
Sierra Leone	O	Y	Y	A	A	A	Y	A	A	Y
Somali Republic	A	N	Y	A	A	A	Y	Y	O	Y
Sudan	A	A	A	A	A	A	Y	Y	Y	A
Tanganyika	A	N	Y	A	O	A	Y	Y	O	O
Togo	A	A	O	O	A	A	A	N	N	Y
Tunisia	A	A	Y	A	A	A	Y	Y	A	A
Uganda	O	–	O	O	O	A	Y	Y	O	O
Upper Volta	A	N	N	Y	Y	A	N	N	A	Y
Jamaica	Y	–	N	Y	A	Y	A	N	N	Y
Trinidad and Tobago	Y	–	O	O	Y	Y	N	A	N	Y
Burma	A	A	Y	A	A	A	Y	Y	Y	A

*Y = Yes, in favor
 N = No, against
 A = Abstained
 O = Absent
 NP = Present, but not participating
 – = Vote taken prior to United Nations membership

Country	Issue Number									
	23	24	25	26	27	28	29	30	31	32
Cambodia	A	N	Y	A	A	A	Y	Y	Y	A
Ceylon	A	N	Y	A	A	A	Y	Y	Y	A
Indonesia	A	N	Y	A	A	A	Y	Y	Y	A
Laos	A	N	O	O	Y	A	Y	Y	O	O
Malaysia	Y	Y	N	Y	Y	Y	A	N	N	Y
Mongolia	N	N	Y	N	N	N	Y	Y	Y	N
Pakistan	Y	Y	O	O	O	Y	Y	Y	A	Y
Philippines	Y	Y	N	Y	Y	Y	N	N	N	Y
Cyprus	A	A	A	Y	Y	Y	A	N	N	Y
Israel	Y	A	A	Y	Y	Y	A	A	A	Y
Jordan	Y	A	A	Y	Y	A	N	N	A	O
Kuwait	–	–	–	–	–	–	–	A	O	O
Afghanistan	A	A	Y	A	A	A	Y	Y	Y	A
Ethiopia	A	N	Y	A	A	A	Y	O	Y	A
Liberia	Y	A	A	Y	Y	A	N	N	A	Y
Greece	Y	A	N	Y	Y	Y	N	N	N	Y
India	Y	NP	A	Y	Y	Y	Y	Y	A	Y
Iran	Y	A	N	Y	Y	Y	N	N	A	Y
Iraq	A	N	Y	A	A	A	Y	Y	A	A
Lebanon	A	A	O	O	O	A	A	A	O	A
Nepal	A	A	Y	A	A	A	Y	Y	A	A
Saudi Arabia	A	N	O	O	O	O	A	A	O	O
Syria	A	N	Y	A	A	A	Y	Y	Y	A
Turkey	Y	Y	N	Y	Y	Y	N	N	N	Y
United Arab Republic	A	N	Y	A	A	A	Y	Y	Y	A
Yemen	A	A	A	A	Y	A	N	Y	O	O
South Africa	Y	Y	N	Y	Y	Y	N	N	N	O
Australia	Y	Y	N	Y	Y	Y	N	N	N	Y
China	Y	Y	N	Y	Y	A	N	N	N	Y
Japan	Y	Y	N	Y	Y	Y	N	N	N	Y
New Zealand	Y	Y	N	Y	Y	Y	N	N	N	Y
Thailand	Y	Y	N	Y	Y	Y	N	N	N	Y
Argentina	Y	Y	N	Y	Y	Y	N	N	N	Y
Bolivia	Y	O	N	Y	Y	Y	N	N	N	Y
Brazil	Y	Y	N	Y	Y	Y	N	N	A	Y
Chile	Y	Y	N	Y	Y	Y	N	N	N	Y
Colombia	Y	Y	N	Y	Y	Y	N	N	N	Y
Costa Rica	Y	Y	N	Y	Y	Y	N	N	N	Y
Cuba	O	N	O	O	N	N	Y	Y	O	N
Dominican Republic	Y	Y	N	Y	Y	Y	N	N	N	Y

| | Issue Number | | | | | | | | | |
Country	23	24	25	26	27	28	29	30	31	32
Ecuador	Y	Y	N	Y	O	Y	N	N	N	Y
El Salvador	Y	Y	N	Y	Y	Y	N	N	N	Y
Guatemala	Y	Y	N	Y	Y	Y	N	N	N	Y
Haiti	Y	Y	N	Y	Y	Y	N	N	N	Y
Honduras	Y	Y	N	Y	Y	Y	N	N	N	Y
Mexico	Y	Y	N	Y	Y	Y	N	N	N	Y
Nicaragua	Y	O	N	Y	Y	Y	N	N	N	Y
Panama	O	Y	N	Y	Y	Y	N	N	N	Y
Paraguay	Y	Y	N	Y	Y	Y	N	N	N	Y
Peru	Y	Y	N	Y	Y	Y	N	N	N	Y
Uruguay	Y	Y	N	Y	Y	Y	N	N	N	Y
Venezuela	Y	Y	N	Y	Y	Y	N	N	N	Y
Austria	Y	Y	A	A	Y	Y	A	A	A	Y
Belgium	Y	Y	N	Y	Y	Y	N	N	N	Y
Canada	Y	Y	N	Y	Y	Y	N	N	N	Y
Denmark	Y	Y	N	Y	Y	Y	Y	Y	N	Y
Finland	A	A	A	A	A	A	Y	Y	A	A
France	A	Y	N	Y	Y	Y	N	N	N	Y
Iceland	Y	Y	N	Y	Y	Y	A	A	N	O
Ireland	Y	Y	N	Y	Y	Y	N	N	N	Y
Italy	Y	Y	N	Y	Y	Y	N	N	N	Y
Luxembourg	Y	Y	N	Y	Y	Y	N	N	N	Y
Netherlands	Y	Y	N	Y	Y	Y	A	A	N	Y
Norway	Y	Y	N	Y	Y	Y	Y	Y	N	Y
Portugal	Y	O	N	Y	A	A	A	A	O	O
Spain	Y	Y	N	Y	Y	Y	N	N	N	Y
Sweden	Y	Y	A	A	Y	Y	Y	Y	A	Y
United Kingdom	Y	Y	N	Y	Y	Y	Y	Y	N	Y
United States	Y	Y	N	Y	Y	Y	N	N	N	Y
Albania	N	N	Y	N	N	N	Y	Y	Y	N
Bulgaria	N	N	Y	N	N	N	Y	Y	Y	N
Byelorussian S.S.R.	N	N	Y	N	N	N	Y	Y	Y	N
Czechoslovakia	N	N	Y	N	N	N	Y	Y	Y	N
Hungary	N	N	Y	N	N	N	Y	Y	Y	N
Poland	N	N	Y	N	N	N	Y	Y	Y	N
Romania	N	N	Y	N	N	N	Y	Y	Y	N
Ukrainian S.S.R.	N	N	Y	N	N	N	Y	Y	Y	N
U.S.S.R.	N	N	Y	N	N	N	Y	Y	Y	N
Yugoslavia	A	N	Y	A	A	N	Y	Y	Y	A

Issue Number	Issue

23 Resolution 1762B(XVII). Sponsored by the United States and the United Kingdom, it calls for a nuclear test ban treaty with effective international controls. 6 November 1962 (51-10-40).

24 Document A/5230, 21 September 1962. Placing the question of Hungary on the agenda. 24 September 1962 (43-34-19).

25 U.S.S.R. motion in the First Committee to seat the representatives of both North and South Korea. First Committee, 11 December 1962 (29-56-11).

26 United States motion in the First Committee to seat only the representatives of South Korea. First Committee, 11 December 1962 (65-9-26).

27 Resolution 1855(XVII). Extension of the mandate for the United Nations Commission for the Unification and Rehabilitation of Korea. 19 December 1962 (65-11-26).

28 Resolution 1857(XVII). United States sponsored draft giving the Secretary-General responsibility for the Hungarian question and affirming the objectives of the previous resolutions on Hungary. 20 December 1962 (50-13-43).

29 Document A/L.395, 18 October 1962. Soviet draft resolution to remove the Republic of China and to seat the People's Republic of China. 30 October 1962 (42-56-12).

30 Document A/L.427, 11 October 1963. Albania and Cambodia draft to remove the Republic of China and to seat the People's Republic of China. 21 October 1963 (41-57-12).

31 Document A/C.1/L.334, 9 December 1963. Mongolian sponsored draft to invite the representatives of North Korea to participate in discussion. First Committee, 9 December 1963 (25-54-20).

32 Resolution 1964(XVIII). Requests North Korea to accept United Nations objectives and extends mandate of the United Nations Commission on the Unification and Reconstruction of Korea. 13 December 1963 (65-11-24).

United Nations Vote Tally on Selected East-West Issues at the Twentieth–Twenty-second Sessions of the General Assembly*

State	33	34	35	36	37	38	39	40	41	42	43	44	45	46	47	48	49	50
									Issue Number									
Algeria	Y	N	Y	N	Y	N	N	N	N	Y	N	N	N	N	Y	N	Y	N
Botswana	–	–	–	–	–	–	–	–	Y	A	N	Y	–	Y	N	A	N	Y
Burundi	A	A	O	O	O	O	O	N	O	N	Y	N	A	A	N	Y	N	Y
Cameroon	A	A	O	O	O	O	Y	A	O	A	A	A	A	A	Y	N	A	A
Central African Republic	Y	N	N	Y	N	Y	A	O	Y	N	N	Y	A	Y	N	N	N	Y
Chad	A	A	O	O	N	Y	A	O	A	A	A	Y	A	Y	N	N	A	Y
Congo (Brazzaville)	Y	N	O	O	O	N	N	N	N	Y	N	N	N	N	Y	N	Y	N
Congo (Leopoldville)	O	Y	N	Y	O	Y	O	O	Y	N	Y	A	A	Y	N	N	O	O
Dahomey	O	O	O	O	O	Y	A	A	Y	N	Y	Y	Y	Y	N	N	N	Y
Gabon	N	Y	N	Y	N	Y	A	O	Y	N	A	Y	A	Y	N	A	N	Y
Gambia	N	Y	O	O	O	O	O	O	Y	N	N	O	O	Y	N	Y	O	Y
Ghana	Y	N	Y	N	Y	A	A	A	N	Y	N	Y	A	N	A	A	A	A
Guinea	Y	N	Y	N	Y	A	N	N	N	Y	N	N	A	N	Y	N	Y	N
Ivory Coast	N	Y	A	Y	A	Y	A	A	Y	N	N	Y	Y	Y	N	N	N	Y
Kenya	Y	N	O	O	O	A	A	O	N	Y	N	A	A	N	Y	A	Y	A
Lesotho	–	–	–	–	–	–	–	–	Y	N	A	Y	–	Y	N	N	A	Y
Libya	A	Y	A	A	A	A	A	O	Y	N	Y	A	A	Y	A	Y	A	A
Madagascar	N	Y	N	Y	N	Y	A	Y	Y	N	N	Y	Y	Y	N	A	N	Y
Malawi	N	Y	N	Y	N	Y	A	O	Y	N	Y	Y	Y	Y	N	N	N	Y
Mali	Y	N	Y	N	Y	O	N	N	N	Y	N	N	N	N	Y	N	Y	O
Mauritania	Y	N	Y	N	Y	A	A	O	N	Y	N	N	N	N	Y	N	Y	N
Morocco	Y	N	A	A	Y	A	A	N	N	A	Y	A	A	N	A	Y	O	A
Niger	N	Y	N	Y	A	Y	A	O	Y	N	Y	Y	Y	N	N	N	N	Y
Nigeria	Y	N	A	A	Y	A	A	O	N	Y	A	A	A	N	Y	A	Y	A
Rwanda	A	N	O	O	O	A	A	O	Y	N	N	Y	Y	Y	N	N	N	Y
Senegal	A	N	O	O	O	A	A	A	N	Y	N	A	A	N	Y	N	A	A
Sierra Leone	Y	N	A	A	A	A	A	A	A	N	A	A	A	Y	N	Y	A	A
Somali Republic	Y	N	O	O	O	A	N	O	N	Y	N	A	O	N	Y	O	Y	A

*Y = Yes, in favor
N = No, against
A = Abstained
O = Absent
NP = Present, but not participating
– = Vote taken prior to United Nations membership

| | | | | | | | Issue Number | | | | | | | | | | |
State	33	34	35	36	37	38	39	40	41	42	43	44	45	46	47	48	49	50
Sudan	Y	N	Y	A	Y	A	A	N	N	Y	N	A	A	N	Y	N	Y	N
Tanzania	Y	N	Y	N	Y	A	A	N	N	Y	N	A	A	N	Y	N	Y	A
Togo	N	Y	N	Y	N	Y	A	Y	Y	N	N	Y	Y	Y	N	A	N	Y
Tunisia	A	N	A	A	A	A	A	A	N	A	Y	A	A	N	A	Y	A	A
Uganda	Y	N	Y	N	Y	A	A	O	N	Y	N	A	A	N	Y	A	Y	A
Upper Volta	N	Y	N	Y	A	Y	A	Y	Y	N	N	Y	Y	Y	N	N	A	A
Zambia	Y	N	O	O	O	A	A	O	N	Y	N	A	A	N	Y	O	Y	N
Barbados	–	–	–	–	–	–	–	–	–	–	–	O	–	Y	N	A	N	Y
Guyana	–	–	–	–	–	–	–	–	Y	N	A	O	A	Y	N	A	N	Y
Jamaica	A	A	A	A	A	A	A	A	Y	A	Y	Y	Y	Y	A	Y	A	Y
Trinidad and Tobago	A	Y	O	O	O	Y	A	O	Y	A	Y	Y	Y	Y	A	A	O	Y
Burma	Y	N	Y	A	Y	A	N	N	N	Y	N	A	A	N	Y	N	Y	Y
Cambodia	Y	N	O	O	O	O	N	O	N	Y	N	N	N	N	Y	N	Y	N
Ceylon	Y	N	O	O	O	O	Y	A	N	Y	N	A	A	N	Y	N	Y	A
Indonesia	–	–	–	–	–	–	–	–	Y	Y	A	A	O	Y	Y	A	Y	A
Laos	O	Y	O	Y	O	Y	A	O	Y	O	A	Y	O	Y	O	Y	A	Y
Malaysia	N	Y	N	Y	N	Y	Y	Y	Y	N	A	Y	O	Y	N	A	N	Y
Maldive Islands	A	A	O	O	O	A	O	A	Y	A	A	Y	O	Y	A	A	O	O
Mongolia	Y	N	Y	N	Y	N	N	N	N	Y	N	N	N	N	Y	N	Y	N
Pakistan	Y	N	A	A	A	A	N	N	Y	N	A	A	N	Y	N	Y	A	
Philippines	N	Y	N	Y	N	Y	Y	Y	Y	N	N	Y	Y	Y	N	N	N	Y
Singapore	Y	N	O	O	O	A	A	A	N	A	N	A	A	N	A	N	O	A
Cyprus	A	A	O	O	O	O	A	O	A	A	A	A	Y	Y	A	Y	A	A
Malta	N	Y	O	O	O	Y	Y	Y	Y	N	Y	Y	O	Y	N	Y	N	Y
Israel	N	Y	N	Y	A	Y	Y	Y	Y	N	Y	Y	O	Y	N	Y	N	Y
Jordan	N	Y	A	A	A	A	A	Y	Y	N	N	Y	A	Y	N	N	A	A
Kuwait	A	A	N	A	A	A	A	A	N	A	A	A	A	N	A	A	O	A
South Yemen	–	–	–	–	–	–	–	–	–	–	–	–	–	–	–	–	–	–
United States	N	Y	N	Y	N	Y	Y	Y	Y	N	Y	Y	Y	Y	N	Y	N	Y
U.S.S.R.	Y	N	Y	N	Y	N	N	N	N	Y	N	N	N	N	Y	N	Y	N

Issue Number	Issue

33 Document A/L.469, a resolution deciding to recognize the representatives of the People's Republic of China as the only lawful representatives of China and to expel the representatives of Chiang Kai-shek from the UN. Plenary, 17 November 1965 (47-47-20).

Issue Number	Issue

34 Resolution 2025(XX) affirming the validity of the Assembly's 1961 decision that any proposal to change the Representatives of China in the United Nations is an "important question." Plenary, 17 November 1965 (56-49-11).

35 Tanzanian motion to give priority to a draft resolution inviting both North Korean and R.O.K. representatives to participate in discussion of the Korean Question. First Committee, 20 December 1965 (26-45-16).

36 Document A/C.1/L.356 which invited representatives of R.O.K. to take part in discussions of the Korean Question. First Committee, 20 December 1965 (50-20-20).

37 Document A/C.1/L.630 a draft resolution inviting both North Korean and R.O.K. representatives to participate in discussion of the Korean Question. First Committee, 20 December 1965 (28-39-22).

38 Resolution 2132(XX) calling upon North Korea to accept UN objectives and requesting continuation of UNCURK. Plenary, 21 December 1965 (61-13-34).

39 Document A/5988 requesting the inclusion on the agenda of the question of Tibet. Plenary, 24 September 1965 (41-26-46).

40 Resolution 2079(XX) renewing the call for a cessation of all practices which deprive Tibetans of their human rights and fundamental freedoms. Plenary, 18 December 1965 (43-26-22).

41 Resolution 2159(XXI) affirming again the validity of the Assembly's 1961 decision that any proposal to change the representation of China in the UN is an "important question." Plenary, 29 November 1966 (66-48-7).

42 Document A/L.496/Add.1 a draft resolution deciding to recognize the representatives of the P.R.C. as the only lawful representatives of China to the UN and to expel forthwith Chiang Kai-shek's representatives from the UN. Plenary, 29 November 1966 (46-57-17).

43 Document A/L.500 a draft resolution deciding to establish a committee to study the question of Chinese Representation in the UN and to make recommendations to the 22d General Assembly. Plenary, 29 November 1966 (34-62-25).

44 Resolution 2224(XXI) reaffirming UN objectives in Korea. Plenary, 19 December 1966 (67-19-32).

45 Document A/6395 concerning the inclusion of the question of Korea on the agenda. Plenary, 24 September 1966 (57-17-34).

46 Resolution 2271(XXII) affirming again the validity of the Assembly's 1961 decision that any proposal to change the representation of China in the UN is an "important question." Plenary, 28 November 1967 (69-48-4).

47 Document A/L.531/Add.1 a draft resolution deciding to recognize the representatives of the P.R.C. as the only lawful representatives of China to the UN and to expel the representatives of Chiang Kai-shek from the UN. Plenary, 28 November 1967 (45-58-17).

48 Document A/L.533 a draft resolution deciding to establish a committee to study the question of Chinese representation in the UN and to make recommendations thereon to the 23rd Assembly. Plenary, 28 November 1967 (32-57-30).

Issue *Number*	*Issue*
49	Document A/C.1/L.400/Rev. 1 an amendment to operative paragraph 1 of draft resolution A/C.1/L.399/Rev. 1 to provide for a simultaneous and unconditional invitation to both the R.O.K. and North Korea to participate in UN consideration of the North Korean question. First Committee, 31 October 1967 (37-50-24).
50	Resolution 2269 (XXII) reaffirming UN objectives in Korea. Plenary, 16 November 1967 (68-23-26).

Bibliography

Books and Pamphlets

Alker, Hayward R., Jr., and Russett, Bruce M. *World Politics in the General Assembly.* New Haven, Conn.: Yale University Press, 1965.

Asher, Robert, et. al. *The United Nations and Economic and Social Co-operation.* Washington, D.C.: The Brookings Institution, 1957.

Bailey, Sydney D. *The General Assembly of the United Nations, A Study of Procedure and Practice.* Rev. ed. New York: Frederick A. Praeger, 1964.

Bloomfield, Lincoln P. "The New Diplomacy in the United Nations" in *The United States and the United Nations.* Edited by Francis O. Wilcox and H. Field Haviland, Jr. Baltimore, Md.: The Johns Hopkins University Press, 1961.

Brecher, Michael. *The New States of Asia, A Political Analysis.* London: Oxford University Press, 1963.

Cott, Suzanne. "The Public Image of Africa as Expressed by the Permanent Missions to the United Nations of the African States (South of the Sahara)." Unpublished Master's Essay, Columbia University, 1963.

Crabb, Cecil V., Jr., *The Elephants and the Grass, A Study of Nonalignment.* New York: Frederick A. Praeger, 1965.

Dahl, Robert A. *Modern Political Analysis.* Englewood Cliffs, N.J.: Prentice-Hall, 1963.

de Seynes, Philippe. "Developing New Attitudes in International Economic Relations" in *The Quest for Peace.* Edited by Andrew W. Cordier and Wilder Foote. New York: Columbia University Press, 1965.

Easton, David. *A Framework for Political Analysis.* Englewood Cliffs, N.J.: Prentice-Hall, 1965.

———. *A Systems Analysis of Political Life.* New York: John Wiley & Sons, 1965.

Farajallah, Samaan Boutros. *Le Groupe Afro-Asiatique dans le Cadre des Nations Unies.* Genève: Librairie Droz, 1963.

Fawcett, J. E. S. "The New Nations and the United Nations" in *The New Nations in International Law and Diplomacy, The Yearbook of World Polity.* Vol. III. Edited by William V. O'Brien. New York: Frederick A. Praeger, 1965.

Gardner, Richard N. *In Pursuit of World Order: U.S. Foreign Policy and International Organizations.* New York: Frederick A. Praeger, 1964.

Good, Robert C. "Congo Crisis: The Role of the New States" in *Neutralism.*

Edited by Lawrence W. Martin, Washington, D.C.: the Washington Center of Foreign Policy Research, School of Advanced International Studies, The Johns Hopkins University, 1961.

Goodwin, Geoffrey. "The Political Impact of the Developing Nations in the United Nations" in *The Evolution of the United Nations*. Edited by G. R. Bunting and M. J. Lee. Oxford: Pergamon Press, 1964.

Gordon, King. *The United Nations in the Congo: A Quest for Peace*. New York: Carnegie Endowment for International Peace, 1962.

Governor's Conference on the United Nations, 2d, 1962. *The United Nations and the Emerging African Nations*. (Number 2: Global Focus Series.) Milwaukee, Wisc.: The Institute for World Affairs Education, The University of Wisconsin, 1962.

Haas, Ernst B. "Dynamic Environment and Static System: Revolutionary Regimes in the United Nations" in *The Revolution in World Politics*. Edited by Morton A. Kaplan. New York: John Wiley & Sons, 1962.

Hadwen, John G., and Kaufmann, Johan. *How United Nations Decisions Are Made*. 2d ed. rev. New York: Oceana Publications, 1962.

Hall, H. Duncan. *Mandates, Dependencies, and Trusteeships*. Washington, D.C.: Carnegie Endowment for International Peace, 1948.

Hovet, Thomas, Jr. *Africa in the United Nations*. Evanston, Ill.: Northwestern University Press, 1963.

———. *Bloc Politics in the United Nations*. Cambridge, Mass.: Harvard University Press, 1960.

Laswell, Harold D., and Kaplan, Abraham. *Power and Society, A Framework for Political Inquiry*. New Haven, Conn.: Yale University Press, 1950.

Lefever, Ernest W. *Crisis in the Congo: A United Nations Force in Action*. Washington, D.C.: Brookings Institution, 1965.

McKay, Vernon. *Africa in World Politics*. New York: Harper & Row, 1963.

Moore, Raymond A., Jr. (ed.) *The United Nations Reconsidered*. Columbia, S. C.: University of South Carolina Press, 1963.

Nicholas, H. G. *The United Nations as a Political Institution*. 2d ed. London: Oxford University Press, 1962.

Nielsen, Waldemar A. *African Battleline: American Policy Choices in Southern Africa*. New York: Published for the Council on Foreign Relations by Harper & Row, 1965.

Padelford, Norman J. *Elections in the United Nations General Assembly, A Study in Political Behavior*. Cambridge, Mass.: Center for International Studies, Massachusetts Institute of Technology, 1959.

Riggs, Robert E. *Politics in the United Nations, A Study of United States Influence in the General Assembly*. Urbana, Ill.: The University of Illinois Press, 1958.

Russell, Ruth B. *A History of the United Nations Charter, The Role of the United States 1940–1945*. Washington, D.C.: The Brookings Institution, 1958.

Russett, Bruce M. *Trends in World Politics.* New York: The Macmillan Company, 1965.

Sady, Emil J. *The United Nations and Dependent Peoples.* Washington, D.C.: The Brookings Institution, 1956.

Schlesinger, Arthur M., Jr. *A Thousand Days: John F. Kennedy in the White House.* Boston, Mass.: Houghton Mifflin Company, 1965.

Slim, Taieb. "The Work of the Committee of 24" in *Annual Review of United Nations Affairs 1963-1964.* Edited by Richard N. Swift. New York: Oceana by arrangement with New York University Press, 1965.

Sorensen, Theodore C. *Kennedy.* New York: Harper & Row, 1965.

Stoessinger, John G., et al. *Financing the United Nations System.* Washington, D.C.: Brookings Institution, 1964.

Swift, Richard N. (ed.). *Annual Review of United Nations Affairs 1960–1961. New York:* Oceana by arrangement with New York University Press, 1960.

Toussaint, Charmian Edwards. *The Trusteeship System of the United Nations.* New York: Frederick A. Praeger, 1956.

Vincent, Jack Ernest. *The Caucusing Groups of the United Nations—An Examination of Their Attitudes toward the Organization.* [Arts and Science Studies, Social Studies Series No. 12.] Stillwater, Okla.: Oklahoma State University, 1965.

Wadsworth, James J. *The Glass House, the United Nations in Action.* New York: Frederick A. Praeger, 1966.

Wainhouse, David W. *Remnants of Empire: The United Nations and the End of Colonialism.* New York: Published for the Council on Foreign Relations by Harper & Row, 1964.

Walters, F. P. *A History of the League of Nations.* London: Oxford University Press, 1952.

Articles and Periodicals

Alker, Hayward R., Jr. "Dimensions of Conflict in the General Assembly," *American Political Science Review,* 58, (Sept. 1964), 642–57.

Anabtawi, Samir N. "The Afro-Asian States and the Hungarian Question," *International Organization,* 17, No. 4 (Autumn 1963), 872–900.

Babaa, Khalid. "The 'Third Force' and the United Nations," *The Annals,* 362, (Nov. 1965), 81–91.

Ball, M. Margaret. "Bloc Voting in the General Assembly," *International Organization,* 5, No. 1 (Feb. 1951), 3–31.

Blough, Roy. "The Furtherance of Economic Development," *International Organization,* 19, No. 3 (Summer 1965), 562–80.

Boulding, Kenneth E. "Organization and Conflict," *Journal of Conflict Resolution,* 1 (1957), 122–34.

Brohi, A. K. "Five Lectures on Asia and the United Nations," *Recueil des*

Cours, Vol. 102. (Académie de Droit International.) Leyde: A. W. Sijthoff, 1962, 1961(I), 122–212.

Brykin, V. "Africa and the United Nations," *International Affairs* (Moscow), Aug. 1965, 38–45.

Clark, William. "New Forces in the United Nations," *International Affairs* (London), 36 (July 1960), 322–29.

Claude, Inis L., Jr. "The Political Framework of the United Nations' Financial Problems," *International Organization*, 17, No. 4 (Autumn 1963), 831–59.

Cohen, Sir Andrew. "The New Africa and the United Nations," *International Affairs* (London), 36, No. 4 (Oct. 1960), 476–88.

Dixon, Sir Pierson. "Diplomacy at the United Nations," *International Relations*, 1, No. 10 (Oct. 1958), 457–66.

Falk, Richard A. "The South-West Africa Cases: An Appraisal," *International Organization*, 21, No. 1 (Winter 1967), 1–23.

Frank, Isaiah. "Issues before the U.N. Conference," *Foreign Affairs*, 42 (Jan. 1964), 210–26.

Frankel, Max, "U.S. Switched Its Tactics," *New York Times*, Mar. 17, 1961, p. 4.

Frye, William R. "Afro-Asian Bloc: Center Stage at U.N.," *Foreign Policy Bulletin*, 40 (Oct. 15, 1960), 17–18.

Gardner, Richard N. "The United Nations Conference on Trade and Development," *International Organization*, 22, No. 1 (Winter 1968), 99–130.

Goodwin, Geoffrey. "The Expanding United Nations, I—Voting Patterns," *International Affairs* (London), 36 (Apr. 1960), 174–87.

———. "The Expanding United Nations, II—Diplomatic Pressures and Techniques," *International Affairs* (London), 37 (Apr. 1961), 170–80.

Gregg, Robert W. "The Economic and Social Council: Politics of Membership," *Western Political Quarterly*, XVI (Mar. 1963), 109–32.

Gross, Ernest A. "The South-West Africa Case: What Happened?" *Foreign Affairs*, 45, No. 1 (Oct. 1966), 36–48.

Haas, Ernst B. "The Comparative Study of the United Nations," *World Politics*, 12, No. 2 (Jan. 1960), 298–322.

———. "The Reconciliation of Conflicting Colonial Policy Aims: Acceptance of the League of Nations Mandate System," *International Organization*, 6 (Nov. 1952), 521–36.

Hamilton, Thomas J. "Gain Made in U.N. on Peace Forces," *New York Times*, June 18, 1963, p. 3.

———. "U.S. Will Give U.N. Extra $2 Million," *New York Times*, June 4, 1963, p. 3.

———. "Arabs in U.N. Call for Cost Changes," *New York Times*, June 7, 1963, p. 3.

———. "Bloc in U.N. Asks Assessment Cut," *New York Times*, June 14, 1963, p. 4.

————. "Gain Made in U.N. on Peace Forces," *New York Times*, June 14, 1963, p. 3.

————. "Colonialism at the U.N.," *New York Times*, Section IV, Dec. 18, 1960, p. 9.

————. "U.S. Joins Assembly Vote to Spur Fight on Colonies," *New York Times*, Nov. 28, 1961, p. 1.

Henkin, Louis. "The United Nations and Human Rights," *International Organization*, 19, No. 3 (Summer 1965), 504–17.

Higgins, Rosalyn. "The International Court and South-West Africa: The Implications of the Judgment," *International Affairs* (London), 42, No. 4 (Oct. 1966), 573–99.

Hoskyns, Catherine. "The African States and the United Nations 1958–1964," *International Affairs* (London), 40 (July 1964), 466–80.

Hovet, Thomas, Jr. "The Role of Africa in the United Nations," *The Annals of the American Academy of Political and Social Science*, 354 (July 1964), 122–34.

————. "United Nations Diplomacy," *Journal of International Affairs*, 17, No. 1 (1963), 29–41.

Hunt, Richard P. "At the U.N.—13,000,000 Words a Year," *New York Times Magazine*, Dec. 9, 1962, 31–33.

Hyde, James N. "United States Participation in the United Nations," *International Organization*, 10, No. 1 (Feb. 1956), 22–34.

"Issues before the Nineteenth General Assembly," *International Conciliation*, No. 550 (Nov. 1964).

"Issues before the Sixteenth General Assembly," *International Conciliation*, No. 534 (Sept. 1961).

"Issues before the Twentieth General Assembly," *International Conciliation*, No. 554 (Summer 1965).

Jacobson, Harold Karan. "The United Nations and Colonialism: A Tentative Appraisal," *International Organization*, 16, No. 1 (Winter 1962), 37–56.

Jordon, William J., "State Department Divides over U.S. Vote on Angola," *New York Times*, Mar. 17, 1961, p. 1.

Karefa-Smart, John. "Africa and the United Nations," *International Organization*, 19, No. 3 (Summer 1965), 764–73.

Keohane, Robert Owen. "Political Influence in the General Assembly," *International Conciliation*, No. 557 (Mar. 1966), 42–64.

Kotschnig, Walter M. "The United Nations as an Instrument of Economic and Social Development," *International Organization*, 22, No. 1 (Winter 1968), 16–43.

Kuebler, Jeanne. "Afro-Asians in the United Nations," *Editorial Research Reports*, 1963-II (Sept. 18, 1963). Edited by Richard M. Boeckel. (Washington, D.C.: Congressional Quarterly Service, 1963), 685–701.

Lall, Arthur. "The Asian Nations and the United Nations," *International Organization*, 19, No. 3 (Summer 1965), 728–48.

Lijphart, Arend. "The Analysis of Bloc Voting in the General Assembly:

A Critique and a Proposal," *The American Political Science Review,* 57, No. 4 (Dec. 1963), 902–17.

Little, Tom. "Mr. Khrushchev and the Neutrals at the United Nations," *The World Today,* 16, No. 12 (Dec. 1960), 510–19.

Lvov, M. "United Nations: Results and Prospects," *International Affairs* (Moscow), No. 9 (Sept. 1965) 3–10.

MacKirdy, K. A. "The United Nations: Some Thoughts on Changing Perspectives," *Queen's Quarterly,* 67 (Winter 1960–1961), 557–67.

Mannes, Marya. "U. N.: The Fine Art of Corridor Sitting," *The Reporter,* Jan. 12, 1956, 30–32.

Manno, Catherine Senf. "Problems and Trends in the Composition of Nonplenary U. N. Organs," *International Organization,* 19, No. 1 (Winter 1965), 37–55.

March, James G. "An Introduction to the Theory and Measurement of Influence," *American Political Science Review,* 49 (1955), 431–51.

Mazrui, Ali A. "The United Nations and Some African Political Attitudes," *International Organization,* 18 (Summer 1964), 499–520.

Michie, Allan A. "The Growth of an African Power Bloc," *The Reporter,* 22 (Mar. 17, 1960), 25–28.

Mower, A. Glenn, Jr. "The Sponsorship of Proposals in the United Nations General Assembly, *Western Political Quarterly,* 15 (Dec. 1962), 661–66.

Nicholas, H. G. "The United Nations in Crisis," *International Affairs,* 41, No. 3 (July 1965), 441–50.

Ogley, Roderick C. "Voting and Politics in the General Assembly," *International Relations,* 2, No. 3 (Apr. 1961), 156–67, 183.

Pedersen, Richard F. "National Representation in the United Nations," *International Organization,* 15, No. 2 (Spring 1961), 256–66.

Rubin, Ronald. "The U. N. Correspondent," *Western Political Quarterly,* 17 (Dec. 1964), 615–31.

Rusk, Dean. "Parliamentary Diplomacy—Debate vs. Negotiation," *World Affairs Interpreter,* 26 No. 2 (Summer 1955), 121–22.

Shonfield, Andrew. "Trade as a Tool of Development—The Issues at Geneva," *International Affairs* (London), Apr. 1964, 219–31.

Soward, F. H. "The Changing Balance of Power in the United Nations," *Political Quarterly,* 28, No. 4 (Oct.-Dec. 1947), 316–27.

Spencer, John H. "Africa at the U. N.: Some Observations," *International Organization,* 16 (Spring 1962), 375–86.

Stevenson, John R. "Judicial Decisions," *American Journal of International Law,* 61, No. 1 (Jan. 1967), 116–210.

Triska, Jan F. and Koch, Howard E., Jr. "Asian-African Coalition and International Organization: Third Force or Collective Impotence?" *Review of Politics,* 21, No. 2 (Apr. 1959), 417–55.

Wilcox, Francis O. "U. N. and the Nonaligned Nations," *Headline Series,* No. 155 (Sept. /Oct. 1962).

Public Documents

Great Britain. *Hansard's Parliamentary Debates* (5th Series). (Commons),
    653 (1962).
International Court of Justice Reports 1962 (The Hague: International
    Court of Justice, 1962).
United Nations General Assembly. *Official Records*, 15th-21st Sessions
    (1960–1966).
United Nations Office of Public Information. *Yearbook of the United Na-
    tions, 1960.* New York: United Nations, 1961.
United Nations Office of Public Information. *Yearbook of the United Na-
    tions, 1961.* New York: United Nations, 1963.
United Nations Office of Public Information. *Yearbook of the United Na-
    tions, 1962.* New York: United Nations, 1964.
United Nations Office of Public Information. *Yearbook of the United Na-
    tions, 1963.* New York: United Nations, 1965.
United Nations *Permanent Missions to the United Nations,* 1960–1968.
United Nations Yearbook 1962. New York: Published by Columbia Uni-
    versity Press in cooperation with the United Nations, 1964.
United States Senate, Committee on Foreign Relations. *The United States
    in the United Nations, 1960—A Turning Point.* Report by Senator
    George D. Aiken (Rep., Vt.) and Senator Wayne Morse (Dem., Ore.).
    87th Congress, 1st session, Feb. 1961.

Index